First World War
and Army of Occupation
War Diary
France, Belgium and Germany

29 DIVISION
Divisional Troops
455 (1/1 West Riding) Field Company Royal Engineers
1 March 1916 - 28 October 1919

WO95/2293/1

The Naval & Military Press Ltd
www.nmarchive.com
Published in association with The National Archives

Published by

The Naval & Military Press Ltd

Unit 10 Ridgewood Industrial Park,

Uckfield, East Sussex,

TN22 5QE England

Tel: +44 (0) 1825 749494

www.naval-military-press.com

www.nmarchive.com

This diary has been reprinted in facsimile from the original. Any imperfections are inevitably reproduced and the quality may fall short of modern type and cartographic standards.

© Crown Copyright
Images reproduced by permission of The National Archives, London, England, 2015.

Contents

Document type	Place/Title	Date From	Date To
Heading	WO95/2293 455 (1/1 Wear Redy) Field Company Royal Engineers		
Heading	29th Division Divl Engineers 1-1st (W.R.) Fld. Coy R.E. 1916 Mar 455th (W.R.) Fld Coy R E. 1916 Mar To Oct 1919		
Heading	29th Divisional Engineers Arrived Marseilles From Egypt 20.3.16 1/1st West Riding Field Company R.E. March 1916		
War Diary	El Kubri	01/03/1916	02/03/1916
War Diary	Suez	03/03/1916	13/03/1916
War Diary	H M T. Miltiades	14/03/1916	20/03/1916
War Diary	Train	21/03/1916	22/03/1916
War Diary	Surcamps	23/03/1916	30/03/1916
War Diary	Ampliers	31/03/1916	31/03/1916
Heading	29th Divisional Engineers 1/1st West Riding Field Company R.E. April 1916		
War Diary	Ampliers	01/04/1916	03/04/1916
War Diary	Mailly Maillet	04/04/1916	30/04/1916
Heading	29th Divisional Engineers 1/1st West Riding Field Company R.E. May 1916		
War Diary	Mailly-Maillet	01/05/1916	31/05/1916
Heading	29th Divisional Engineers 1/1st West Riding Field Company R.E. June 1916		
War Diary	Mailly-Maillet	01/06/1916	30/06/1916
Heading	Q 29th Divisional Engineers 1/1st West Riding Field Company R.E. July 1916		
Heading	War Diary of 1/1st West Riding Field Company R.E. (T.F.) From 1st To 31st July 1916 Volume XV		
War Diary	Auchonviller Sector	01/07/1916	24/07/1916
War Diary	Louvencourt	25/07/1916	27/07/1916
War Diary	Wormhoudt	28/07/1916	28/07/1916
War Diary	Vlamertinge	29/07/1916	31/07/1916
Heading	29th Divisional Engineers 1/1st West Riding Field Company R.E. August 1916		
War Diary	Vlamertinghe	01/08/1916	31/08/1916
Heading	29th Divisional Engineers 1/1st West Riding Field Company R.E. September 1916		
War Diary	Vlamertinghe and Ypres	19/09/1916	30/09/1916
War Diary	Vlamertinghe And Ypres	01/09/1916	18/09/1916
Heading	29th Divisional Engineers 1/1st West Riding Field Company R.E. October 1916		
War Diary	Vlamertinghe and Ypres	01/10/1916	03/10/1916
War Diary	Houtkerque	04/10/1916	08/10/1916
War Diary	Douars	09/10/1916	09/10/1916
War Diary	Dernancourt	10/10/1916	13/10/1916
War Diary	Fricourt	14/10/1916	20/10/1916
War Diary	Longueval	21/10/1916	30/10/1916
War Diary	Fricourt	31/10/1916	31/10/1916
Heading	29th Divisional Engineers 1/1st West Riding Field Company R.E. November 1916		

War Diary	Fricourt	01/11/1916	03/11/1916
War Diary	Daours	04/11/1916	16/11/1916
War Diary	Trones	17/11/1916	30/11/1916
Heading	29th Divisional Engineers 1/1st West Riding Field Company R.E. December 1916		
Heading	War Diary of 1/1st West Riding Field Company Royal Engineers (T.F) From December 1st 16 To December 31st/16 (Volume 1)		
War Diary	Trones Wood	01/12/1916	10/12/1916
War Diary	Trones	10/12/1916	11/12/1916
War Diary	Citadel	12/12/1916	12/12/1916
War Diary	Mericourt	13/12/1916	14/12/1916
War Diary	Dreuil-les-Molliens	15/12/1916	18/12/1916
War Diary	Molliens Vidame	19/12/1916	27/12/1916
War Diary	Pont Remy	28/12/1916	31/12/1916
Heading	War Diary of 455th (W. Riding) Fld Coy R.E. From 1st January 1917 To 31st January 1917 Volume I		
War Diary	Pont Remy	01/01/1917	07/01/1917
War Diary	Molliens Vidame	08/01/1917	09/01/1917
War Diary	Daours	10/01/1917	14/01/1917
War Diary	Meaulte	15/01/1917	15/01/1917
War Diary	Trones Wood	16/01/1917	25/01/1917
War Diary	Trones	26/01/1917	31/01/1917
Heading	War Diary of 455th (West Riding) Field Co Royal Engineers (T) From 1/2/17 To 28/2/17 Volume I		
War Diary	Trones Wood S 30 A Central	01/02/1917	02/02/1917
War Diary	Trones Wood	03/02/1917	07/02/1917
War Diary	Heilly	08/02/1917	18/02/1917
War Diary	Mansel Camp	19/02/1917	19/02/1917
War Diary	Combles Catacombs	20/02/1917	20/02/1917
War Diary	Combles	21/02/1917	28/02/1917
Heading	War Diary of 455th (West Riding) Field Co., R.E. From 1st March 1917 To 31st March, 1917 Volume I		
War Diary	Combles	01/03/1917	01/03/1917
War Diary	Combles Catacombs	02/03/1917	02/03/1917
War Diary	Combles	03/03/1917	03/03/1917
War Diary	Meaulte	04/03/1917	04/03/1917
War Diary	Heilly	05/03/1917	18/03/1917
War Diary	Saisseval	19/03/1917	28/03/1917
War Diary	Flesselles	29/03/1917	29/03/1917
War Diary	Montrelet	30/03/1917	31/03/1917
Heading	War Diary of 455th (West Riding) Field Co., R.E. From 1st April 1917 To 30th April 1917 Volume XIV		
War Diary	Le Quesnel Farm nr Outre Bois	01/04/1917	01/04/1917
War Diary	Le Gros Tison Farm Nr Mondicourt	02/04/1917	02/04/1917
War Diary	Le Gros Tison	03/04/1917	04/04/1917
War Diary	Etree Wamin	05/04/1917	06/04/1917
War Diary	Grand Rullecourt	07/04/1917	07/04/1917
War Diary	Bavincourt	08/04/1917	11/04/1917
War Diary	Maison Rouge Cambrai Road	12/04/1917	13/04/1917
War Diary	Maison Rouge	13/04/1917	14/04/1917
War Diary	Monchy	14/04/1917	14/04/1917
War Diary	Maison Rouge	15/04/1917	17/04/1917
War Diary	Cambrai Road	18/04/1917	18/04/1917
War Diary	H 32 C 05 B 5	18/04/1917	18/04/1917
War Diary	Thilloy Quarry	18/04/1917	24/04/1917

War Diary	Duisans	25/04/1917	25/04/1917
War Diary	Noyellette	26/04/1917	26/04/1917
War Diary	La Herliere	27/04/1917	30/04/1917
Heading	War Diary of 455th (West Riding) Field Co. R.E. From 1st May 1917 To 31st May 1917 Volume XV		
War Diary	Wanquetin	01/05/1917	01/05/1917
War Diary	Arras	02/05/1917	07/05/1917
War Diary	Dainville	08/05/1917	12/05/1917
War Diary	Arras	13/05/1917	14/05/1917
War Diary	Tilloy Quarry	15/05/1917	19/05/1917
War Diary		16/05/1917	17/05/1917
War Diary	Proven (in The Train)	18/05/1917	19/05/1917
War Diary	A 11 A 35	20/05/1917	30/05/1917
War Diary	Vacquerie	12/05/1917	16/05/1917
War Diary	Vacquerie	06/05/1917	11/05/1917
Heading	War Diary of 455th (West Riding) Field Co. R.E. From 1st June 1917 To 30th June 1917 Volume XVI		
War Diary	Thilloy	01/06/1917	02/06/1917
War Diary	Arras	03/06/1917	03/06/1917
War Diary	Berneville	04/06/1917	04/06/1917
War Diary	Lucheux	05/06/1917	05/06/1917
War Diary	Tilloy Quarry	19/06/1917	22/06/1917
War Diary	Thilloy	23/06/1917	31/06/1917
Heading	War Diary of 455th (West Riding) Field Co. R.E. From 1st July 1917 To 30th July 1917 Volume XVII		
War Diary	A 10 B 63 Sheet 28 Belgium	01/07/1917	02/07/1917
War Diary	A 10 B 63	03/07/1917	31/07/1917
Heading	War Diary of 455th (West Riding) Field Co. R.E. From 1st August 1917 To 31st August 1917 Volume XVIII.		
War Diary	A 10 B 63	01/08/1917	06/08/1917
War Diary	Elverdinghe	07/08/1917	21/08/1917
War Diary	Elverdinghe Defence	22/08/1917	25/08/1917
War Diary	Pilgrim Camp E 4C St Pu Au W Of Probin	26/08/1917	27/08/1917
Heading	War Diary of 455th (West Riding) Field Co. R.E. From 1st September 1917 To 30th September 1917 Volume XIX		
War Diary	Pilgrim Camp	01/09/1917	01/09/1917
War Diary	N.R. Proven	01/09/1917	11/09/1917
War Diary	Pilgrim Camp	12/09/1917	12/09/1917
War Diary	P4 Aux W of Proven	12/09/1917	18/09/1917
War Diary	Elverdinghe Chateau	19/09/1917	30/09/1917
Heading	War Diary 455th (W.R.) Field Coy R.E. Volume XX		
War Diary	Elverdinghe 25 N W U15 C 27	01/10/1917	09/10/1917
War Diary	Rutlowes Camp 27/F10 A 52	10/10/1917	14/10/1917
War Diary	In The Train	13/10/1917	13/10/1917
War Diary	Blairville 9 Kilos S.W Of Arras	16/10/1917	19/10/1917
War Diary	Blairville	20/10/1917	31/10/1917
Heading	War Diary of 455th (West Riding) Field Coy. R.E. Volume 21 (November 1917)		
War Diary	Blairville	01/11/1917	14/11/1917
War Diary	Bethune	15/11/1917	15/11/1917
War Diary	Surel Les Fins	16/11/1917	16/11/1917
War Diary	Sorel	17/11/1917	19/11/1917
War Diary	Bivouac Pest W. Of Gouzeaucourt Front No 1 The Road L Fins	19/11/1917	19/11/1917
War Diary	Marcoing	20/11/1917	30/11/1917

Heading	War Diary of 455th (West Riding) Field Co RE (T) From Dec 1st 1917 To Dec 31st 1918 Volume XXII		
War Diary	Marcoing	01/12/1917	03/12/1917
War Diary	Hindenburg Line at R 3 A 32 57 C NE	04/12/1917	04/12/1917
War Diary	Sorel	05/12/1917	05/12/1917
War Diary	Berlencourt	05/12/1917	16/12/1917
War Diary	Aubrometz (Lens II)	17/12/1917	17/12/1917
War Diary	Bemencourt (Lens II)	18/12/1917	18/12/1917
War Diary	Bealencourt	18/12/1917	18/12/1917
War Diary	Coupelle Neuve (Hazelinet)	19/12/1917	19/12/1917
War Diary	Coupelle Neuve	20/12/1917	30/12/1917
War Diary	Elnes	31/12/1917	31/12/1917
War Diary	Maison Blanche	01/01/1918	01/01/1918
War Diary	Hardifort X Roads	02/01/1918	02/01/1918
War Diary	Putney Camp	03/01/1918	04/01/1918
War Diary	Elverdinghe Chateau	05/01/1918	13/01/1918
War Diary	Eofile Camp	14/01/1918	18/01/1918
War Diary	Ypres	19/01/1918	31/01/1918
Heading	War Diary of 455th (W. Riding) Field Coy R.E. From 1/2/18 To 28/2/18 Volume XIV		
War Diary	Ypres	01/02/1918	28/02/1918
Heading	War Diary From Mar 1st To Mar 31st/18 Volume XXIV		
War Diary	Ypres	01/03/1918	30/03/1918
War Diary	Somme Dugout	30/03/1918	31/03/1918
Heading	29th Divisional Engineers 455th (West Riding) Field Company R.E. April 1918		
Heading	Original War Diary From 1st April To 30th April 1918 Volume No XXVI		
War Diary	Somme Dug-Out	01/04/1918	08/04/1918
War Diary	St Jan-Ter-Biezen	08/04/1918	09/04/1918
War Diary	St Jan-Ter-Biezen L.3.a.5.8. Sheet 27	09/04/1918	09/04/1918
War Diary	Neuf Berquin L.7.a.6.1. Sheet 36A	10/04/1918	10/04/1918
War Diary	Neuf Berquin	10/04/1918	11/04/1918
War Diary	Pisec Bois E.9.c.9.1 Sheet 36A	12/04/1918	12/04/1918
War Diary	Pisec Bois	12/04/1918	12/04/1918
War Diary	Petit Sec Bois	12/04/1918	12/04/1918
War Diary	Strazeele W 22 d.9.8 Sheet 27	13/04/1918	13/04/1918
War Diary	Strazeele	13/04/1918	13/04/1918
War Diary	Strazeele St Sylvestre P 36 a.6.6 Sheet 27	14/04/1918	16/04/1918
War Diary	St Sylvestre	16/04/1918	19/04/1918
War Diary	Hondeghem V.8.d.2.6 Sheet 27	19/04/1918	20/04/1918
War Diary	Hondeghem	21/04/1918	26/04/1918
War Diary	Au Souverain	27/04/1918	30/04/1918
Heading	War Diary of 455th (W Riding) Fd Coy RE From 1/5/18 To 31/5/18 Volume No Vol 28		
War Diary	Au Souverain	01/05/1918	12/05/1918
War Diary	Au Souverain	05/05/1918	08/05/1918
War Diary	Au Souverain	13/05/1918	15/05/1918
War Diary	Hazebrouck	15/05/1918	31/05/1918
Heading	War Diary 455th (W. Riding) Field Company R.E. From 1/6/18 To 30/618 Volume No XXVIII		
War Diary	Hazebrouck	01/06/1918	22/06/1918
War Diary	Bandringhem	23/06/1918	30/06/1918

Heading	War Diary (Original) Volume No XXVIII For July 1918 Unit 455th (W.R.) Field Coy R.E. (T.F.) B.E.F. Vol 30		
War Diary	Bandringhem	01/07/1918	17/07/1918
War Diary	Eecke Hout Castell	18/07/1918	21/07/1918
War Diary	Korten Loop (Area)	22/07/1918	26/07/1918
War Diary	Godewaersvelde	27/07/1918	31/07/1918
Heading	Original War Diary of 455th (W.R.) Field Coy. R.E. (TF) For August 1918 Volume 29		
War Diary	Goed	01/08/1918	04/08/1918
War Diary	Le Peuplier	05/08/1918	07/08/1918
War Diary	Hazebrouck	08/08/1918	22/08/1918
War Diary	Congo Corner	23/08/1918	31/08/1918
Heading	Original War Diary of 455th (W.R.) Field Coy R.E. (T.F.) For Month Of September 1918 Volume 30		
War Diary	Merris	01/09/1918	03/09/1918
War Diary	Verity Crossing F 5 C 2.6.	04/09/1918	04/09/1918
War Diary	Steenwerk	05/09/1918	11/09/1918
War Diary	Hazebrouck	12/09/1918	17/09/1918
War Diary	Dirty Bucket	18/09/1918	21/09/1918
War Diary	Machine Gun Sidings	22/09/1918	28/09/1918
War Diary	Glencorse Wood	29/09/1918	30/09/1918
Heading	War Diary of 455 WR. Field Coy R.E. (T.F.) For Month Of October 1918 Volume 31		
War Diary	Glencorse Wood	01/10/1918	04/10/1918
War Diary	Glencorse Wood J 14 a 9.6	05/10/1918	10/10/1918
War Diary	Glencorse Wood	11/10/1918	14/10/1918
War Diary	Dadizeele	15/10/1918	17/10/1918
War Diary	G3d 0.2.	18/10/1918	18/10/1918
War Diary	H1d 33	19/10/1918	20/10/1918
War Diary	Staceghem H.29. Central Sheet 29	21/10/1918	26/10/1918
War Diary	Tourcoing X.30 Central Sheet 28	27/10/1918	27/10/1918
War Diary	Siandre K.8.d.10.15 Sheet 36	28/10/1918	30/10/1918
War Diary	Croix L.18.d.0.5 Sheet 36	30/10/1918	31/10/1918
Heading	Original War Diary of 455th (West Riding) Field Coy. RE. (TF) For Month Of November 1918 Volume 32		
War Diary	Croix (near Roubaix) L.10.c.0.5 Sheet 36	01/11/1918	03/11/1918
War Diary	Croix L.10.c.0.5 Sheet 36	04/11/1918	06/11/1918
War Diary	Tourcoing	07/11/1918	08/11/1918
War Diary	Farm O.25.c.8.3 Sheet 29	08/11/1918	09/11/1918
War Diary	Farm 29/O.25.c.8.3	09/11/1918	09/11/1918
War Diary	Farm 37/U 23.b.6.7	09/11/1918	11/11/1918
War Diary	Buile E.30.b.7.4	11/11/1918	11/11/1918
War Diary	37/F.20.c.6.4 Farm	11/11/1918	17/11/1918
War Diary	Tribouriau	18/11/1918	30/11/1918
Heading	Original War Diary of 455th. (W.R.) Field Coy. R.E. (T.F.) For Month Of December 1918 Volume 33		
War Diary		01/12/1918	14/12/1918
War Diary	Burscheid	15/12/1918	31/12/1918
Heading	Rhine Army Southern Division Late 29th Division 455th (W.R.) Fld Coy R.E. Jan-Oct 1919 Box 2065 & 2084		
Heading	Original War Diary of 455th (W.R.) Field Coy R.E. (T.F.) For Month Of January 1919 Volume 34		
War Diary		01/01/1919	04/01/1919
War Diary	Burscheid	05/01/1919	31/01/1919

Heading	War Diary of 455 (W.R.) Field Company R.E. (T) For Month Of February 1919 Volume 35		
War Diary	Burscheid	01/02/1919	04/02/1919
War Diary	Burscheid Germany	05/02/1919	28/02/1919
Heading	War Diary of 455th Field Coy R.E. From 1/5/19 To 31/5/19 Volume No 38		
War Diary	Burscheid	01/05/1919	31/05/1919
Heading	Original War Diary of 455th Field Coy. R.E. For Month Of June 1919 Volume 39		
War Diary	Burscheid	01/06/1919	18/06/1919
War Diary	Burscheid Germany	19/06/1919	30/06/1919
Heading	Original War Diary of 455th Field Coy RE. (T) For Month Of July 1919 Volume 40		
War Diary	Burscheid (Germany)	01/07/1919	31/07/1919
Heading	Original War Diary of 455th Field Coy. R.E. For Month Of August 1919 Volume 41		
War Diary	Burscheid	01/08/1919	31/08/1919
Heading	Original War Diary of 455th. Field Coy R.E. (T) For Month Of September 1919 Volume 42		
War Diary	Burschied (Germany)	02/09/1919	28/09/1919
Heading	Original War Diary of 455th Field Coy R.E. (T) For Month Of October 1919 Volume 43		
War Diary	Burschied (Germany)	02/10/1919	28/10/1919

WO/95/2293

1, 455(I) workshops field
Company Royal Engineers

29TH DIVISION
ROYAL ENGINEERS

1-1ST (W.R.) FLD. COY R.E.
1916 MAR —
455TH (W.R.) FLD COY R.E.

1916 MAR to OCT 1919

29th Divisional Engineers

Arrived MARSEILLES from EGYPT 20.3.16.

1/1st WEST RIDING

FIELD COMPANY R. E.

MARCH 1 9 1 6

WAR DIARY or INTELLIGENCE SUMMARY.

Army Form C. 2118.

MARCH TO MAY 1916

1/1 West Riding Field Coys. MARCH – MAY 1916

Place	Date	Hour	Summary of Events and Information	Remarks and references to Appendices
EL KUBRI	1.3.16		Work on Canal defences. Training Staff: Drawing equipment.	
	2.3.16		Company marched back to SUEZ. Casualties 2 O.R. rejoined	
SUEZ	3.3.16		Company training. Drawing stores. 1 O.R. Sick	
	4.3.16		" " " "	
	5.3.16		" " Strength. 8 officers 142 O.R.	
	6.3.16		Sunday. Capt. J.K.B. LANGLEY and 26 O.R. (hand) left for Alexandria for embarkation on H.M.T. MANITO – this party arrived MARSEILLES 12.3.16 & proceeded to ABBEVILLE arriving 14.3.16. Divers horses (wagons) & went into billets at OLR CAMP. 17.3.16. Casualties 5 O.R. rejoined	
	7.3.16		Company training. 10 O.R. rejoined from BASE at SIDI BISHR.	
	8.3.16		" " 1 O.R. rejoined	
	9.3.16		" " 1 O.R. Sick	
	10.3.16		" " 1 O.R. Sick	
	11.3.16		" " 2 O.R. to BASE for being sent home for Jurisdiction. 2 O.R. Sick	
	12.3.16		2 O.R. rejoined. Strength 8 Officers 183 O.R.	
	13.3.16		Sunday. 3 O.R. Sick 2 O.R. rejoined. Orders received to embark on 13.3.16 at SUEZ DOCKS. Baggage sent to Docks 7 a.m. Company marched to Docks at 11.30 am. Embarked on H.M.T.	
H.M.T. MILTIADES	14.3.16		MILTIADES at 1 p.m. Sailed 5 p.m. Casualties 1 O.R. Sick 1 O.R. rejoined	
	15.3.16		Arrived PORT SAID 7 am. Coaled. Sailed at 9.30 p.m.	
	16.3.16		} at Sea. 1 O.R. Sick 17.3.16 1 O.R. Sick 19.3.16 Thurs Fri 18 3.16. 8 officers 180 O.R. entrained 2 p.m.	
	20.3.16		Arrived MARSEILLES 9 a.m. disembarked 12.15 p.m.	
TRAIN	21.3.16		in the train	
	22.3.16		Arrived PONT REMY 12.30 p.m. Unloaded, marched off 2.15/3.0 to billets at SUR CAMPS. Casualties. 1 interpreter joined.	
SUR CAMPS	23.3.16		Overhauling Horses equipment etc.	

Army Form C. 2118.

WAR DIARY
or
INTELLIGENCE SUMMARY.
(Erase heading not required.)

1/1 West Riding F. Coys.

Place	Date	Hour	Summary of Events and Information	Remarks and references to Appendices
SURCAMPS.	24.3.16		Overhauling equipment, harness etc. Personal kits. Putting teams together.	
	25.3.16		" " "	Strength 8 officers; 8 subalterns; 180 O.R.
	26.3.16		Packing wagons. Turned out full marching order. 10.R. begun ad.	
	27.3.16		Marching order-parade & route march.	
	28.3.18		" " " "	
	29.3.16		Company training. 1 O.R. attached to VIII Corps	
	30.3.16		Company paraded 7.15 am marched to 87th Bde. rendezvous at 6 am. at DOMART - marched to AMPLIERS & went into huts. 2 O.R. attached to A.S.C.	
AMPLIERS	31.3.16		Company training.	

A Clay Major R.E.
OC 1/1 W.R. F.Coy R.E.

29th Divisional Engineers

1/1st WEST RIDING

FIELD COMPANY R. E.

APRIL 1 9 1 6

Army Form C. 2118.

WAR DIARY or INTELLIGENCE SUMMARY.
(Erase heading not required.)

1/1 West Riding Field Coy R.E.

Place	Date	Hour	Summary of Events and Information	Remarks and references to Appendices
AMPLIERS	1.4.16		Company Training. Strength 8 officers, 1 interpreter. 177 O.R.	
	2.4.16		" "	
	3.4.16		Company marched at 2 p.m. to MAILLY-MAILLET + went into billets. 1 O.R. Sick.	
MAILLY-MAILLET	4.4.16		Took over Water Supply + work in the area from Fd.Co. of 31st DIVISION.	
	5.4.16		Taking over work in area	
	6.4.16		Work in area. 2/Lt. Grogan + 1 section to Tauderlor for work on first line entire Brigade. 1 O.R. attached C.R.E.	
	7.4.16		Work in area. Water Supply, Improvements to trenches, Reg. dug outs. Strutting Roads etc	
	8.4.16		Work in area. 1 O.R. Sick. 4 O.R. rejoined. 2/Lt. BUCKLEY attached L/3 West Ridings	
	9.4.16		Strength 7 officers, 1 interpreter 176 O.R.	
	10.4.16		Work in area. Company went through practical gas protective test.	
	11.4.16		Work in area. 1 O.R. Sick. 2 O.R. rejoined	
	12.4.16		Work in area	
	13.4.16		" " "	
	14.4.16		" " "	
	15.4.16		" " " Strength 7 officers 1 interpreter 179 O.R.	
	16.4.16		" " "	
	17.4.16		" " "	
	18.4.16		" " "	
	19.4.16		" " "	
	20.4.16		" " " Lieut V. GORDON / KOSB + 61 O.R. Inf. attached for dug out work	
	21.4.16		" " " 1 O.R. attached sick. 20 O.R. Inf. attached.	
	22.4.16		" " " Strength 7 officers. 1 interpreter 179 O.R. attached 1 Officer 80 O.R.	
	23.4.16		" " " 1 O.R. Sick	
	24.4.16		" " " 1 O.R. rejoined.	

Army Form C. 2118.

WAR DIARY
or
INTELLIGENCE SUMMARY.
(Erase heading not required.)

1/1 West Ridings Pioneers 49 Corps

Instructions regarding War Diaries and Intelligence Summaries are contained in F. S. Regs., Part II. and the Staff Manual respectively. Title pages will be prepared in manuscript.

Place	Date	Hour	Summary of Events and Information	Remarks and references to Appendices
MAILLY-MAILLET	25.4.16		Work in area. 10 O.R.(attached) left. 25 O.R. LONDON R.E. attached for work on Huts.	
	26.4.16		2 O.R. Sw.B. attached for instruction in BANGALORE TORPEDOES. 10 O.R. attached GR's 2 Lt. H JENISON Border R. + 26 O.R. 2y attached for instruction	
	27.4.16		Work in area. 2 O.R. Sick. 1 O.R. Sick. 9 O.R. LONDON RE left.	
	28.4.16		" " "	
	29.4.16		" " " 30 O.R. 2y Sick. 2 Lt. H. JENISON + 10 O.R. 2y beyond their unit	
Sports			2 Sw.B. O.R. rejoined their unit. Strength 5 officers 1 Interpreter 750 O.R. (attached) 1 officer. 108 O.R.	
	30.4.16		Work in area	

a Rigby Major R.E.
O.C. 1/1 WR 49 Corps

29th Divisional Engineers

1/1st WEST RIDING

FIELD COMPANY R. E.

M A Y 1 9 1 6

Army Form C. 2118.

WAR DIARY
or
INTELLIGENCE SUMMARY.
(Erase heading not required.)

1/1 West Riding Ft Co RE

Place	Date	Hour	Summary of Events and Information	Remarks and references to Appendices
MAILLY- MAILLET	1.5.16		Work in area. 4 O.R. rejoined.	
	2.5.16		" " " 1 O.R. rejoined	
	3.5.16		" " "	
	4.5.16		" " "	
	5.5.16		" " " 4 O.R. Inf Sick. 16 O.R. LONDON R.E. rejoined at their unit.	
	6.5.16		" " " Strength 7 officer 180 O.R. 1 Interpreter. Attached. 1 officer 88 O.R. Capt W.G. SALE + 1 O.R. 2/Monmouth Regt attached.	
	7.5.16		Work in area. 2 O.R. rejoined.	
	8.5.16		" " "	
	9.5.16		" " " 1 O.R. Inf Sick. 2 O.R. rejoined.	
	10.5.16		" " "	
	11.5.16		" " "	
	12.5.16		" " "	
	13.5.16		" " " Strength 7 officers 1 Interpreter 184 O.R. attached 9 officer 88 O.R.	
	14.5.16		" " "	
	15.5.16		" " "	
	16.5.16		" " " 2 O.R. attached Dist H.Q.	
	17.5.16		" " " 2 O.R. Inf rejoined 1 O.R. Inf sick.	
	18.5.16		" " "	
	19.5.16		" " " Strength 7 officers. 1 Interpreter 181 O.R. attached 2 officers. 89 O.R.	
	20.5.16		" " " Sunday 2nd off. Capt W.G. SALE + 1 O.R. rejoined Regt. Lt. G.F. FOSTER. 1 O.R. 2/Monmouth R. attached	
	21.5.16		1 O.R. Sick. 1 off attached 1 O.R. sick	

Army Form C. 2118.

WAR DIARY
or
INTELLIGENCE SUMMARY. 1/1 West Riding S. & T. Corps.
(Erase heading not required.)

Instructions regarding War Diaries and Intelligence Summaries are contained in F. S. Regs., Part II. and the Staff Manual respectively. Title pages will be prepared in manuscript.

Place	Date	Hour	Summary of Events and Information	Remarks and references to Appendices
MAILLY-MAILLET	22.5.16		Work in Area. 2 O.R. Sick.	
	23.5.16		" " " 1 O.R. Sick	
	24.5.16		" " "	
	25.5.16		" " " 1 O.R. Sick. 1 O.R. Inf. Sick.	
	26.5.16		" " "	
	27.5.16		Instr " " 1 O.R. rejoined. Strength 7 officers. 1 at hospital 177 O.R. attached 2 officers 89 O.R.	
	28.5.16		Sunday Rest. 1 O.R. Sick	
	29.5.16		Work in Area 3 O.R. Inf. rejoined. 1 O.R. Inf. sick.	
	30.5.16		" " " 1 O.R. Sick. 2 O.R. rejoined.	
	31.5.16		" " " 1 O.R. Sick. 2 O.R. rejoined. 1 O.R. Inf. rejoined.	

A E Bagley Major R.E.
O.C. 1/1 W.R. F.C. R.E.

1577 Wt. W10791/1773 500,000 1/15 D. D. & L. A.D.S.S./Forms/C. 2118.

29th Divisional Engineers

1/1st WEST RIDING

FIELD COMPANY R. E.

JUNE 1916

WAR DIARY or INTELLIGENCE SUMMARY

Army Form C. 2118.

Vol 5
1/1 West Riding Fd Coy RE.

Place	Date	Hour	Summary of Events and Information	Remarks and references to Appendices
MAILLY-MAILLET	1.6.16		Work in area. 2 O.R. rejoined. 2 O.R. 2/ sick.	
	2.6.16		" " " 1 O.R. 2/ wounded.	
	3.6.16		" " " Strength 7 officers 1 in hospital 180 O.R. attached 2 officers 87 O.R.	
	4.6.16		Sunday Rest. 2 O.R. rejoined. 10 O.R. 2/ rejoined.	
	5.6.16		Work in area. 2/Lt G.F. FOSTER & 10 O.R. rejoined regt.	
	6.6.16		" in area. 1 Sapper rejoined.	
	7.6.16		" " " 3 O.R. 2/ rejoined	
	8.6.16		" " " 2/Lt T.H. SIMPSON joined unit.	
	9.6.16		" " " 2 Sappers evacuated sick	
	10.6.16		" " " Strength 8 officers 1 in hospital 181 O.R. attached 1 officer 90 O.R.	
	11.6.16		Sunday " "	
	12.6.16		" " " 1 officer 23 O.R. London Fd R.E. attached for learning work in front line	
	13.6.16		15 Sappers attached to London Fd Co. Work in area. 1 Sapper killed (shell) 15 Sappers attached under C.R.E. rejoined - now in formation received that Artillery bombardment would commence on morning 20.6.16. all work to be hurried on.	
	14.6.16		Work in area including preparing front line for Cylinders, APM's shelter, bridging forward roads, R.A. observation posts & dugouts. Heavy T.M. Bty emplacements. 18 London R.E. attached.	
	15.6.16		Work in area. 1 Sapper away sick. 3 London RE attached. Bapt. 150 animals 2 and 7 remitted Sappers joined	
	16.6.16		Work in area.	

1577 Wt.W10791/1773 500,000 1/15 D.D.&L. A.D.S.S./Forms/C. 2118.

WAR DIARY
or
INTELLIGENCE SUMMARY.
(Erase heading not required.)

Army Form C. 2118.

Instructions regarding War Diaries and Intelligence Summaries are contained in F. S. Regs., Part II. and the Staff Manual respectively. Title pages will be prepared in manuscript.

Place	Date	Hour	Summary of Events and Information	Remarks and references to Appendices
MAILLY-MAILLET	17.6.16		attached R.E.S.R. Strength 8 officers 1 interpreter 202 O.R. attached. 1 officer 42 R.S. 1 officer 90 B.R. w/ work in area	
	18.6.16		1 Sapper evacuated Sick. Information received that artillery bombardment postponed for 4 days. Forward R.E. dumps made. Tramlines from MAILLY-MAILLET-AUCHONVILLERS completed.	
	19.6.16		work in area. 1 Sapper evacuated sick - orders received showing that there would be an Artillery bombardment lasting 5 days i.e. U.V.W.X.Y. Days. Z to be day of attack	
	20.6.16		work in area	
	21.6.16		work in area	
	22.6.16		work in area	
	23.6.16		1 officer 42 O.R. R.S. rejoined.	
	23.6.16		1 officer + 20 O.R. inf. 1 officer & Co. 1 officer + 20 O.R. inf. reported their units. 1 officer evacuated Lt. RONKSLEY + Lt. MATHEWS + 5 S.O.R. went to dug outs in 88th trench for maintenance preparation of forward road bridges tramlines, water supply during bombardment in front line. 2/Lt. BALL + 2 cyclists attached to C.R.E. as orderly officer orderlies. All transport to Acheux except 4 GS. carts, 1 water cart + 4 mules during day (4 mules killed) maintenance work in line. Strength 8 officers. 1 interpreter 200 O.R.	
	24.6.16		" " Northern O.P. - direct hit on top of 5"x3" girders covered 1ft. earth. by 5.9" shell	
	25.6.16		" "	
	26.6.16		Girders under in post destroyed. New O.P. constructed 1 Sapper evacuated maintenance work bridge constructed over Broadway on AUCHONVILLERS-ENGELBELMER Road. Tee O.P. made	
	27.6.16		maintenance work. Unit affiliated to 81st Bde. Orders received. Operations postponed 48 hours	
	28.6.16			

1577 Wt. W10791/1773 500,000 1/15 D.D.&L. A.D.S.S./Forms/C. 2118.

Army Form C. 2118.

WAR DIARY
or
INTELLIGENCE SUMMARY.

(Erase heading not required.)

Place	Date	Hour	Summary of Events and Information	Remarks and references to Appendices
MAILLY-MAILLET	29.1.16		Maintenance work in line. Unit joined with 86th Bde + attached to G.O.C. 29th Division. 2 O.R. evacuated sick.	
	30.1.16		Maintenance work in line.	

Aubrey Inyo 1/2
O.C. 1/1 West Riding F.Coys.

Q29th Divisional Engineers

1/1st WEST RIDING

FIELD COMPANY R. E.

JULY 1916

CONFIDENTIAL

WAR DIARY

OF

1/1ST WEST RIDING FIELD COMPANY R.E.(T.F.)

from 1st to 31st JULY, 1916

VOLUME XV

WAR DIARY
INTELLIGENCE SUMMARY

Army Form C. 2118.

1/6 West Riding F.A.R.E.

Place	Date	Hour	Summary of Events and Information	Remarks and references to Appendices
AUCHONVILLERS Sector.	1.7.16	6.30 a.m.	Moved off from NAILLY-MAILLET to take up position in trenches preparatory to advancing to BEAUMONT HAMEL should the attack at 7.30 a.m. succeed. (Reached 20½ trench 7.30 a.m.)	
		8.10 a.m.	Orders given to stand fast as attack had not succeeded.	
		1.30 p.m.	Company distributed in sectors to clear trenches of dead & wounded. The unwounded carried stretchers for carrying stores forward were invaluable for this purpose. A lot of clearing was done. Stream found that dugouts were severely shelled with much wounded.	
		4.30 p.m.	Orders received to cover in the approach to SUNKEN ROAD in front of BEAUMONT HAMEL, erect barricades at two steps & barricade the ends. Men were taken in from clearing the trenches & engaged for this work. This work arrived at midnight, but a good deal of delay caused by the removal of dead & wounded. All men were equipped with a load of useful tools for carrying forward — picks, shovels, adzes, felling axes, hand axes, & cut saws, hand saws, hammers, heavy chisels, mauls, chisels rather small, carpenters tools, hand saws, blocks, cordage & tripods for raising water from deep wells, hooks, carried a pair of wire cutters & a pair of hedging gloves. Casualties 1 O.R. wounded. 1 O.R. joined.	Off. 8 officer 1 Lt. 198 O.R. attached 10 O.R.
			The unit remained in the trenches.	

WAR DIARY or INTELLIGENCE SUMMARY

Army Form C. 2118.

Place	Date	Hour	Summary of Events and Information	Remarks and references to Appendices
	2.7.16		During the day the Comm: trench to sunken road were deepened & widened. Light - work on sunken road. The Comm: trench covered in. M.G. emplacement made. Barricades improved. M.G. emplacements made in each. Fire steps made & improved. Dugouts made. Wires improved. Casualties night 2/3. Lieut. J.H. SIMPSON killed. 3 O.R. wounded.	
	3.7.16		Remaking & cleaning front line on August front.	
	4.7.16		Remaking & cleaning support line. Orders received in afternoon. Maintenance of water etc. Section on relief by the 4th Division. New trench between MARY REDAN & R. ANCRE reconnoitred & taped out thro' during the night by Lt. RONKSLEY & GROGAN. A line staked 18" long was used & found ideal for rapid taping. The Company picked up transport & marched into billets at MARTINSART.	
	5.7.16		New forward line 800 x long N of MARY REDAN reconnoitred & taped out same night by Lt. HOWARTH. Billet fairly shelled in MARTINSART so went moved into bivouac on the MARTINSART - ENGELBELMER road. 1 O.R. wounded.	
	6.7.16		Orders received to wire new front line N of MARY Redan. Stores carried up during afternoon & wiring done that night along front. — 2 twin screw pickets, 2 twin trench rail, apron & barbed. 3 O.R. gassed.	

WAR DIARY
or
INTELLIGENCE SUMMARY.
(Erase heading not required.)

Army Form C. 2118.

Place	Date	Hour	Summary of Events and Information	Remarks and references to Appendices
	7.7.16		Work on Bivouac. Afternoon wiring stores carried up. Night a second line of wire same as night before put up. 10* in rear of 1st Line. 4 officers 4100 men each night.	
	8.7.16		Work on Bivouac. Training METNIL - KNIGHTSBRIDGE road + bridge constructed. Night - thickening of wire done two previous nights. 1 O.R. Killed. Strength 7 officers, 1 Int. 197. O.R. attached 10.O.R.	
	9.7.16		Work on METNIL Road. 10 O.R. evacuated sick.	
	10.7.16		" " Training of wiring parties, Jacob ladder, Communic. Bde dugouts. METNIL. Commenced work on Screening ENGELBELMER - METNIL Road.	
	11.7.16		Work as on 10.7.16. 10 O.R. evacuated sick. 1 O.R. wounded. 6 O.R. joined.	
	12.7.16		Work as on 11.7.16. 1 O.R. evacuated sick.	
	13.7.16		Work as on 12.7.16.	
	14.7.16		Work as on 13.7.16. 2 sunken M.G. emplacements Commenced.	
	15.7.16		Work as on 14.7.16. Work by Coys on H on Engthening Jacob Ladder. By on M. Charles Avenue yft. Strength 7 officers. 1 Int. O.R. 199. attached 10.O.R.	
	16.7.16		Work as on 15.7.16. " " + on Charles Avenue dugouts	
	17.7.16		2/Lt R.A. CHRISTISON joined. 1 O.R. rejoined. Work as on 16.7.16. Coys B. Lengthening Jacob ladder - Charles Avenue wght 3 O.R. RDF attached for Lewis Gun. 10 O.R. RDF attached for trench list.	

WAR DIARY
or
INTELLIGENCE SUMMARY

Army Form C. 2118.

Place	Date	Hour	Summary of Events and Information	Remarks and references to Appendices
A8.	18.7.16		Work as on 17.7.16. Cas./20 Ors +4 O.Rs. or Cmm.	
	19.7.16		Work on MESNIL Road - Charles Avenue - Jacob's Ladder - Constitution Hill - Officers to have supplies in 5. Esplanade. Casualties Begin to Bosch behind our support line commenced hard interfered with by fire. Casualties 1 OR killed, 1 OR wounded. 6 OR joined.	
	20.7.16		Work as on 19.7.16. Heavy shelling on dug out work at night. Casualties 2Lt. J. HOWARTH wounded 3 OR killed, 10 OR wounded, 15 OR evacuated sick.	
	21.7.16		Work as on 20.7.16. Casualties 1 OR wounded.	
	22.7.16		Work on Mesnil Road - Brigade dug out - M.G. emplacements - Jacob's Ladder. Placed ruts rests from Blocking Conc. to new Support Line. 1 OR evacuated sick. Strength 7 officers, 1 interpreter 199 OR. attached 19 OR.	
	23.7.16		Orders rec'd to hand over to 105 Fd. C.R.E. on 24.7.16 + to proceed to LOUVENCOURT same day.	
	24.7.16		Work on Mesnil Road, M.G. emplacement + Jacob's Ladder. Took officers of 105 G.R.E. round the works. Marched off from Bienvac at 9.50 am. arrived LOUVENCOURT at 10 pm. + went into Bivouac. Orders received to entrain at DOULLENS. Notation at 2334 on 27.7.16 to join 2nd Army	
LOUVENCOURT	25.7.16		1 N.C.O. proceeded to obtain billets or cantonment. Inspection of kit etc. short march.	
"	26.7.16		Short march.	

Army Form C. 2118.

WAR DIARY
or
INTELLIGENCE SUMMARY.

(Erase heading not required.)

Instructions regarding War Diaries and Intelligence Summaries are contained in F. S. Regs., Part II. and the Staff Manual respectively. Title pages will be prepared in manuscript.

Place	Date	Hour	Summary of Events and Information	Remarks and references to Appendices
LOUVENCOURT	27.7.16		Unit marched to DOULLENS at 4.30 p.m. arrived 8 p.m. Train arrived for loading 9.30 p.m. loading completed 10.45 p.m. Train left 11.34 p.m.	
WORMHOUDT	28.7.16		Train arrived HAZEBROUCK 5 a.m. - ordered to proceed to ESQUELBEC arrived 6.45 a.m. detrained marched off 7.45 a.m. & went into billets 3½ miles E of WORMHOUDT - orders received to proceed to VLAMERTINGE on 29.7.16 & take over from 2/2 West Riding Fd Co R.E. an advance party (L.F.) going ahead.	
VLAMERTINGE	29.7.16		2 officers & 14 men went forward at 7.30 a.m. on bicycles to take over. Unit marched at 9 a.m. halted at WATOU for water + feed. Arrived 4.45 p.m. 8 O.R. attached Inf (L.F.) rejoined their unit at WORMHOUDT 2 officers + 110 R went into billets in YPRES remainder in the Huttons. Strength 7 officers 1 Br. 199 O R attached 11. O R.	
"	30.7.16		½ WR Fd Co R.E. marched out. Took over huts + stables. Cleaning + fixing up	
"	31.7.16		morning drill + inspection. afternoon fatigues & work on camp 33 O R went into billets at YPRES.	

A H Mayhoe? R.E.
O.C. 1/1 West Riding Fd Co R.E.

29th Divisional Engineers

1/1st WEST RIDING

FIELD COMPANY R. E.

AUGUST 1 9 1 6

WAR DIARY or **INTELLIGENCE SUMMARY**

1/1 West Riding F. Co. R.E.

Vol 7   Army Form C. 2118.

Place	Date	Hour	Summary of Events and Information	Remarks and references to Appendices
VLAMERTINGE	1.8.16		Work on Camp. Cellars at ECOLE & MENIN ROAD. Orders received as to making POTIJZE & surrounding farms into strong point & providing shell proof accommodation. Interpreter EMILE VANLOO joined.	
	2.8.16		Work on Camp. Lt BALL 20 O.R. 2 double tent carts proceeded to billets YPRES. Commenced work on POTIJZE as strong point. Work on heavy T.M. emplacement. Interpreter FELIX PIETREMENT left unit.	
	3.8.16		Work on Camp. POTIJZE T.M. emplacement. Camouflaging roads. 9 O.R. joined unit.	
	4.8.16		Work as on 3.8.16. 20 O.R. went into billets at YPRES	
	5.8.16		Work as on 4.8.16. Strength 7 officers 1 interpreter 209 O.R. attached 11 O.R. Lt MATHEWS to YPRES	
	6.8.16		Day parties resting. Night - work on POTIJZE T.M. Emplacement - 1 O.R. to YPRES.	
	7.8.16		Work in Camp. POTIJZE T.M. emplacement. Screening roads.	
	8.8.16		Work as on 7.8.16. Accidental water supply etc for attack by enemy about 10 p.m. Casualties YLt E.E. LOFTING joined 20 R wounded (gas) 10 R joined	
	9.8.16		Work as on 8.8.16. (1 O.R. died (gas))	
	10.8.16		" " 9.8.16.	
	11.8.16		" " 10.8.16.	
	12.8.16		" " 11.8.16. Strength 8 officers 1 interpreter 218 O.R. attached 11 O.R.	
	13.8.16		Parties Resting. Reports. Casualty 1 O.R. to c/s (evacuated)	

1/1 West Riding Field Co RE 26(T)

WAR DIARY
or
INTELLIGENCE SUMMARY.
(Erase heading not required.)

Army Form C. 2118.

Instructions regarding War Diaries and Intelligence Summaries are contained in F. S. Regs., Part II. and the Staff Manual respectively. Title pages will be prepared in manuscript.

Place	Date	Hour	Summary of Events and Information	Remarks and references to Appendices
VLAMERTINGHE	14.8.16		Work as on 13.8.16 – 3 NCOs went for course to Divisional School.	
	15.8.16		" " " 14.8.16. 1 O.R. evacuated sick.	
	16.8.16		" " " 15.8.16. 1 O.R. evacuated sick.	
	17.8.16		" " " 16.8.16	
	18.8.16		" " " 17.8.16	
	19.8.16		" " " 18.8.16. 1 O.R. evacuated sick. Strength 8 officers 1 O.R. 214	
	20.8.16		Not working. Lieut F.H. RONKSLEY sick.	
	21.8.16		Work as on 19.8.16	
	22.8.16		" " 21.8.16. 1 O.R. sick (evacuated)	
	23.8.16		" " 22.8.16. 1 O.R. evacuated sick	
	24.8.16		" " 23.8.16. Commenced work on Royal emplacements front line 104.	
			evacuated sick.	
	25.8.16		" " 24.8.16. Bases for Royal emplacements. Difficulties from experience here in the Somme. It would seem that emplacements from experience made in with are always preferable to boxes owing to the difficulty of taking up	
	26.8.16		work as on 25.8.15. Emplacements completed work started on English strong strength 7 officers 1 Inf. 211 O.R. 11 O.R. attached	
	27.8.16		work as on 26.8.16	
	28.8.16		" " 27.8.16	
	29.8.16		" " 28.8.16. + Commenced work Signal Dugout Head Qrs. 1 O.R. evacuated sick	
	30.8.16		" " 29.8.16	
	31.8.16		" " 30.8.16. Commenced work on Railway works.	

Anthony Major R.E.
O.C. 1/1 WRFCoRE

29th Divisional Engineers

—————

1/1st WEST RIDING

FIELD COMPANY R. E.

SEPTEMBER 1 9 1 6

Army Form C. 2118.

WAR DIARY
or
INTELLIGENCE SUMMARY.

(Erase heading not required.)

1/1 West Riding Ft. Tps.

Instructions regarding War Diaries and Intelligence Summaries are contained in F. S. Regs., Part II. and the Staff Manual respectively. Title pages will be prepared in manuscript.

Place	Date	Hour	Summary of Events and Information	Remarks and references to Appendices
VLAMERTINGHE and YPRES.	18.9.16	7.7	6 O.R. evacuated sick	
	19.9.16		" " 19.9.16	
	20.9.16		" " 20.9.16 Commenced work on Potijze Defences	
	21.9.16		" " 21.9.16	
	22.9.16		" " 10 O.R. evacuated sick	
	23.9.16		" " Strength 7 officers 1 R. 208 O.R. attached 11 O.R.	
	24.9.16		all forward work as usual to be back work in rear wing.	
	25.9.16		" " 23.9.16. 1 O.R. wounded	
	26.9.16		" " 25.9.16. Enfield Farm handed over to 38th Division.	
	27.9.16		" " 26.9.16. 1 O.R. evacuated sick	
	28.9.16		" " 27.9.16. 1 O.R. wounded sick	
	29.9.16		" " 28.9.16 Commenced work near Crump Farm	
	30.9.16		" " 29.9.16 Strength 7 officers 1 R. 205 O.R. attached 11 O.R.	

A E Clay Major
O.C. 1/1st West Riding Ft. Tps.

Army Form C. 2118.

1/1st West Riding F.C.R.E.

Vol 6

WAR DIARY
or
INTELLIGENCE SUMMARY.

(Erase heading not required.)

Instructions regarding War Diaries and Intelligence Summaries are contained in F. S. Regs., Part II. and the Staff Manual respectively. Title pages will be prepared in manuscript.

Place	Date	Hour	Summary of Events and Information	Remarks and references to Appendices
VLAMERTINGHE and YPRES	1.9.16		Work on Potijze strong point. English Farm. T.M. Emplacement. Railway Wood – making new trenches with Vfranen. Reclaiming old timber. Putting Bunkers in Bean Aramp. repairing wagons. Improving roads to stables. Sigrid Dugout Dead End.	
	2.9.16		Work as on 1.9.16. 1 O.R. wounded (evacuated) Strength 7 Officers 1 Sgt 210 O.R. attached 11 O.R. work on Railway wood. Remainder resting. 7 O.R. evacuated sick.	
	3.9.16		work as on 2.9.16. light work very difficult due to rain & extreme darkness	
	4.9.16		work as on 4.9.16. commenced using railway for taking up stores to Railway wood.	
	5.9.16		work as on 5.9.16	
	6.9.16		" " " " Strength 7 Officers 1 Sgt. 203 O.R. attached 11 O.R.	
	7.9.16		" " " "	
	8.9.16		" " " "	
	9.9.16		work on Railway wood remainder resting.	
	10.9.16		work as on 9.5.16	
	11.9.16		" " " "	
	12.9.16		" " " " 7 O.R. joined. 2 O.R. evacuated sick	
	13.9.16		" " " " 1 O.R. evacuated sick	
	14.9.16		" " " " Commenced Potijze Drying room.	
	15.9.16		" " " "	
	16.9.16		" " " " Strength 7 Officers 1 Sgt 207 o.r. attached 11 O.R.	
	17.9.16		Night work only on Railway wood	
	18.9.16		work as on 16.9.16. New trenches on Railway wood broken in in some cases by trench mortar bombardment. 10 O.R. rejoined 7 O.R. joined.	

29th Divisional Engineers

1/1st WEST RIDING

FIELD COMPANY R. E.

OCTOBER 1 9 1 6

WAR DIARY
INTELLIGENCE SUMMARY

1/1st West Riding Fd Co. R.E.
Vol 9

Army Form C. 2118.

Place	Date	Hour	Summary of Events and Information	Remarks and references to Appendices
VLAMERTINGHE and YPRES	1.10.16		Work on CRUMP FARM and POTIJZE defences. Two lorries out early morning in foundry Battle dump, due either to procuring of our own sand or to enemy shells on the sandbag store. 2/Lieut O.H.E BRIDGEN RE(T) joined 10R rejoined.	
	2.10.16		Work on CRUMP FARM. RAILWAY WOOD. POTIJZE defences. Orders received to move to HOUTKERQUE on 3.10.16 & to hand over work camps & billets to a Field Co. of 55th Division on relief. 2 OR wounded sick	
	3.10.16		Unit marched to HOUTKERQUE & went into billets. Handing over parties left at VLAMERTINGHE and YPRES. Orders received to entrain from PROVEN on 8th inst. for SALEUX.	
HOUTKERQUE	4.10.16		Fatigues in billets. Weather very wet. 1 Officer & 1 OR left from POPERINGHE to take over billets at new destination. Small advanced party of 1/1st West Lancashire FD CO RE arrived VLAMERTINGHE & took over camp billets & work.	
	5.10.16		Shot into work cleaning hour vehicles. Fatigues.	
	6.10.16		Inspection by Gen Sir C.G. Hunter-Weston. Return in hrs reading Compass bearings - bridging wagons & road staff. 2/Lt E.Van. Loo left. 2/Lt G. Fiebber joined.	
	7.10.16		Shot into work Inspection of kit arms etc. Packing wagons - strength 8 officers 1 2/Lt. 204 OR. Attached now	

WAR DIARY

INTELLIGENCE SUMMARY.

1/1 West Riding F.C.R.E.

Army Form C. 2118.

Place	Date	Hour	Summary of Events and Information	Remarks and references to Appendices
HOUTKERQUE	8.10.16		Marched off at 7.30 am. Arrived PROVEN 9.30 am. Commenced entrainment 11 am. Completed entrainment of unit complete 11.45 am. Train left PROVEN 1.20 pm.	
DOUARS	9.10.16		Arrived SALEUX 1.30 am. Commenced detrainment 2.30 am. Completed detrainment 3.45 am. Issued a/c'd breakfasts, marched off 5.45 am. arrived DOUARS 9.45 am. + went into billets	
DERNANCOURT	10.10.16		Marched off 9.40 am with 86th Bde. Arrived DERNANCOURT 3 pm + went into billets. 3 O.R. evacuated sick.	
	11.10.16		General fatigues cleaning up. Instrns to all officers & senior NCO's in construction of strong points. Orders received at 7.30 pm to be in readiness to move in 1 hour if necessary. All ranks instructed in construction of strongpoints. Projects for officers Bill. Orders received to march with 87th Bde + be attached to them + to march off at 3 pm on 13th for FRICOURT	
	12.10.16		5 OR joined from Base. The unit marched at 4.15 pm + went into Bivouac at FRICOURT.	
FRICOURT	13.10.16			
	14.10.16		Received orders to work under CRE XV Corps. Commenced work on erecting a Bivouac hutment camp. Staff. 8 officers 1 wt. 306 OR attached 11 OR	
	15.10.16		Work on Brigade Hutments. 1 OR evacuated sick	
	16.10.16		Work on Brigade Hutments. Artillery screens + M.G.A.C. hutmts/s. 2 OR evacuated sick	
	17.10.16		Work on huts making road from Fricourt to Montauban with 87th Bde. Orders received to be prepared to move at 2 hours notice. 1 OR evacuated sick	

Army Form C. 2118.

WAR DIARY
or
INTELLIGENCE SUMMARY.
(Erase heading not required.)

1/2 West Riding Field Co R.E.

Place	Date	Hour	Summary of Events and Information	Remarks and references to Appendices
FRICOURT	18.10.16		Work on huts. Road. Party sent to BUIRE to remove ammunition huts	
	19.10.16		Work on huts. Party to POMMIER redoubt to erect ammunition huts. Orders received to proceed on 20.10.16 to S.23.a.4.5. South of LONGUEVAL & take over from 69th Fd Coy R.E. Very wet weather	
	20.10.16		16 men proceeded to MONTAUBAN to take over R.E. Dump. Ponton. Left at Fricourt & exchanged. Unit marched to LONGUEVAL & went into dugouts with stores of 69 F.C. took over Ammunition huts at Pommier. Screens erected near Longueval Arena. 1.O.R. joined	
LONGUEVAL	21.10.16		Work with Cavalry Party on Longueval - Flers road. 1.O.R. evacuated sick. Strength 8 officers, 1 St. 202 O.R. attached 11 O.R.	
	22.10.16		Work on road. Erecting huts Pommier redoubt (complete). 4.O.R. wounded on road.	
	23.10.16		Work on road. Screening LONGUEVAL - BAZENTIN LE PETIT road.	
	24.10.16		Work on road. Screening on LONGUEVAL - BAZENTIN LE PETIT road. Getty up stores for 87th F.A. Bde. 1 O.R. wounded 2 O.R. evacuated sick	
	25.10.16		Work on road. Taking up stores for 87th F.A. Bde. 1 O.R. evacuated sick	
	26.10.16		Work on road. Taking up stores for 87th F.A. Bde. 3 O.R. evacuated sick.	
	27.10.16		Work as on 26.10.16. 1 O.R. rejoined. 1 O.R. evacuated sick.	

Army Form C. 2118.

WAR DIARY
or
INTELLIGENCE SUMMARY.
(Erase heading not required.)

1/1st West Riding F.A.Rs.

Place	Date	Hour	Summary of Events and Information	Remarks and references to Appendices
LONGUEVAL	28.10.16		Work on 27.10.16. 2 O.R. evacuated sick. Strength 8 officers. 1 N/. 191 O.R. attacked 11. O.R.	
	29.10.16		Work on road. Orders received to move to FRICOURT on 30.10.16 & hand over work & quarters etc to 2nd Australian Fd. Co.R.E.	
	30.10.16		Marched into camp at FRICOURT. Weather very wet & great difficulty in getting wagons over old trenches into camp.	
FRICOURT	31.10.16		Cleaning kit, wagons, harness, horses etc.	

A. Dawley 2nd Lt R.E.
o.c. 1/1st West Riding F.C.R.E.

29th Divisional Engineers

1/1st WEST RIDING

FIELD COMPANY R. E.

NOVEMBER 1 9 1 6

Army Form C. 2118.

VOL 10

4th West Riding Field Coy R.E.

WAR DIARY
or
INTELLIGENCE SUMMARY.
(Erase heading not required.)

Instructions regarding War Diaries and Intelligence Summaries are contained in F. S. Regs., Part II and the Staff Manual respectively. Title pages will be prepared in manuscript.

Place	Date	Hour	Summary of Events and Information	Remarks and references to Appendices
FRICOURT	1.11.16		Drill + inspection of arms equipment etc	
	2.11.16		Drill Transport marched to CORBIE Pontoon equipment left at M.M. Dump.	
	3.11.16		Orders received to be prepared to move at any moment. Sappers left at 3 p.m. in motor lorries & went into billets at DAOURS. Transport joining them there same day.	
DAOURS.	4.11.16		Cleaning up billets, clothing etc. 1 O.R. joined. 1 O.R. evacuated sick. Strength 8 officers 1 Interpreter 191 O.R. attached 11 O.R.	
	5.11.16		Marching order parades, inspection after, fire drills etc.	
	6.11.16		Commenced work on 39th 17th + 8th Divisional schools, erecting huts, making tables etc.	
	7.11.16		Work as on 6.11.16. 4 O.R. joined	
	8.11.16		Work as on 7.11.16	
	9.11.16		Work as on 8.11.16. 1 O.R. evacuated sick. 1 O.R. to Base.	
	10.11.16		Work as on 9.11.16. 2 O.R. to Base.	
	11.11.16		Work as on 10.11.16. 1 O.R. evacuated sick. 2/Lt. D.R. LYNE joined. Strength 9 officers 1 Int. 190 O.R. attached 11 O.R.	
	12.11.16		Resting. Inspection of two helmets & kits	
	13.11.16		Work as on 11.11.16 commenced work on R.A. School	
	14.11.16		Work as on 13.11.16. Wet weather that must would probably have forward on 16.11.16 & proceed to camp near TRONES WOOD	

Army Form C. 2118.

WAR DIARY
INTELLIGENCE SUMMARY.
11th Hotchkiss Field Co. R.E.

(Erase heading not required.)

Place	Date	Hour	Summary of Events and Information	Remarks and references to Appendices
DAOURS	15.11.16		Work as on 14.11.16. 4 O.R. evacuated sick.	
	16.11.16		Transport marched off at 7.30 am. 20 O.R. reported. 70 R. joined from Base. Sappers left at 8.30 am by lorries & arrived at TRONES WOOD at 4 pm.	
TRONES	17.11.16		Work on duckwalk from GINCHY to LES BOEUFS. Baths near MONTAUBAN. S.R.H.A. Bde H.Q. improvements to camp. Took over TRONES Wood dump. 2 O.R. wounded.	
	18.11.16		Work as on 17.11.16. 1 O.R. reported. Strength 9 Officers 1 W.O. 195 O.R. attached 11 O.R.	
	19.11.16		Work as on 18.11.16. 1 O.R. rejoined.	
	20.11.16		Work as on 19.11.16. Commenced work on elephant dugout for Bde H.Q. to Bde.	
	21.11.16		Work as on 20.11.16. 10 O.R. evacuated sick.	
	22.11.16		Work as on 21.11.16. 3 O.R. evacuated sick. 5 O.R. joined from Base.	
	23.11.16		Work as on 22.11.16.	
	24.11.16		Work as on 23.11.16. Commenced work on new cookhouse near GINCHY. Strength 9 Officers. 1 W.O. 197 O.R. attached 11 O.R.	
	25.11.16		Work as on 24.11.16.	
	26.11.16		Work as on 25.11.16. Commenced work on mule track from GINCHY to forward dumps.	

Army Form C. 2118.

WAR DIARY
or
INTELLIGENCE SUMMARY.

1/4 West Riding Fd Co RE

(Erase heading not required.)

Instructions regarding War Diaries and Intelligence Summaries are contained in F. S. Regs, Part II. and the Staff Manual respectively. Title pages will be prepared in manuscript.

Place	Date	Hour	Summary of Events and Information	Remarks and references to Appendices
TRONES	27.11.16		Work as on 26.11.16	
	28.11.16		Work as on 27.11.16	
	29.11.16		Work as on 28.11.16. Commenced work on new Battalion elephants at GUILLEMONT	
	30.11.16		Work as on 29.11.16.	
				A W Loy Lieut RE o.c. 1/1st West Riding Fd Co RE

29th Divisional Engineers

1/1st WEST RIDING

FIELD COMPANY R. E.

DECEMBER 1 9 1 6

Vol XI

Confidential

War Diary
of
1/2 West Riding Field Company Royal Engineers (T.F.)

From December 1st/16 to December 31st/16

(Volume 1)

Army Form C. 2118.

WAR DIARY
or
INTELLIGENCE SUMMARY.   1/4 West Riding R.E. T.F.
(Erase heading not required.)

Instructions regarding War Diaries and Intelligence Summaries are contained in F. S. Regs., Part II. and the Staff Manual respectively. Title pages will be prepared in manuscript.

Place	Date	Hour	Summary of Events and Information	Remarks and references to Appendices
TRONES WOOD	1.12.16		Work on mule track to Les Boeufs – Tea Kitchen at GINCHY, Sack drying room near MORVAL – maintenance of duck walk forward – putting up elephants for 2 battalions GUILLEMONT – Bath house near BERNAFAY WOOD – erection of new dugouts in Camp.	
	2.12.16		Work as on 1.12.16 4 OR evacuated sick Strength 9 officers 1 Lt. 197 OR attached 11 OR	
	3.12.16		Work on GUILLEMONT elephants – Carrying forward stores for drying room. Took over French 9th A.C. RE Park + hut stores round	
	4.12.16		Work as on 2.12.16	
	5.12.16		Work as on 4.12.16 1 OR joined	
	6.12.16		Work as on 5.12.16 drying room completed	
	7.12.16		Work as on 6.12.16	
	8.12.16		Work as on 7.12.16. Night defences drawn of 2 strong points near MORVAL. 3 OR evacuated sick + one joined.	
	9.12.16		Work as on 8.12.16. Reg[t]l – further work on strong points – 2 Lieut G.W. BALL struck off strength from 3.11.16 Strength 8 officers 1 int 197 OR attached 11 OR	
	10.12.16		Completing Tea Kitchen. Making Cookery road into camp. Orders received to march to	

Army Form C. 2118.

WAR DIARY
or
INTELLIGENCE SUMMARY.

(Erase heading not required.) 1/ West Riding Field Co R.E.

Instructions regarding War Diaries and Intelligence Summaries are contained in F. S. Regs., Part II. and the Staff Manual respectively. Title pages will be prepared in manuscript.

Place	Date	Hour	Summary of Events and Information	Remarks and references to Appendices
TRONES	10.12.16 (cont)		CITADEL Camp on 11.12.16 on relief by 84th Field Co R.E. To march to MERICOURT L'ABBÉ on 12.12.16 & to entrain there with 88 & 1 Bde on 14.12.16.	
"	11.12.16		Unit marched to CITADEL Camp & went into camp.	
CITADEL	12.12.16		Unit marched to MERICOURT-L'ABBÉ & went into billets.	
MERICOURT	13.12.16		Pontoons & trestles taken to DAOURS & left there. General fatigues	
	14.12.16		Transport proceeded by road to DREVIL-lès-MOLLIENS (28½ miles) started 7.20 am arrived 5.30 p.m. Sappers entrained EDGEHILL at 4 p.m., detrained at LONG PRÉ at 8 p.m. then marched to DREVIL, arriving 1.30 am 15.12.16	
DREVIL-lès-MOLLIENS	15.12.16		Cleaning billets, billet yards & roads in front. Making latrines etc. B.O.R joined	
	16.12.16		Inspection & checking of kits after the march. Cleaning up village generally. Strength 8 officers, 1 Inft. 305 O.R. attached 11 O.R.	
	17.12.16		Orders received to proceed to MOLLIENS-VIDAME - party sent to take over billets	
	18.12.16		Marched to MOLLIENS-VIDAME & went into billets in morning. Cleaning up billets, putting in latrines etc. afternoon.	
MOLLIENS-VIDAME	19.12.16		Squad Drill all ranks. Rifle exercises, inspection kit & billets. Cleaning harness & chaffing foot carts, cleaning.	

WAR DIARY
or
INTELLIGENCE SUMMARY

Army Form C. 2118.

1/1st West Riding Fd. C.R.E.

Place	Date	Hour	Summary of Events and Information	Remarks and references to Appendices
MOLLIENS-VIDAME	20.12.16		Work as on 19.12.16. Orders received for 2 sections to proceed to PONT REMY to take over work from 15th Field Co. R.E.	
	21.12.16		Work as on 20.11.16. Special instruction parade for all NCOs. Capt. LANGLEY proceeded to PONT REMY to take over. 2 O.R. evacuated sick.	
	22.12.16		3 & 4 sections proceeded by march route to PONT-REMY.	
	23.12.16		Work as on 22.12.16. Squad Drill, Rifle Inspection, Kit inspection, fatigues. MOLLIENS-VIDAME.	
	24.12.16		Squad Drill, Musketry, cleaning wagons, fatigues. Capt Langley returned.	
	25.12.16		Major A. E. Bagley left unit to report to R.E. School of Instruction G.H.Q. Troops. Inspection Parade. Captain J.M. Langley took over command. 2 O.R. evacuated sick.	
	26.12.16		Physical drill, musketry, route march. Received orders for remainder of Coy to proceed Pont Remy.	
	27.12.16		No 1 & 2 sections left Molliens Vidame 10AM arrived Pont Remy 4PM.	
Pont Remy	28.12.16		No 1 & 2 sections squad drill, cleaning wagons, fatigues. No 3 & 4 work on South Army Musketry Camp.	
	29.12.16		No 1 & 2 sections squad drill, musketry, lecture on trato by Lt Loftus. No 3 & 4 sections on works.	
	30.12.16		No 1 & 2 " " " " . Lecture storing tools, bases, no 3 & 4 " " .	
	31.12.16		Strength 10 off, 1 interpreter, 199 O.R. 11 attached. Casualties 1 O.R. evacuated sick. Inspection arms, equipment, gas helmets, ammunition. No 3 & 4 sections on works.	

J M Blagley Capt R.E.
O.C. 1/1st W.R. Fd. Co. R.E.
29th Division.

COVER FOR A.F.C. 2118.

Vol 12

CONFIDENTIAL.

WAR DIARY OF

455ᵀᴴ (W. Riding) F'LD COY R.E.

FROM 1ˢᵗ JANUARY 1917.

TO 31ˢᵗ JANUARY 1917.

VOLUME I

WAR DIARY
or
INTELLIGENCE SUMMARY.
(Erase heading not required.)

Army Form C. 2118.

1/0 1st W.R. Sdf. Co. R.E. (T)

Place	Date	Hour	Summary of Events and Information	Remarks and references to Appendices
Port Regis	1.1.19		Squad Drill. Rifle exercises. Billet inspection, lecture on Esprit de Corps by O.C. & gun drill. No 3 & 4 sections on works for South Army Musketry Camp.	
"	2.1.19		Squad Drill Musketry. Lecture on Trench feet for Nos 1 & 2 Sections. No 3 & 4 sections on Works as above. Casualties. 1 O.R. proceeded to Base for release for munitions.	
"	3.1.19		Squad Drill. Rifle exercises. Lecture on Discipline. Casualties. 1 O.R. joined from Base.	
"	4.1.19		Squad Drill. Musketry. Lecture & practical demonstration on rapid wiring. 2nd Lt. E.H. Le Bridgeman proceeded to 4th Army Infantry School for course. No 1 & 2 sections on Works for South Army Musketry Camp. No 3 & 4 " "	
"	5.1.19		Squad drill, rifle exercises, lecture on Trench feet. No 1 & 2 sections on works as above. No 3 & 4 Squad Drill. Musketry lecture firing strongpoints. Sergt. Officer & 1 interpreter 1, O.R. 205. Started 11. Unit moved back to Mulieux Vidame, moved off 10 AM arrived Mulieux Vidame 4 PM	
"	6.1.19			
"	7.1.19		Casualties. 6 O.R. joined from Base.	
Mulieux Vidame	8.1.19		Coy Drill. fatigues. Orders received to proceed to Daours on 9th for Huntingdon course.	

Army Form C. 2118.

WAR DIARY
or
INTELLIGENCE SUMMARY.
(Erase heading not required.)

1/ & R. Field Co. R.E.

Instructions regarding War Diaries and Intelligence Summaries are contained in F.S. Regs., Part II. and the Staff Manual respectively. Title pages will be prepared in manuscript.

Place	Date	Hour	Summary of Events and Information	Remarks and references to Appendices
Molliens Vidame	9.1.19		Dismounted ranks marched to Prouzel & proceeded by lorries to Daours. Left Molliens Vidame 7.30 AM, arrived Prouzel 10.30 AM, arrived Daours 1. PM. Mounted section moved off 9.30, proceeded by road to Corbie, arrived Corbie 4. PM	
DAOURS.	10.1.19		Pontoon Drill on Somme, 8.30 to 12.30 & 12.30 to 4.30, Casualties 3 O.R. rejoined from Base	from Base
"	11.1.19		Work as on 10.1.19. Casualties 2 O.R. evacuated sick	
"	12.1.19		All dismounted ranks pontooning under Lieut O.C. Casualties 1 O.R. evacuated sick	
"	13.1.19		All dismounted ranks proceeded to Corbie on Battrix funds, all cycles cleaned & handed in to No 4 pontoon park. Strength 7 off., 1 interpreter, 211 O.R. attached 11.	
	14.1.19		Unit marched to Meaulte joining mounted section at Corbie, marched off 9 AM. arr. Meaulte 3. PM. Casualties Interpreter & Serjeaker proceeded to A.H.Q.	
Meaulte	15.1.19		Unit marched off at 9 AM & proceeded by road to Trones Wood East arriving 1. PM. Took over from 93rd Field Co. R.E.	
Trones Wood	16.1.19		Fatigues - unpacking waggons, clearing camp. Casualties 1 O.R. evacuated sick	
"	17.1.19		Work on Guillemont camp, trenches etc.	
"	18.1.19		Erecting camouflage. Other work as on 17th. 16 Ridge London University O.T.C. attached	
"	19.1.19		Work as on 18th.	

1577 Wt. W10791/1773 500,000 1/15 D.D. & L. A.D.S.S./Forms/C. 2118.

WAR DIARY or INTELLIGENCE SUMMARY

Army Form C. 2118.

1/. W.R. Fd. C. R.E.

Place	Date	Hour	Summary of Events and Information	Remarks and references to Appendices
Trones Wood	20.1.17		Erecting camouflage, making & hutting Guillemont Camp. strength Off 7. O.R. 210. attached 11.	
"	21.1.17		Having Nos 1 & 2 sections hutting, hutmise, etc at Guillemont; Nos 2 & 3 sections erecting elephants in camp, all sections night work, informing frontline. Casualties 1 O.R. wounded.	
"	22.1.17		Coy arrived back to camp early morning & rested half day. Worked on Guillemont Camp improving the huts &c – casualties 1 O.R. Capt: B.T. WILSON joined & took over Command of Coy.	
"	23.1.17		Work on GUILLEMONT CAMP and erecting new elephants in camp – preparing barbed wire Concertina entanglements – Casualties 1 O.R. evacuated sick.	
"	24.1.17		Work during morning as on 23.1.17. All sappers night work wiring front-line with knife-rest entanglements. Casualties 2 O.R. evac'd sick.	
"	25.1.17		Sappers rested till 13.00 and work in afternoon as on 23.1.17 received W.O. letter No 9/Engineers/7611 (A.G.7) of 6/1/17 notifying new title of Coy, viz: 455th (W. Riding) Fd. Coy from 1.2.17	

Army Form C. 2118.

WAR DIARY
or
INTELLIGENCE SUMMARY.
(Erase heading not required.)

1/0 W.R. Field Co. R.E.

Place	Date	Hour	Summary of Events and Information	Remarks and references to Appendices
Trones	26.1.17		Work as on 23.1.17	
"	27.1.17		Work as on 26.1.17 and erected elephants for 87th Field Ambulance A.D.S at FLANK AVENUE. Strength 8 Off. 206. O.R. 11 attached	
"	28.1.17		Work as on 23.1.17 and making wiring frames until 15.00.	
"	29.1.17		2 Off: and 32 O.R proceeded to front line to wire during the night. Night party resting until 13.00. Others worked as on 23.1.17 Casualties 1 O.R killed 4 O.R wounded 5 O.R evacuated sick. 2 Off: and 32 O.R and 10 Drivers (as carrying party) proceeded to front line and carried on as per previous night.	
"	30.1.17		Night party resting. 4 Off: and 40 O.R proceeded to front-line and carried on wiring. Casualties II LT: R.L.R GROGAN killed, 1 O.R wounded	
"	31.1.17		Night party resting. Others worked as on 23.1.17 - 2nd Lieut GROGAN buried at CITRONT cemetery 3 P.M.	

Brinton
Major R.E.
O.C. 1/0 W.R Field Co R.E.

Vol 13

Confidential

War Diary

of

455 (West Riding) Field Co Royal Engineers (T)

From 1/2/17 to 28/2/17

Volume I

WAR DIARY
or
INTELLIGENCE SUMMARY.

Army Form C. 2118.

455th (H.R. Army) Field Coy R.E.

Place	Date	Hour	Summary of Events and Information	Remarks and references to Appendices
TRONES WOOD S.30.A Central	Feb 1st	—	Work proceeded in GUILLEMONT camp of which both huts are lined except its Officers mess consisting in its hasty to highest mining in N 36 C. Machining the placing of Figs and Pipe centrelines — There were 14 sick — Ambition of mining hanover & pill pipe by day met in BERTHA TRACE proceeded at limit — There appear within the RE in GUILLEMONT CAMP MOBILE BRIGADE in washing & paint Service — LELLE relieved him Cpl Dobson thinking the mining section working on the night of the 30th/31st in their attempt mad in spite of Rifle shelling. Salvage of CGS hours GUILLEMONT Continued. Successful night mining in N 36 C by Liouts LINE and CHRISTIAN including reconnaissance Brigade.	
	Feb 2nd		Work in Guillemont camp right camp for practically complete — all elephants except one bounded — Mining hanover & pill pipe continued — German dug out hanover reamined Rd by Cpl Maxfield — Dug dry mt TIG & Du measured up — Mining section 46, 67th 87th Brigade all at work at TII D, TIIC & UIC continued respectively — 2Lieut MATHEWS 1st RDF joined 85th B Mining Section. This day he took — work in camp Journey by the Unit Elephants to 67th Br F.A. Sent to FRANK AVENUE — Driver BUXTON handed at CHRIST CURCH	

WAR DIARY or INTELLIGENCE SUMMARY

Army Form C. 2118.

Place	Date	Hour	Summary of Events and Information	Remarks and references to Appendices
TRONES WOOD	Feb 3rd		Work proceeding as usual – GUILLEMONT ROAD finishing up 3rd Relief – Party detailed for the dug-outs at TIZA 59, 2 relief – 8 each to live at site of work – Experiment with ammunit in burning ground in dugouts beneficial – Successful – 3 no Ammunit in an angle bite into 18" deep one per yard – FLANK MENUS. 87th Fy Pk blew elephants AT159 – Salvage of 2 T.M.s by Capt Mayden continued. Installation in Construction of Footbridges Continued to the B[n] lines in GUILLEMONT Camp – Reconnaissance FLANK AVENUE stretchers met by Major CHRISTISON – keep to avoid the own Artillery – B[n] dugout TIZA 59 started by 258th Tunnelling Co continues by the Co[y] – Two parties for hutments began ground with Appendices proceeded to TIZA 59 for hut at Vaux Ceding heart – Support was garnished field. Strength 7 African 19 ors CE 11 attached, 1 or wounded.	
TRONES WOOD	Feb 4th		Divr Boot received Military Medal for Gallantry during the mining operation on the night of the 29th/30th. Work proceeded as on 3rd Feb. Major Manit 53rd Field Co 20th Division arrived to inspect work in progress – Conference GPS J" hut in Trench Area. Seven hot. 1 or evacuated sick.	

WAR DIARY
INTELLIGENCE SUMMARY

Place	Date	Hour	Summary of Events and Information	Remarks and references to Appendices
Trenches Wood	Feb 5th		Work on standing patrols – CRE visited camp – Attempt by enemy to link up with the new mi of the Cantle Stellt – Punitive bombardment by Artie the work of which was accomplished without incident – Lt Stapell returned sick from C.C.M.S Carrot Avenue – Pte Lewis Armourers Regimentnt in this unit was killed on morning of the 5th inst – Buried near Mervel – Les Boeufs between Brick & Plank Avenue. Grave marked with his name – Govt Inspector Br MR T12 A 59 4" array of chambridged in 2 days 6' only removed to the Bank – T.Mortars Bosch 19,6 2 successfully silenced – Visited Somme Rd TIO A TIOE with CRE – Brigadier new drunk walk at Lie the Granary near this Hd Cavalry, hard up the line at night with Col. Bosch-walk recommended for work tomorrow. Only 68st Battalion.	
	Feb 6th		Breakfasten at lie shop started and hogged out. Carried up some stones in 60th. Project Camp to level Trench Army. By attacked carrier. Preparations for more Shared an map to Lieut Day. 83rd Field Co. the O.C. transferred to Rifle an actual mechanic. Return of Cpl Brown & 15 O.R. from Br MR Depot at TRAOSQ. Topotaii handed over to 5 N.Z.O's. Visited Carrières Carriage Corner.	

Army Form C. 2118.

WAR DIARY
or
INTELLIGENCE SUMMARY.
(Erase heading not required.)

Instructions regarding War Diaries and Intelligence Summaries are contained in F. S. Regs., Part II. and the Staff Manual respectively. Title pages will be prepared in manuscript.

Place	Date	Hour	Summary of Events and Information	Remarks and references to Appendices
TRAVEL WARD	7th		Moved this day to HEILLY. Sappers in motor lorries. Transport by road.	
HEILLY.	8th		Billet with Officer Mess. Billet 26 to Tillers O.C. Coy. Work on No 36. 38. C.S.S. Sgt Huning Section to RATIN VILLE. Visited Bois Escadanaine. Two sections at work in hospitals one going into baths, cleaning camp etc.	
	9th		Work in hospitals continued. CAE arrived HEILLY from BERNAFAY RAINNEUILLE markings.	
	10th		Work on Wells to 9th. Visited Dugouts with CAE in afternoon. 2/Lieut BRIDGEN returned from Army School FELIXSTOWE. Took over dump material from CAE's Mess. Strength 7 Officers 192 O.R. 11 attached. Captain LANGLEY with from ROUEN.	
	11th		Church Parade 9.30. CAE parade Military Medal driver POTT. Football match afternoon v. Kent Bristol R.E. No Riding run by S-2 Scouts	

Army Form C. 2118.

WAR DIARY
or
INTELLIGENCE SUMMARY.
(Erase heading not required.)

Instructions regarding War Diaries and Intelligence Summaries are contained in F. S. Regs., Part II. and the Staff Manual respectively. Title pages will be prepared in manuscript.

Place	Date	Hour	Summary of Events and Information	Remarks and references to Appendices
HEILLY	12th		Hospital work on his hospitals continues. No 36 C.C.S. OC tells me that No 36 are moving and that No36 will occupy his camp – i. that no men took in No 38. Lieuts Loftus and Stone to Amiens with instruction and CO Everyday in state.	
	13th		Work on No 36 C.C.S. to shutdown. Work as usual. Inspected Mounted section in detail. Lieut CHRISTISON on leave to Paris	
	14th		Work continued on C.C.S. 36 and 38. Gun huts (2) being erected for Divn Gas Officer.	
	15th		Captain LANGLET returned from leave. Work as usual.	
	16th		Lieut Christison returned from Paris – Work as usual.	
	17th		Small bridge over the ANCRE in the village just SW of The Corps Baths erected by parties – Visit of the R.E. Band to HEILLY. – Drivers detachment taken to HEILLY with Lieutenant MATHEWS RE. – Work on CCS continued. Fascine brought in from LA HOUSSOYE. Work on baths at RIBEMONT-VILLE completed.	

Army Form C. 2118.

WAR DIARY
or
INTELLIGENCE SUMMARY.
(Erase heading not required.)

Place	Date	Hour	Summary of Events and Information	Remarks and references to Appendices
HEILLY	18th		O.C. Coy to Division HQrs AARON HEAD CAMP to arrange billets for mining section in CORBIE. Advance party 21st Light rSpers to proceed to CORBIES. CATACOMBS stations at MANSER CAMP. 2 O.R. evacuated sick.	
MANSER CAMP	19th		Coy marched to MANSER CAMP. Coy. waited loop siding to entrain about Employed by Field Co Sappers there. Coy left HEILLY at 0800 arrived Manser Camp 1330.	
CORBIES CATACOMBS	20th		Coy moved CORBIES CATACOMBS at 1230. Transport at WEDGE WOOD with No 2 section. Handing over arrangements by 17th Division RE yielded indifferent. No. 1 section and HQ in the CATACOMBS No 2, 3 sections in cellars. 60th Mining Section HAIE WOOD 67th Mining Section MAMETZ WOOD and 88th Mining Section HAIE WOOD pard. Immediate work started on clearing falls in the CATACOMBS & attending to the main air shaft.	

1577 Wt.W10791/1773 500,000 1/15 D. D. & L. A.D.S.S./Forms/C. 2118.

Army Form C. 2118.

WAR DIARY
or
INTELLIGENCE SUMMARY.
(Erase heading not required.)

Instructions regarding War Diaries and Intelligence Summaries are contained in F. S. Regs., Part II. and the Staff Manual respectively. Title pages will be prepared in manuscript.

Place	Date	Hour	Summary of Events and Information	Remarks and references to Appendices
COMBLES	21st		No 1 Section ypening Duckwalk out of HAIE WOOD. No 2 section installed huts and started clearing air shaft with it. No 3 section building sleeping accommodation above tunnel for Officers as the catacombs are unhealthy, also clearing away rung & putting down Duckwalk at the entrance to CATACOMBS. – Lieut. CHRISTISON reconnoitred OP. SAILLISEL CH. Various reconnaissances initiated of dug outs to be put to CRE – CO. Reconnoitred duckwalks so far as the CHATEAU. Took on HAIE WOOD DUMP. Visited CRE at ARROW HEAD COPSE in the evening. 2 OR. evacuated sick.	
	22nd		5 OR. joined from Base. Reconnoitred to BAPAUME-PERONNE road with CRE. Visited Left Brigade HQ. Work of sections continues as stated on 21st. Two sections of 93rd Field Co RE and York and Lancs Pioneers at work on Duckwalks, Dugouts and tunneling.	

Place	Date	Hour	Summary of Events and Information	Remarks and references to Appendices
CAMBLES	23rd		Lieut Mathews reconnoitred front line from U8D06 to U14B39 for laying a tape line for troops to form up on for attack. OC reconnoitred position of barricade at U8C6.5 across BAPAUME - PERONNE road. Also duck board switch N. of the CHATEAU grounds & 2 bayonets - Milly morning very useful for this work. — No 2 section & 87th Mnr/Coy carried up materials for camouflaging the road at this point. CO practiced Bgde HQs & continued orders of barricade, switch to dispersal trench from barricade to front line. Night work 100 infantry carrying duck boards from withered head dump South COPSE to switch. 87th r 88th Mnr Coy erected barricade across road as ordered. No 3 section carried on building one portion of which was occupied. No 1 section carried on repair of duck boards March discipline of the unit commended by XIV Corps & was not to troops in manner.	

WAR DIARY
or
INTELLIGENCE SUMMARY

Army Form C. 2118.

(Erase heading not required.)

Place	Date	Hour	Summary of Events and Information	Remarks and references to Appendices
COMBLES	24th		Slight frost at night colder + clearer in the morning — 88th minira digging C.T. East of BAPAUME - PERONNE road — No 2 section camouflage + laying of duckboards in shifts under Lieut MATHEWS. No1 section No 3 section on leave. No 2 section HARDECOURT CAMP and improving section on leave. Night work — 87th, 88th minira buttressing the barricade. HEDGE WOOD. Night work — 87th, 88th minira buttressing the barricade. Lieut OTTRASTISON shrinking out duckboards along the shift from 200 x W. of the CHATEAU SP. to the barricade. 100 W. of CHEESE SUPPORT. OC reconnoitred CHEESE support to the North Apex bomb to bombs method U8c88 with lick running back to barricade at U8c65. Field left flank of attack Strength Officers 7 OR. 169. 1 OR hammered 15 57th (London) FSTU RE	
	25th		Very misty morning — No2 section and 2Lieut Mathews continued levelling duckboard shift. No1 section half day on duck boards. No 3 section half day hauling retails hench with CRE — Night work — Saw Pigot at Lappage HQ — No1 section finished duck board stretch to barricade. No2 section finished camouflage, prepared lick to wiring during with bombite steps — Section bombs placed at U8.3 . U8.2 . U8.1.	

Army Form C. 2118.

WAR DIARY
or
INTELLIGENCE SUMMARY.
(Erase heading not required.)

Instructions regarding War Diaries and Intelligence Summaries are contained in F.S. Regs., Part II. and the Staff Manual respectively. Title pages will be prepared in manuscript.

Place	Date	Hour	Summary of Events and Information	Remarks and references to Appendices
COMBLES	25th		U.14.9, U.14.8 & one in U.14.7. Fire was opened to the enemy. No 3 section dug. Wired trenches the W. end of the C.T. running East from the dug. There was considerable artillery activity on both sides barricade to the firing line. There was considerable artillery activity on both sides at dusk. Quiet later, a few rifle shots - Gas shell fired into the valleys by Gers. Evacuated sick. Hostile Barrage opened at 1600	
	26th		Quiet morning - no work before 1300 hours - O.C. Coy. went out with Lieut. MATTHEWS to recce right flank of the impending attack at 0230, which was found with some difficulty and felt in the bombing front at U.14.B.82 - Return was much at dawn - Hostile Barrage at 1800 - Lieut. LYNE got the wiring dumps all ready for laying the left flank of the attack of incasshi - Starting rifles completed CATHCART'S air shaft carrying placed in position. Night work, placing of Jute line tapes for attack morning of 28th - This was done by Lieut. MATHEWS and O.C. Coy. starting from COMBLES at 1800 and returning at	
	27th		the same hour following morning - The whole line of attack was traversed six direction tapes put out and we laying up tape - Tape was laid from the bombing post on the right to the dump in U.14.7, which was other wise not linked up	

1577 Wt.W10791/1773 500,000 1/15 D. D. & L. A.D.S.S./Forms/C. 2118.

WAR DIARY
or
INTELLIGENCE SUMMARY.
(Erase heading not required.)

Army Form C. 2118.

Place	Date	Hour	Summary of Events and Information	Remarks and references to Appendices
CAMBRES	29th Cut.		No hostile barrage this day. Duck walk laid light but burries up to the hut were prepared, half used and properly camouflaged. Line at U6C 94. The burries were supplied, half used and properly camouflaged to this house at U6D18	
	28th		Misty morning. CHATEAU duck walk repaired in the morning from Battereur yard to this house at U6D18. The attack took place at 0515 and was successful. The left flank was successfully moved as arranged by LIEUT LINE's (No 4) section with Corporal Brown. LIEUT BADGERS section (No 3) was in support — 120 yards accomplished concealment B.W. with supporting rifle in half also knife roll 30 No. LIEUT LINE wounded (with grenade) this the shoulder. Germans very quiet, only anxious at first only the noise made by the carrying party — Very dark at 0300 good light before them. Rgts informed at the retreat of progress made — Gen. Williams sick Private Mayor wounded. Reports wages at hint, but situation quite clear about 2200 before we went to bivi. No.3 etc section harassed the CHATEAU duckwalk from the Battereurs. Reinforced boys the Motor store during the morning & repaired. damage caused by shell fire. Battalion. Major R.E. OC 45th (W. Riding) Free TCo.	

CONFIDENTIAL.

WAR DIARY

OF

455th (West Riding) Field Co.,R.E.

From 1st March, 1917 To 31st March, 1917

(VOLUME I)

WAR DIARY
or
INTELLIGENCE SUMMARY

Army Form C. 2118.

ASS/MorRudry/7thACB

Place	Date	Hour	Summary of Events and Information	Remarks and references to Appendices
COMBLES	March 1st		No 3 in section who opp light wing — No 2 section continued work in the air chaft at the CATACOMBS in the morning. Night work wiring the lights. C.T. Night work wiring the lights. C.T. at V8.D.5.D. chg by the Monmouth Previous — Party in Wham No 2 section and Lieut. MATHEWS, 5D or. Kent F.C. carrying under Lieut BUCKLEY and BOYCE, 19 or. Moving skeletons under Lieut JAMES NFZD — Scheme worked out in new book 2 how of booked F.W. obstacles 200x — Tape hitch laid to carrying party lights up L side of work — this is invaluable. Troops picked up + chiid — Bombing in PH22 trench started a brisk barrage at 1030, but everybody was in a trench at the time and no casualties were suffered — Germans evidently not very apprehensive + but comparable to. There he had to contend with in the LEFT DIVISION of the Corps in January. No Minenwerfer — slight M.G. fire some sniping before the work blew up with the barrage. Beautiful moon ideal conditions for wiring — No2 section much Knit up's in the afternoon in our Mynuid just W. of the took up of the CHEESE SUPPORT SWITCH	

WAR DIARY
or
INTELLIGENCE SUMMARY

Army Form C. 2118.

Place	Date	Hour	Summary of Events and Information	Remarks and references to Appendices
CONTAI̅S BRINCOURT	March 2nd 3rd		Morning No 3 & 4 sections repairing CHATEAU BUCKWORK and CHEETHA SUPPORT SWITCH as far as the top of the hill to the N.E. — No 2 section pushing — No 1 section repairing — No 1 section preparing 36 knife rests in the afternoon. Orders received for mining the front of POTSDAM 300–350x at 12 noon. Polls No 2, 3 sections, 40 OR KENT FE, 66th & 68th Miners (40 OR + 2 Officers.) LIEUT MATTHEWS R/LIEUT BUCKLEY were R.E. (W.R.) (KENT.) subalterns in charge — Work on POTSDAM accomplished also the mining of the C.T. on the S. as far as the German wire in front of PARZ TRENCH for about 100x. Seventy KR & knife rests remainder double row of barbed F.W. — Bosche has been vigilant & corners of the duckboard shifted and hit 5x of the KENT F.E. who were carrying — all seriously wounded. W.Riding Lot CO's nobody killed + 2 OR wounded. Found Colonel Brown's body of the Monmouthshire Fusion, who has sniped opposite POTSDAM also a wounded R.D.F. who had been lying out 3 days — Sgt him to the dressing station. Reconnoitred Bombing Post to the S. in PARZ TRENCH which is to be held at least. Clear moon at night many snipers misty but steady wind keeping & working — our artillery firing very short. Officer shot & POTSDAM. W.R.

WAR DIARY
INTELLIGENCE SUMMARY
(Erase heading not required.)

Army Form C. 2118.

Place	Date	Hour	Summary of Events and Information	Remarks and references to Appendices
CORBIES	March 3rd		No 2 . 3 section naking offic twing – No 4 section repairing duckwalk thro' the CHATEAU – Preparation for march – Sapper Stoveley trained in CORBIES MILITARY CEMETERY MANNERS MUD ROAD – Mining Section R.E. 87 AB to march with no arms or tools to MÉAULTE	
MÉAULTE	March 4th		Section marched to WEDGE WOOD exit independently so to avoid long range shelling at LEUZE WOOD – Formed up and marched thro' GUILLEMONT about 1000 . MÉAULTE old billets by 1200 – Snowing at night – wagons got ready for the pull out in the morning.	
HEILLY	March 5th		Marched at 0945 to HEILLY, which was reached at 1200 . Scattered billets in the village. Scout branch – Officers room No 24 – Excellent orderly room. Parade for truths at 1100 and 1400 .	
"	March 6th			
"	7th		Coy parade for company drill light musketry etc at 0900 . 1015 Two sections repairing river bank to prevent inundation, has sections clearing out orchard below CHATEAU to make stable for 12 horses. Afternoon 1330 to 1630 Work Company completed work on preventing inundation . Sandbag wall needed to complete – Coys. party at night	

WAR DIARY
or
INTELLIGENCE SUMMARY

Army Form C. 2118.

(Erase heading not required.)

Instructions regarding War Diaries and Intelligence Summaries are contained in F.S. Regs., Part II. and the Staff Manual respectively. Title pages will be prepared in manuscript.

Place	Date	Hour	Summary of Events and Information	Remarks and references to Appendices
HENCY	8th		Section paraded in billets to check Officers C.S.M. of kit and look into the state of the men generally — 10.45 clean linens and continue look on the stable archway. 11.00 Coy. parade for Coy drill. — C.M.E. presented notifying made to — 476 OSD Corporal ARTHUR BROWN. 15.45 – 16.45 clean wagons & stable archway. Coy 2	
	9th		Section — Snow during day with spells of sunshine. Noy section to stoves to set postern & turths. No. 1, 2, 3 section drill hard sound drill light marching order 9 – 10 — 10.45 – 11.45 Fatigues washing wagons & cleaning out stable nob-nay. – 14.00 – 16.00 Inspecting marching order parade in billets. Old & snow	
	10th		Marching order parade with transport at 10.00 till 12.00 – Did various manoeuvres calisthenicly. – 13.30 – 17.00 No 3 & 4 slipped the look in the Barn on the Avenue left track 2nd up Stream from HEULY mill. No 1 & 2 sections cleaning wagons — Capts BROWN and RODGERS to Divisional Bombing school. Drizzling jam afternoon lunch hours.	

WAR DIARY
or
INTELLIGENCE SUMMARY.

Army Form C. 2118.

Place	Date	Hour	Summary of Events and Information	Remarks and references to Appendices
HELLY	11th		Mild weather continues. Inspection of kits in the morning – One section M Aubrey with one section Hunt F.E. under 2/Lieut. BADGEN were employed on the Jam work on the R. ANCRE 250x above the mile left bank – In the afternoon the whole company was employed & finished the 1st + 2nd line temps. Conference of COs with CRE at lunch.	
	12th		Practice Parade. On Inspection by GOC Division at 0900 – Practiced march past. Fire between BUIRE and ROBERMONT – Intensive digging for a light strong point seemed successful – 57 men took out 75×of ditch 3'×2' in 1½ hour = 23 C.F. per hour per man = 18½ C.F. per man hour – Covered bag some check in parts – Took out haversack which + coats – Reinforcement 10 drivers & sappers – Removed 3 charges & 2.D. mines. Arranged with the demonstration with Bangalore torpedo – 18' long – Mounted section done well. Some shower + overcast. Glass high.	
	13th		Inspection of all three field companies by GOC at 0930. Companies marched past.	

WAR DIARY
or
INTELLIGENCE SUMMARY.
(Erase heading not required.)

Army Form C. 2118.

Place	Date	Hour	Summary of Events and Information	Remarks and references to Appendices
HENLY	13th		after the General Salute – after march past & dividing of unit – Mr Riding Fired to died standard string point with millimetre defects 1 man really 2 men digging 2' rounds – Also blew up a Bangalore torpedo 1½" piping three 12' of thick wire home made explosion – C.O. will pleased with inspection.	
	14th		Two sections under Lieut CHRISTENSEN battle bridging at BURE – No 2 & B sections drill – Cleaning wagons – Marking out standards string point – O.C. Coy & Lieut LEFEVRE on leave to PARIS – Morrilès section ¾ clock work exercising horses and road work	
	15th		No 2, 3 sections battle bridging – No 1-4 Wagon – string points – drill	
	16th		Whole Coy to BURE for practice in rapid wiring under Lieut CHRISTENSEN – not satisfactorily done – visit of C.R.E, who ordered further practice	
	17th		Morning – lectured in route march HENLY – FRANC VILLERS – BONNAY – HENLY. Afternoon sections to HENLY Cross to 2/Lieut DR.LYNE Military Cross to 2/Lieut DR.LYNE for gallantry when hiving at LE TRANSLOY and SAILLY-SAILLISEL – Italian Silva for military valour (sic) Major BT.WILSON – Rapid wiring by sections much improved – C.O. and 2/Lieut LeFèvre returned from Paris leave	

Army Form C. 2118.

WAR DIARY
or
INTELLIGENCE SUMMARY.
(Erase heading not required.)

Instructions regarding War Diaries and Intelligence Summaries are contained in F. S. Regs., Part II. and the Staff Manual respectively. Title pages will be prepared in manuscript.

Place	Date	Hour	Summary of Events and Information	Remarks and references to Appendices
ITEAULT	18th		Received orders for Company to move to SASSEVAZ to SASSEPONT – Lieut CHRISTISON sent on with advance guard to billets – Transport with all remaining Officers except Lieut LOFFRE moved off at 1330 hr ARGOEUVES, when Lieut BRIDGEN learned excellent billets – O.R.s comfortable at lunch – Sappers to move by latest train on 19th.	
SASSEVAZ	19th		Transport arrived SASSEVAZ 1230. Sappers arrived 2000 by good hire transport the delivering point – All reminds made over to the billets since December last delivering point –	
	20th		Applicant men parade for section drill standard sling point 10' snapping machine – Reconnoitred unit march to REVEILLE – Riding school for officers.	
	21st.		O.P.E. held conference H.R. orderly room. Drill, allotment of tasks, 10' snapping practice, sharpening shovel, cleaning magma, kit inspection. Riding school – jumps made – leg raining & lunging – By night Lieutt CHRISTISON, BUCKLEY BRIDGEN laid out sling points in combat training – Senior N.C.O.s did exercise with P. Company & patrols – Lieut Matthews & No 2 section supplied hostile opposition & bombing – Investigation of shortage of rations shown some shortage	

WAR DIARY
or
INTELLIGENCE SUMMARY.
(Erase heading not required.)

Army Form C. 2118.

Instructions regarding War Diaries and Intelligence Summaries are contained in F. S. Regs., Part II. and the Staff Manual respectively. Title pages will be prepared in manuscript.

Place	Date	Hour	Summary of Events and Information	Remarks and references to Appendices
SASSEVAL	21st		Route march to NEVELLES and examination of strong point for defence of that village to the south — Instruction in advance guards, marine work & company transport billeting in shanty village — left SASSEVAL 0930, about 17.0 Haversack rations and cook's cart accompanied —	
	23rd		Instruction by lectures in jupid mining, bombing, digging out strong point, snapping musketry drill — 2/Lieut LOFTUS to DREUIL to investigate rates stoppage — lecture by 2/Lieut BLAGDEN — the latest development of modern war as visualed at FLIXECOURT — Riding school afternoon — Conference on the work on the night 22nd/23rd. Snow on ground — Frost last night — Sunny pleasant day —	
	24th		Route march to PICQUIGNY, where men all bathed. Started 0900 returned 1530. CRE lectured on modern pontoon bridges.	
	25th		Church Parade 1100. Conference at CRE's room at 1430. 2nd marching reinforcement out.	

1577 Wt.W10791/1773 500,000 1/15 D. D. & L.   A.D.S.S./Forms/C. 2118.

Army Form C. 2118.

WAR DIARY
or
INTELLIGENCE SUMMARY.
(Erase heading not required.)

Instructions regarding War Diaries and Intelligence Summaries are contained in F. S. Regs., Part II. and the Staff Manual respectively. Title pages will be prepared in manuscript.

Place	Date	Hour	Summary of Events and Information	Remarks and references to Appendices
SAILLY SUR LA LYS	26th		Lt Matheson and No 2 section went border guides briefs over 36' gap other sections kicking - Asst all sections out at 12 bay cut - stout 8'fry cleaned stony front made short caparison Football match v. Monmouthshire Pioneers - lost by 2 - 1	
	27th		Enunstum Ing huts by Lieut. Matheson. Senior went to Great Priestley seeking Nos 1 r 3 sections mining - Football match Mrs Officers v Men's won v Mens dust - won by 2 - 0 - Blizzard during match Preparing to march 15 horses - Gale made it rather hard on intents - O.S. cur sharpening pickaxe chisels - Sections huddle to keep well	
	28th		March 10 - Heavy fall in PLEVEMENT - O.C. insisted company kept short of CARRIERS - expensed his satisfaction at the march - Good billets in	
PLESSELLES	29th		March 12 miles = Heavy snow in PREVENT - dittance 12 miles = Near East stayed march 2 PLESSELLES all animals under cover. Drew Reserve Rations on the head and left behind	

1577 Wt.W10791/1773 500,000 1/15 D. D. & L. A.D.S.S./Forms/C. 2118.

Army Form C. 2118.

WAR DIARY
or
INTELLIGENCE SUMMARY.
(Erase heading not required.)

Place	Date	Hour	Summary of Events and Information	Remarks and references to Appendices
MONTAGNE	30th		Marched to MONTAGNE at 1015 from PERSIAUX Otherway morning 1330 — Rain — Ground better — all animals harder cover — Roads very heavy	
"	31st		Morning Divl parade inspection of arms before inspection of whole afternoon marching order parade of horses turn out animals & kits. Fine at night.	

B.T. Wilson
Major RE
OC 458th (West Riding) Fd Co RE

31/1/17

CONFIDENTIAL

War Diary

of

455th (West Riding) Field Co., R.E.

From 1st April, 1917   To 30th April, 1917.

VOLUME XIV.

-o-o-o-o-

WAR DIARY or INTELLIGENCE SUMMARY

Army Form C. 2118.

A.S.S.(W. Riding) Fd. C. R. E.

Place	Date	Hour	Summary of Events and Information	Remarks and references to Appendices
LE QUESNEL FARM nr OUTRÉBOIS	April 1st		Marched from MONTRELET at 1000. Guns & transport on village road. FIENVILLERS met C.O. late at the starting point, on the hill also the slope hill – Pontoons guard & horses to bring them up – not sleeping at all sleep. Advance Party 63rd BRIGADE – M. Phillippe the interpreter. LEQUESNE FARM – men in Nissen huts – Officers in the farm – horses in the farm – the courtyard. Wagons on the approach road, land under cultivation. Sub. Jad, who has had his many journeys transferred on him. Cold bleak weather – arrived 1330. Distance 7 miles.	
LE GROS TISON FARM nr MONDICOURT	April 2nd		Marched at 1015 to LE GROS TISON FARM. Distance 12 miles. Passed thro' OUTRÉBOIS. DOULLENS. GROUCHES. LUCHEUX. Brigadier 62th Brigade inspected men in DOULLENS. Snow storm commenced N. of LUCHEUX – LE GROS TISON Farm very full but all arrivals received some sort – Men in' barns – Officers mess MONDICOURT – all counted. The LUCHEUX–MONDICOURT hill was specially arranged for an wagon had extra teams. Dismounted party arrived 1700. Transport 1800 – Very cold with commencement of Blizzard.	

Army Form C. 2118.

WAR DIARY
or
INTELLIGENCE SUMMARY.
(Erase heading not required.)

Instructions regarding War Diaries and Intelligence
Summaries are contained in F. S. Regs., Part II.
and the Staff Manual respectively. Title pages
will be prepared in manuscript.

Place	Date	Hour	Summary of Events and Information	Remarks and references to Appendices
LE GPT TILLOY	April 3rd		General Fatigues at 10.30. Arranged to dump pontoons at No 5 A.E. Park MONDICOURT. Dyer picks shovels + shunting slats + carry on pontoon + trestle wagons; also timber from LAHERLIERE for superstructure to augment. Clearing bicycles. C.R.E. visited MONDICOURT in the afternoon. Orderly officer to see clean to men's billets.	
"	April 4th		Rain abated. Superstructure to pontoon + wagons hired. Brake to MS pontoon wagon repaired. Machines also handle for suspension driven. Lechini to man at 17.30 on various schools.	
ETRÉE WAMIN	April 6th		Seven mile march to ETRÉE WAMIN to find billets – animals all under cover. Grazing – Bright sunny day. Three miniature lake at the studding'ins S.E. of LUCHEUX.	
"	6a		Halt. Rifle inspection + drill. Inspection of harm vehicles and oil bottles + pull throughs. Billet signs. held barracks. Visited C.R.E.	
GRAND RULLECOURT	7th		March to GRAND RULLECOURT. Excellent billets in CHÂTEAU. Bridges for any lopping for mens stove – Fine day.	
BAVINCOURT	8th		March to BAVINCOURT 5 Miles – Clean billets but all animals under cover. Weather cascade.	

WAR DIARY
or
INTELLIGENCE SUMMARY.
(Erase heading not required.)

Army Form C. 2118.

Instructions regarding War Diaries and Intelligence Summaries are contained in F. S. Regs., Part II. and the Staff Manual respectively. Title pages will be prepared in manuscript.

Place	Date	Hour	Summary of Events and Information	Remarks and references to Appendices
BOUNINCOURT	9th		Halt - Packing, Arranging stores - Pack mules - Pumps - Filled pick heads - Successful attack by 3rd Army E. of ARRAS starts at 0500 - Snow sleet.	
"	10th		Halt - Under six hour notice to march. Snow, sleet. Saw the German prisoners at GOUY - hundreds of them. Snow, sleet interval of sunshine but cold generally	
"	11th		Halt. Marching order boots at 0900 - 2½ hrs notice to march - Sergt Stanley goes sick - Snow & sleet	
MAISON ROUGE	12th		Marched to ARRAS at 0945. Fine day cold. Arrival ARRAS 1400. Camp near Inundations has No 3 BOULEVARD CRESPEL. Received orders from CRE to carry forward kit & mess pots from the RITZ DUMP in producer + trestle wagons, which we did - March outside at 1700 to continue march to MAISON ROUGE 400* short of FEVENT CROSS ROADS. Passed starting point at 2030 arrived MAISON ROUGE 0600 13th - Bivouac. Relieved 57th KOYLI - 12th Division. Long tiresome march with little sleep at the end.	
CAMBRAI ROAD	13th		Fine day. Settling in Camp - Three sections went out with one section London Fd. Co. I hut MONCHY LE PREUX in state of defence under O.C. 455th Coy, who went ahead. I MONCHY to reconnoitre ground going across country from Bgh Brigade Hd at H34A. Section sent round by LA BERGÈRE (was MINT) lands in the CATTISRAH road. Barricade made at the N.E. exit from the village in line with the CHATEAU hall running from NW & SE. The gap in this took was made by the London Fd Coy.	

WAR DIARY or INTELLIGENCE SUMMARY

Army Form C. 2118.

Place	Date	Hour	Summary of Events and Information	Remarks and references to Appendices
MAISON ROUGE	13th		Shelling of the village was fairly steady, but mostly in the hollow just W. of the Church. Received 4 counting changers + split these. Shells fell & 2nd country huts. and one dead. A few German dead in the square. Returned via the brick and the LA BERGÈRE Crossroads CATTERN - ARRAS Road — No casualties, although heavy shell between LA BERGÈRE + MAISON ROUGE, chiefly gas. London F.O. Co had a man wounded by the SW/3	
	14th		Three sections Nos 2,3,4 went in the morning — No 1 section looking up dump Wksat Co: Gravelin white bands under supply arrangement at the MAISON ROUGE well. Alt. tricks + shovels brought + SLE Colls carried in tandem — Limbs wagons carried up MAISON ROUGE DUMP. Transport animals organized. Oak Company 14 so an 1/2 mile in independent of infantry carrying parties — 88th Brigade attacked at 0530 this morning. Sections from MONCHY LE PREUX — Md (2) Brs got far ahead + were either killed or isolated. Gatherings — Counter attack of the enemy came in behind the attack + isolated it. Communications [illegible] Sergeant Coote guided up a Kent R.E. working party + Sapper Stedman the Co. Kent R.E. to bring up men in the [illegible] Square. Quiet night in camp — gas shells only. Lieut Brackley + men seeking look up the first convoy to the brick on The LA BERGÈRE road. Forty two mules in loads of Shells in all	ESSEX. NFLD
	Monday			

WAR DIARY
or
INTELLIGENCE SUMMARY
(Erase heading not required.)

Army Form C. 2118.

Place	Date	Hour	Summary of Events and Information	Remarks and references to Appendices
MAISON ROUGE	15th		Four sections Nos 1, 2, 3 & 4 went up to MONCHY LE PREUX to swing with a ration convoy & 2 strong under Lieutenant MATTHEWS. Lieut BUCKLEY was in section lifted to 07 A 4 of the LA BERGERE road, which had not been carried earlier to the light spot by the convoy on the previous day. These were then used by 2 section of the LONDON F.D. Coy going from the point O1 D 40 to the north — The trucks convoy had difficulty in getting to MONCHY and & shell	MONCHY CAT reconnoitred MONCHY including barricades costerly trenches BILLETS BMMA other mts.
			his, but after much delay the R.E. dump was successfully established at O1 D 28. BILLETS were found for Nos 1 & 2 sections for 2 nights, in the former a called at about O1 D 04, the latter in a German dug out nearby. Picked army at O1 A 70 in a corner of the CHATEAU grounds — An unfortunate burst of shelling wounded eleven men — Officers in the square about O345 including Lieut CHRISTISON, Sergeant GILLOTT, Sergeant CASTLE — two of the wounded were serious unamage slightly — four men were brought	
			when Sergeant GILLOTT "Alfie" wounded behaved with characteristic cooldress — Little this contretemps by their the trampe marched on at 0345, had died away, they were treating. Lieut MATTHEWS remained on as R.E. Officer in MONCHY & the CO stepped out home. Sent walking wounded on a quiet sunny Spring morning with larks in the hum song. The contrast of the mined homes sad men Dead horses with the freshness of the morning was striking.	

WAR DIARY
or
INTELLIGENCE SUMMARY
(Erase heading not required.)

Army Form C. 2118.

Place	Date	Hour	Summary of Events and Information	Remarks and references to Appendices
MAISON ROUGE	16th		Nos 1 & 2 sections in MONCHY LE PREUX — No 3 sections landed hunks for the evening convoy. Completed CO's dugout. Shelled just E ⟶ ENEMY. Solved timber. Enlarged strong points, Nos 1-2 sections built strong points at 01 B 57. Nos 1-2 sections hunts the strong points at 01 B 57 with Fed and Bn's. Steam pickets there. CO visited them at (abt) 00.30, which had then finished. Lieut BUCKLEY relieved Lieut MATTHEWITZ schemes. No casualties in MONCHY during day.	
"	17th		No 3 section as per 16th. Started making bridge. No 1 - 2 sections built tramroad between strong points at 01B57 on the front running N.E. Also did some camouflage in the village. Erected white boards. Widened the walls of the château in the M.E. hundred ran to 2 section of the London Regt to reinforce 1st BATTALION ROYAL abt 00.30. Corporal BROWN took up hunts for MAUDES & JADEN successfully. Dark wet night. Shelling of MAISON ROUGE camp became unpleasant in the afternoon. 5 men kit — 1 killed 4 wounded. During night his direct hit hit WALLS in a dug, hit the CSM's dugout, which shattered Sergt Smith's bed, he fortunately having decided to leave it earlier in the evening. De Gruson shaken up by the hit, served not WILLIAM WILLIS N. WALLIS land.	

Army Form C. 2118.

WAR DIARY
or
INTELLIGENCE SUMMARY
(Erase heading not required.)

Instructions regarding War Diaries and Intelligence Summaries are contained in F.S. Regs., Part II and the Staff Manual respectively. Title pages will be prepared in manuscript.

Place	Date	Hour	Summary of Events and Information	Remarks and references to Appendices
MAISON ROUGE	17th		Dunning Day or MUHCHY a Bosch S.O.S. scored a direct hit on the men's cellar but did not explode - only wounded 2 men with brickbats	
CAMBRAI ROAD H32 c.6. b.t.	18th		In view of shelling + probable further losses moved camp at 0900 to new location on the margin + spent rest of the day securing shelter in the huts & making frames in German dugouts - very comfortably off --	
TRILLOY QUARRY			No. 1 Section Convoy — Officer i/c the section — Captain LANGLEY 2" MONTCHY with men along with trucks with ammunition — F/W. Steepn + Labour in the LONDON Fire Coy. Evening Convoy of 12 lorries with some. This makes 3rd at the old camp at Left 1800 returned 2045 mostly done — New Dump shelled — artily from MAISON ROUGE returned to MORENS to forefront — New Dump shelled along the CAMBRAI road in old M.C. Emplacement at the Back 400x hitt. E. along the CAMBRAI road Pol. Conte. Little + A.E. Dump at MAISON ROUGE left with Grand + L.C. ATKINSON - New camp at must smell after Dump but shell almost next them — Some sick including STEEDMAN Co's orderly.	
	19th		Landed convoy of lorries which brought Lieut. Buckley took up to the new MOTICHY dump at N.6.D.9.5. with no casualty. Sgt Gosling who apparently got a broken arm	

1577 Wt.W.10791/1773 500,000 1/15 D.D.& L.   A.D.S.S./Forms/C. 2118.

Army Form C. 2118.

WAR DIARY
or
INTELLIGENCE SUMMARY.
(Erase heading not required.)

Instructions regarding War Diaries and Intelligence Summaries are contained in F. S. Regs., Part II. and the Staff Manual respectively. Title pages will be prepared in manuscript.

Place	Date	Hour	Summary of Events and Information	Remarks and references to Appendices
WAILLY QUARRY	19th		Rest of company engaged in making a camp, cooking shelter & the new dump. Intermittent shelling during the day accounted for 2 wounded. The total no. of killed & wounded since coming into the ARRAS battle has been 20th & 30th & 10th of the individual total strength – most of the wounded are fortunately but very slight. The Daily sick of the company is but their number which is constant is slight.	
	20th		Moved Nos 2 & 3 sections and the orderly room into dug outs in EOLIENNE CHATEAU to avoid "Quick Dick" whose shells spasmodically from the direction of ROEUX. There was German aeroplane excellently made chiefly occupied by A/A – ann'n Telephonic communication with CRE thro' 147th H.A. Group, whose headquarters are in The Quarry. Communicate with VIIth Corps. Sent No. 1 section up the night to be billeted and given a comfortable night with us – a good breakfast the following day. Time was a great success in every of much E MONCHY dump to all.	
	21st		Completed yet to all the personnel of the company. No 2 & 3 sections to ARRAS to rest of the night. CRE Inspects in ARRAS at 1800 t-thirties carrying machine loaded his trucks for the London Fd Eng. Shoeing with us in camp.	

1577 Wt.W10791/1773 500,000 1/15 D. D. & L. A.D.S.S./Forms/C. 2118.

WAR DIARY
or
INTELLIGENCE SUMMARY
(Erase heading not required.)

Army Form C. 2118.

Place	Date	Hour	Summary of Events and Information	Remarks and references to Appendices
THILLOY QUESNOY	22.3		Work in Camp - Painted divisional post - Unloaded stores - Salvage of pieces, shovels, rifles, kit German bullets - carted fence for making m/g camp - West of C.O.E. in the morning - Saw Capt 87th Brigade re Lieutenant's work. Conference of Officers & NCOs to explain plan to them at 1500 -	
	23.3		Nari picket paraded to inspect kit for evening's work. Left camp at 1300. Left O/C Kent Fusrs to NE to proceed to 87th Brigade HQ to find out how operations were progressing. Brigade HQ was being considerably shelled. We succeeded in getting in at 1500. Site of Brigade HQ was MONCHY. N63.63 in the village of the jed was hit at the extreme top of the village. Shelling of MONCHY and the front line was very intense all afternoon. Left Bn HQ 1645. Returned to GUNPITS at 1730 and went up situation was I-ORE. Reconnoitred that line to select during the most easterly strong points of the SWB, Grenadiers this to be to the South & East of MONCHY. Went ahead as forward observer at 0103 61.5 due East to ARROW HEAD COPSE and the TWIN COPIES at 0203.15 - Found all 4 Companies of the SWB - information of the NORTH BORDER & INNISKILLINGS forming south from the Twin Copses. The 29th Division had thus secured the 1st objective (BLUE LINE) except in each flank where the divisions on the right flank had failed to come up.	

WAR DIARY or INTELLIGENCE SUMMARY

Army Form C. 2118.

Place	Date	Hour	Summary of Events and Information	Remarks and references to Appendices
TILLOY DUMPIT	24th		The undersigned reported to the Company & the 100 infantry carrying party was met the wounded at 01B 5b. The 20 wounded carrying this material & lined up at the dump at NSA 83 & the company on their route with Lieut MATHEWS and BUCKLEY with 100 infantry carrying party of the LANCS FUSILIERS (Lieut LE MESURIER & CRAWFORD) left at 2045. Everything went well until the head of the column was E. of MERCURY about 02A 00 with the tail about the Tank at 07A 17. A series of shells at 01D 30 wounded 20 of the company 2 being killed on the spot with 5 eleven carts and other horse or less seriously wounded. The infantry in the rear also sustained casualties about this limit of their fire. Lieut LE MESURIER was knocked out. CAPTAIN BEARDY was seriously wounded when with the infantry in rear & was found considerably later by the KENT FLD CoY. The infantry in rear was seriously disorganised & the only firing common of action was L. CALVERT & GENERALS the wounded, which ably done by Lieut MATHEWS. Lieut BUCKLEY reported the position of affairs to the C.O. at the rendezvous who returned to our pits about 0200, reporting at Brigade HQ in the way back. The evacuation of wounded was completed by 0300, company was back in TILLOY by dawn. Lieut MATHEWS C.O. visited station at FEUCHY CHAPEL X roads during afternoon after CAPTAIN BEARDY. General Lossm	

Army Form C. 2118.

WAR DIARY
or
INTELLIGENCE SUMMARY.
(Erase heading not required.)

Place	Date	Hour	Summary of Events and Information	Remarks and references to Appendices
TILLOY QUARRY	24th		to be learned sections the MAN 1.) It is advisable to insist to an hour at least after any considerable barrage before taking a hill of from up to 6 front line jobs. 2.) It would be worth while organising the work in 5 or 6 groups under Nos. each party complete with stores to take & guard the group ahead, first to reconnoitre for their jobs. 3.) While the line taken was to close to the village, which was heavily shelled until 2300 at night. The whole division infantry + supporting artillery + engineers suffered heavy losses this day from artillery. Paraded at 1600 in the afternoon. & then some inspection. Kind had view which other camp — Company made a short visit to march not longer.	
DUISANS	25th		Supper by bus from ARRAS to DUISANS marching from TILLOY QUARRY at 1300 to ARRAS. Transport by road under CAPTAIN LANGLEY. Handed over to Field Co of the 3rd Division with reconnaissance to take over our camp. Anniversary of the landing at GALLIPOLI.	
NOYELLETTE	26th		March to NOYELLETTE. Visited AVESNES LE COMTE.	

1577 Wt. W.10791/1773 500,000 1/15 D. D. & L. A.D.S.S./Forms/C. 2118.

WAR DIARY
or
INTELLIGENCE SUMMARY
(Erase heading not required.)

Army Form C. 2118.

Place	Date	Hour	Summary of Events and Information	Remarks and references to Appendices
LA HERLIÈRE	27th		Marched to LA HERLIÈRE at 1030. Fine day & sunny. Arrived 1445. Roomy billets, which needed cleaning up. Foot inspection.	
" "	28th		Clean wind inspection at 0900 — CSM. sick — Clean waggons — Fixed mechanical transport gar Lt Hardern to throttle lagens — Violet CAR at COUIN and arranged about clothes return for the men — Saw laundry at PAS & worked out details of individual ride for officers.	
	29th		Sent clean clothes from PAS and Russian bath from WARLUS — CO. CAPTAIN LANGLEY, LIEUT MATHEWS and LOFTING inidentichered into PAS — BEAUQUESNE — AMIENS. Midday half BEAUQUESNES — many county cart hacks an terrible halt night AMIENS (25 MILES) Warning order to move from DIVISION. Weather perfect.	
	30th		Daily clothes returned PAS. Drill parade at 0900. Baths by driver. Unable to carry out R.E. reconnaisance by L^{ieut} BUCKLEY and NCOs at PAS as important orders in force orders. Officers ride left AMIENS 1045. BEAUQUESNES 1350. PAS 1715. LA HERLIÈRE 1930 — No One slightly rubbed back. Came across country on cart hacks most of way. Forded QUILIENNE stream at SARTON	

WAR DIARY
or
INTELLIGENCE SUMMARY.

Army Form C. 2118.

Place	Date	Hour	Summary of Events and Information	Remarks and references to Appendices
LA HERLIÈRE	30th		Sgt Stanley returned from hospital. 28th Pecond ypania SAULTY - BARLY 40 men	
		1645	returned. 2100, Finished cleaning Bayonet - Sgt Clifford sick - no	
			reinforcements to ypres. 47 Casualties incurred since beginning of month.	

BJ. Killson
Major RE
OC 453rd (NZ.) Field Coy RE
30/4/17

CONFIDENTIAL

War Diary

of

455TH (WEST RIDING) FIELD CO., R.E.

From 1st May, 1917 to 31st May, 1917.

VOLUME XV.

-o-o-o-o-o-

WAR DIARY
INTELLIGENCE SUMMARY

Army Form C. 2118.
4/5th (W. Riding) 2/W. Co. R.E.

Place	Date	Hour	Summary of Events and Information	Remarks and references to Appendices
WANQUETIN	MAY 1st		Moved from LA HERLIÈRE to WANQUETIN at 0655. Arrived WANQUETIN 1000 – Billets at Schort.	
ARRAS	MAY 2nd		Moved to ARRAS leaving LA HERLIÈRE 1845 arrived ARRAS 2200 – Billets École Maternelle & Rue d'Amiens	
"	MAY 3rd		Clean arms. Sen. Subalt. drill at 1700. C.R.E. indm construction of B.W. concertina at RITZ DUMP at 0945 – Fm section employed made 45' complete with stiffeners & carrying poles by 1700 – Homemade yarn taken	
"	4th		Company making B.W. concertinas – 40 made – Damp fire & sun showers in evenings – Nsty night with his Nev hut billets	
"	5th		Cantine making B.W. concertinas – Capt. Boy's cantina box – Rolls of infantry material in making them in the Place Ripitchie – 60 made – Sergt BUTCHER junior from ROUEN	
"	6th		Sunday – 12 carpenters in the London Co. to assist in making latrine fittings Church Parade 0930 – Capt Rins continues making antenna box – Riot & advancement in R.E. pay in voire – Capt Brown promoted & Sergt. Latrine cleaning & billets during our stay in ARRAS & improved Sanitary measures – CSM sick.	

WAR DIARY or INTELLIGENCE SUMMARY.

Army Form C. 2118.

Place	Date	Hour	Summary of Events and Information	Remarks and references to Appendices
ARRAS	MAY 7th		Marched to Dainville.	
DAINVILLE	8th		Routine work. Clean arms. Gas helmet drill. Company drill. Message writing. Kit inspection.	
	9th		Routine work as above.	
	10th		2/Lieut LOFTUS, 2/Lieut RODGERS, L.C. ATKINSON an 10th were out on a Harry Sharp point job W. of MONCHY walls CRE'S orders - Also 2/Lieut BUCKLEY the O.R. Work was successfully done - Sergeant RODGERS was killed - Sharp point A B C D E of his Raid out at following locations N18C47. N18B09. 07.C.18 N12 B 96. N 6 D03. H 36 C 91. - Sergeant RODGERS was killed at the last named one - It is buried at FEUCHY CHAPEL CEMETERY N. of the Arras road: was intelligence 2/Lieut MATHEWS, 50 O.R. Against the Raid, N. of DAINVILLE. 2/Lieut Buckley proceeded to PARIS on completion of his job on 2 days leave.	

WAR DIARY
or
INTELLIGENCE SUMMARY.
(Erase heading not required.)

Army Form C. 2118.

Place	Date	Hour	Summary of Events and Information	Remarks and references to Appendices
BAVINCOURT	May 11th		OC Coy checked position of string points ABRI DE F with Capt 86th Brigade & G.S.O. (1) - Coy moved in ordinary trek except No 2 section and Lieut. MATTHEWS who laid out Spots marked by 87th Brigade.	
	12th		Manoeuvres of 200 P.W. conducted at RITZ DUMP by Lieut MATTHEWS all the Coy. Sergt RODGERS body brought in here F post by ½ Atkinson party. Lieutenant BATT ynstld for duty from BATE. Lieut LOFTING said not brid. late he in hunt & C D - E for work by 86th Brigade - Sergeant BROWN mounded late he in unit & BAUDIMONT BARRACKS at 14.30.	
ARRAS.	13rd		To CORPS SCHOOL. Draft of 20 men from BATE.	
	14th		Lieut BALL & 60 ok making P.W. enculment at RITZ DUMP - Lieut MATTHEW & Tilloy with advance party - Employers at 87th Brigade HQ. - Two infantry platoons on INNISKILLINGS (Lieut SWINDEAN) and MOSS (Lieut BARNARD) attached to the Company for carrying work. Both reported in the evening.	

WAR DIARY or INTELLIGENCE SUMMARY

Army Form C. 2118.

Place	Date	Hour	Summary of Events and Information	Remarks and references to Appendices
TILLOY QUARRY	18th		Marched to TILLOY QUARRY N. of LATTREM - ARRAS and taking over from 5¼th E. RIDING FIELD COY. Left ARRAS 1000 arrived & settled in by noon. Lieut MATTHEWS reconnoitred front line system	
	15th		The Garrison of the whole Coy objected to make COY collecting wiring & making Knife rests. Lieut BALL reconnoitred ground between the BROWN LINE and S. of MONCHY to MONCHY-BERGERE. OT reconnoitred GRANGE & EAST trenches locating C.D. E.&F. strong points. Three Lewis teams of Bn. carried men (100) C-E strong hut. 36 men carried Pgnr. carrying to E shing hut in ADDISON at 1900	
	17th		All available men including clerks, batmen, drivers, tool cart men, sanitary men & carried Knife rest(ep) to E-Post. 58 Bn. carrying men from E-Post to Junction & CANNISTER & SHRAPNEL TRENCHES. 40 Pgnr. carrying him "E" dump & Junction of GRANGE & EAST TRENCHES. 86 Knife rests were collected during the day & laid. 40 trench nails kinds made MANILLA - Elephant constructed in camp & dugout in ADDISON TR - Bricks made at BEGS MTG	

A5834 Wt. W4973/M687 750,000 3/16 D. D. & L. Ltd. Forms/C.2118/13.

WAR DIARY or INTELLIGENCE SUMMARY

Army Form C. 2118.

Place	Date	Hour	Summary of Events and Information	Remarks and references to Appendices
TILLOY CARENCY	18th		Major & 17th/18th 120 B.W. continued from "E" Dump L. Junction CANNISTER & SHRAPNEL TRENCHES. — Shells & MWBOMBS were lobbed to the CANNISTER & SHRAPNEL TRENCHES & "E" dump.	
	19th		Aftn continued rifle at "E" dump. Completed order of 200 km/h feet at "E" Dump by dusk — Trench mortar bombs sent to Brigade. Thro. Coy. Cmdr of willing material. A number of Saphson sent to each of D E F & G shing panels went to "E" dump. Two Saphson sent to each L & to L SNAFFLE Right Bank - 10 OR went with O.C. 1st to 1st SNAFFLE by O.C.'s orders. Enemy 18th/19th, but whimmed buried in readiness for the attack on the OC & Lieut DISTURNALL owing to enclosing orders received by OC BORDER Regt. OC & Lieut N. of ARRAN reconnoitred EAST TRENCH in Jerusalem, then E. across the line. Considerable enemy shelling between CAPE & SNAFFLE. Twin tank at dusk. Sniping & M.G. hits. One heavy artillery hurls shot at the mound at 0.3.C.16. Canadian that in Lowwood's attack my leading Coy to the tank line took cover so to the NORTH of MOMENT via ORCHARD TRENCH. Cpl. AUDOIRE wounded but remained at duty.	

Army Form C. 2118.

WAR DIARY
or
INTELLIGENCE SUMMARY.
(Erase heading not required.)

Instructions regarding War Diaries and Intelligence Summaries are contained in F. S. Regs., Part II. and the Staff Manual respectively. Title pages will be prepared in manuscript.

Place	Date	Hour	Summary of Events and Information	Remarks and references to Appendices
	16th		Smoker heats not marched M.O. - 3° wire Sergt Clifford R.E. (Open 57th Division) R.E. Diving competition with lost costs r six hrs team 1st prize Cpl HUNT and no 1 section (London Kent + 24th Signals R.E. Riding) - Hot Day	
	17th		General Fatigue moving materials to move in the 18th - CO by car L XIVth Corps HQ with OC London Plates - Msg section dismantled huts in front ground & moving them retuned moving times.	
PROVEN (w/the town)	18th		Marched to LONDON by 1100 Entrained wagon animals Leaving 1757 Arrived PROVEN 0200 - Breakfast PROVEN marched to bivouac at N° 11 A.S.C. SHEET 28 Belgium - Arrived camp 1130 - Tents pitched horse XIV Corps - elected	
	19th		Camp improvement - commenced ex Box Vehicle drill - service recs 1, 1, 2 Section: marched rec 2 new road, round the eastern side of moor with CO	
AMASSE	20th		Work of the CO is making shelter in the new artillery by the XIV Corps Movement the following, Mo6 horses in hardest indistinct no of scraps etc unsuccessful	

WAR DIARY
or
INTELLIGENCE SUMMARY.
(Erase heading not required.)

Army Form C. 2118.

Instructions regarding War Diaries and Intelligence Summaries are contained in F. S. Regs., Part II. and the Staff Manual respectively. Title pages will be prepared in manuscript.

Place	Date	Hour	Summary of Events and Information	Remarks and references to Appendices
A II A 33	21st		NOVARA FARM (2) LUMIVILLE FARM (2) PARKGATE FARM (1) VLM FARM (1) RIOTTO (1)	
			LA TURQUE FARM B 15 B 68 (1) MICHEL FARM (2) EMILIE FARM (1) MARIE JEAN (2) B15C 27	
			MARGUERITE (1) CHATEAU B 14 C 88 STAMFORD FARM A 18 D 86 CAMERON FARM A18 B18	
			Farm shelled ARMENTIERES — NOVARA — Artillery average of 5 hours in the past night	
	22nd		Enemy at STAMFORD — NOVARA	
	23rd		1 Elephant at ARMENTIERES in conduit finished by NZ trellis	
	24th		Work continued	NZ trellis
	25th		1 Elephant at NOVARA	
	26th		⅔ — LA TURQUE	NZ trellis
	27th		Infantry = 300 ⎫ Elephants erected ready to conduit at NOVARA (1)	
	28th		daily ⎬	CARDEEN (1) ARMENS (1)
	29th		trench = 24 ⎭	EMILE (1)
	30th		= 72 hrs of material Excavation ready at	RED HQ EMILE
				B.T. Wilson
				Major [signature]

PR 4554(WC Diary) Paz C.2118

(A7092) Wt. W12839/M1293. 75,000. 1/17. D. D. & L. Ltd. Forms/C.2118/14.

Army Form C. 2118.

WAR DIARY
or
INTELLIGENCE SUMMARY.
(Erase heading not required.)

Instructions regarding War Diaries and Intelligence Summaries are contained in F. S. Regs., Part II. and the Staff Manual respectively. Title pages will be prepared in manuscript.

Place	Date	Hour	Summary of Events and Information	Remarks and references to Appendices
VIEAUFORT	12th		Physical Drill – Company Drill – 2 men to section School led by musing machine Gun – Lecture by Captain RYAN Re "Sanitation" – Sgt Brown returned from Corps School – Lt Jymes from leave.	
	13th		Physical Drill – Company Drill – Coy to ASSAULT FARM and his 5" jumped Quarries and Sergt LETTRIECE gets SOMERSET L.I. Mantle work allotted to 4 days. 10 wounds upon it – Evening training the Sports ground, which is in a great company works – 1/2 hr army – 2/Lieut VINTER. PE(T) joined Coy for duty. Sports about hands – Wagons Parked shell and Carto examined returned.	
	14th		Physical Drill & Coy drill continued – Corps marched to Sports Ground WARLEY aft Games taking note to hospital.	
	15th		Physical drill – Coy drill Bayonet work + practice.	
	16th		2t Brockley RE run to Section but up a Wooden bridge on the Sports Ground with Special combination of The Corps – In the afternoon the whole company went to the Div: Horse Show Following prizes were won Officers' chargers – 3rd Prize Major Killen's "Johnnie" ridden by Captain Lumpry	

WAR DIARY
or
INTELLIGENCE SUMMARY.
(Erase heading not required.)

Army Form C. 2118.

Instructions regarding War Diaries and Intelligence Summaries are contained in F. S. Regs., Part II. and the Staff Manual respectively. Title pages will be prepared in manuscript.

Place	Date	Hour	Summary of Events and Information	Remarks and references to Appendices
VACQUERIE	6th		Coy marched at 0500 f- VACQUERIE arriving 1130 via DOULLENS HEM REM VILLERS	
			Halt from 0900 – 1000 Coys Billets at VACQUERIE – Head Quar Hôpital	
			+ Cleaning toilets	
	7th		Cleaning Equipment clothing &c – After noon past – drill ordu in shirt sleeves	
	8th		Physical Drill 0700 – 0725 – Coy drill + kit inspection 1 OR. from Hospital	
	9th		26 OR. work in 29th Div. Grenade School Remainder drill – Coys mixture hit	
			in hill marching order – NCOs class in physical drill – 9 OR. inoculated	
	10th		Physical drill + Church parade at BEAUVAL – After noon Coy march I-the Sports Ground	
			+ competition pitched for R.E. Sports building Horenon Gazett Capt A/Major BSt William RE IT'LR	
			Brevet Major	
	11th		Physical drill – Sgt Elliott + 20 OR. t- MONDICOURT L- get hundred Equipment from N.E. AS	
			Parks, returning 12th – During march to Divl + R.E Sports	

CONFIDENTIAL.

War Diary

of

455th (West Riding) Field Co., R.E.

From 1st June, 1917   To 30th June, 1917.

VOLUME XVI.

WAR DIARY
or
INTELLIGENCE SUMMARY.

(Erase heading not required.)

Army Form C. 2118.

4/5th (York & Lancs) 2nd R.

Instructions regarding War Diaries and Intelligence Summaries are contained in F. S. Regs., Part II. and the Staff Manual respectively. Title pages will be prepared in manuscript.

Place	Date	Hour	Summary of Events and Information	Remarks and references to Appendices
TINCLEY TITLOY	June 1st June 2nd		Preparing to march – Marched out 1st – 3rd Division 627th E. Rly Field Co R.E. – Co. (Major Wilson) went in Van Guard left TITLOY at 1030 by sections and numbered 2nd ARRAS – Billet BAUDETIMONT BARRACKS 1 to Co. sent on lorries. (MARIN BOVENNELL) – Light detournee & S.O.R. taken out a new lined by night from TWIN COPSE TRENCH – Enemy planes dropped bombs near TRENCH to DOVE TRENCH – the Billet	
ARRAS	June 3rd		General fatigues in Barracks – Shot went march in the afternoon – March when received from Bgde. that W. Riding Co. would march with the Transport of the Bgde with Captain Loneley in command, while E. Riding Infantry march order – Lt BUCKLEY S.D.R. proceeded by 702 to VACAUERIE & return Billets	
BERNEVILLE	June 4th		Lt Cs Lopring & 2 Or P.C. r C. Spencelow have Each Unit in advance to BERNEVILLE at 0900 – Cos marched 1530 arrived BERNEVILLE 1700 – March orders for the Bgde handed in the afternoon – Cos orderly from – Hot weather. Hot weather Advanced Party & Light Loftine to LUCHEUX attend of column	
LUCHEUX	June 5th		On marched at 0600 – arrived LUCHEUX 1300 – Men fatigued owing to heat – Bivouac by side of stream, which was useful to bathing – Route SIMENCOURT – GOUY – FOSSEUX – BARLY – SOMBRIN – COULLEMENT HOMBERCOURT	

WAR DIARY or INTELLIGENCE SUMMARY

Army Form C. 2118.

Place	Date	Hour	Summary of Events and Information	Remarks and references to Appendices
TILLOY DU HART.	Sept 19th		In the evening the attack on BOIS DES AUXPINES - CIGAR - APPLE - MOUND at O.3.C.6. was made by the 87th Brigade, was a division failure - Bn of R.F. Augt but attacked on the left immediately on the right - Lieut Ball - 10 P.S. of this company, incurred orders to go forward with and carry his platoon when the battle became too spirited down - Lieut MATHEWS on ... or with the Inniskillings received the same orders - Lieut Ball R.F. was at the Inniskillings' trenches between SNAFFLE and TWIN TRENCHES - Lieut MATHEWS in Mill trench. Unfortunately Lieut Ball did not stay his orders; he was on top of the trench at 2.10pm the trench having fallen at 2.00pm German trenches at 2.10pm - Competent witnesses say that he was hit by our own shells; his men carried him into the trench, where he died in extreme pain. Lieut MATHEWS, his party when left the little trench, which they had 15 men, for there was scarcely left in the trench line bottom; few German shells hit the trench.	

A5834 Wt. W4473/M687 750,000 8/16 D. D. & L. Ltd. Forms/C.2118/13.

WAR DIARY
or
INTELLIGENCE SUMMARY.
(Erase heading not required.)

Army Form C. 2118.

Place	Date	Hour	Summary of Events and Information	Remarks and references to Appendices
TILLOY QUARRIES	20th		47 German mining shell fired from HOULETTE WORK - carried to Deep Dug-out in D. E. Copse salvage from shells in camp started. P.W. ambulances wounded in lorries. Junction EAST & GRAPPE — CANNISTER - SHRAPNEL 40 — 169. CANNISTER - HE 30 SHRAPNEL & TWIN 20 Awaiting material on MINES carried to EAST TRENCHES by Light DISTURBERS. 16 x am Lieut PAUL's body brought from TWIN COPSES L. FRONT & Trench Bombs. CANNEL X roads & lorries lost at present enemies an 21st & A.E. in D E F & shells past issued — 2 Cyl in DocK L-- hospital injured in the eye with a bomb spring while machining new shaft - Lieut LOFTUS to BREME on leave, shells past commenced at 0800 this morning Dug-Dug-out took in D. E — Mess awaiting wet at EAST TRENCH — former first shift left camp at 0630 — the hills not seeing slight disturbers Arm section Lieut MATTHEWS Sergt MYERS any night & hour in 16 hours Sergt BUTCHER — Both left. Continuous whole ½	
	21st			

WAR DIARY or INTELLIGENCE SUMMARY

Army Form C. 2118.

Place	Date	Hour	Summary of Events and Information	Remarks and references to Appendices
TALLUS QUARRY	21st		100 B.W. concertina carried to "E" Dump arranged in lines ready for carrying. Salving German mini bombs from HOULETTE work continued. 220 lbs of upper salvo. Loaded from stables wood camp. — "Dripping" Economy scheme now well in hand water bottle from stables wood camp. — SHELLS filling in shell holes in camp. Light BUCKET sick to C.C.S. 4/c COOK. — 2 O.R. WOUNDED.	
"	22nd		Continued salvage German mining huts (83 sets). Twenty yards pitching completed in EAST TRENCH. Filling up TITERLEY dump from Ritz dump in MOFFAT — B.W. concertina "E" Dump (100) & upper salvage continued (100 lbs). Knife rests repositioned constructed. Two hundred & eighty yards double row Concertina successfully erected between pegs at O.I.D 23 S. & MONCHY M.M. and the point O.I.C 60 Casualties 2 O.R. — African troops Lieut MATHEWS and DISTURBER. Mess Cpl WYKES Cpl COZENS. Shelling heavy at first with intermittent lulls till break of M.E. for Light DISTURBER has now been posted to the Company. Dry out at E.-D. continued well. Also ENY TRENCH jerking.	

Army Form C. 2118.

WAR DIARY
or
INTELLIGENCE SUMMARY
(Erase heading not required.)

Place	Date	Hour	Summary of Events and Information	Remarks and references to Appendices
THIEPVAL	23rd		Enemy counter Bomb & Coy counter attack was pressed successfully at O.I.C. 5⅔. 2nd Lieut DISTURNAL для work last known night – Coy set work continued. Pont advanced made had 13 L = 18" pieces fixed – the communication trench up. Continued scheme German mini self + copper shining bombs – Purchased all having Copie. Pulling East Trench continued 60" fit for traffic.	
	24th		Twenty five Bosche mining self echoed + mine Expects years to explode to "E" Sump. Construction of Bay trenches terminated in camp. East bursh work ripper + men put on the day fray not at "D" E swing to infantry managing being manufactured. Cont going No 1 + 2 beslins on their job – Wiring of MOMENT completed W. to N 6 D 96 with double you Bay conclusion in Pollan:: ⊗⊗ (2 pieces). These new survivis 150" eastwards to the point O I D 44. (50 pm. concertina) Cotts at CEMETERY (MUSCAR LANE), opposite N° 2 Tank. 116" E of N°2 Tank, at trench to B3rd MG – VINE TRENCH was shelled also. Night was quiet with own M.G. fire – Battr at OIC 93.	

WAR DIARY
INTELLIGENCE SUMMARY

Place	Date	Hour	Summary of Events and Information	Remarks and references to Appendices
TRENCHES	May 24th	—	Chief work of the day was finishing off new share of the mining in front of MERCLEY, which was successfully completed — The sticking was considerable throughout the night — 2 more of B.W. concertina wire were laid. The left saw 2 more strong officer laying in 2 places. Lieut MATTHEWS + DISTURNAL with Cpl THRASHER NESBITT + GLYON shot and main stick - The length of mining line now about 1700. The carrying party of the trenchemerings with 50 coils of B.W. coils also good service every brought up his coil in spite of the party being repeatedly by shells — Only slight scratches where sustained by the working party — Cpl NESBITT's party stuck in the trench from 7pm to 2.40 at the establisher. Day work on 'D' + 'E' half landward work — Salvage of tramway running trams of copper continued + some sanitary work done in camp — Transport — running trams from E + E dump. Total amount of mining done during the night of the 22/23rd 920" of R.W. concertina double wire laid minimum S.P. in each tail at every 10".	
	25th		Continued work on dugouts at D.15 - 2 galleries now down 15' 20" of overhead cover. Salving mining frames Manufacture of R.W. concertina continued.	

WAR DIARY
or
INTELLIGENCE SUMMARY

(Erase heading not required.)

Army Form C. 2118.

Place	Date	Hour	Summary of Events and Information	Remarks and references to Appendices
THILLOY	26th		Settling of camp – Cleaning kitchen lofts – New Draft 34 O.R. arrived from Base.	
	27th		Dry out continued. East Trench work yesterday, but work particular by the instalments of Lewis artillery. Trench Lewis Cont. 5" East Trench 15 in number. 71 gallery of dispatch prosed. 2Lieut BUCKLEY Lewis relief from HOUETTE work + wounded early to day whilst returned from C.C.S. – 2 O.R. killed + no wounded of a relief proceeding to dug outs	
	28th		East Trench work. 2Lieut DISTURNAL + Chief Bayonets. CAF wested dry out work. At much Doss work Bar at East army to dry out at D.E. + F. poste. Infantry below working parties lost men killed wounded – shelling from which infantry below working parties lost men killed + wounded + missing had not Release men much of weapons had been Lost of Salvage working parties continued. Reamer on must of weapons had CCS. back to East with it took at Kent. 10R. no gunners in Horse work. Sammtsap Kent C. EAST TRENCH Sergt GILLOTT wounded / run wounded.	
	29th		Fair progress on EAST TRENCH. Good progress at dry outs. About gunfire have been recovered to the infantry have up D.A. – All gallery now started – 2Lieut BUCKLEY instilled. Homicet, which is now a keep of brown + buckskin and has lost all importance is the town bitte village it our when the Cos hart went up there on the night of April 13th/14th	

WAR DIARY
or
INTELLIGENCE SUMMARY
(Erase heading not required.)

Army Form C. 2118.

Place	Date	Hour	Summary of Events and Information	Remarks and references to Appendices
Trenches	29th		The hostile shelling this day - notably a plant opposite the 87th Brigade. Collective shellfire concentrated behind Brown Line & E Post, amounting to 31 in M. The hostile shelling not intense. "F" Post to in evening their being shells at "E Post" more strong but intervals - yesterday destroyed by a chance shell. Salvos of gallery kannon (3.4 in) contrived - 2/140 + 1in = 5.25. 400 lbs copper wire handed over to the Divl. salvage dump @ Minor culvipoint 56th Brigade did not carry plan. Oak Cross in hand to "West Bull's Grave". Very few replacements. 5D. Prussian marching work entrenched day and "EAST TRENCH" - Lieut MATTHEWS. DISTURBED BUCKLEY since 13th May only his day's	
	30th		Few casualties in the Bumps. Weather has been insignificant rain. 16660 Ptes Trimble slight wound in D + S park.	
	31st		Work continued on dugouts + EAST TRENCH. Will push work forward to having Well but firing very wet after yesterday's thunderstorm. Main practice carr night in front of HILL TRENCH by 88th Brigade unsuccessful.	

CONFIDENTIAL.

War Diary

of

455th (West Riding) Field Co., R.E.

From 1st July, 1917. to 30th July, 1917.

VOLUME XVII.

Army Form C. 2118.

WAR DIARY
or
INTELLIGENCE SUMMARY.
(Erase heading not required.)

Instructions regarding War Diaries and Intelligence Summaries are contained in F. S. Regs., Part II. and the Staff Manual respectively. Title pages will be prepared in manuscript.

Place	Date	Hour	Summary of Events and Information	Remarks and references to Appendices
4.10.B.65 Sheet 28 Pulpitroo	July 1st		Captain Hawtrey went L" Posit on four days leave on evening 30th June – Eleven Lorries of materials sent up the line last night as follows:— Red House { 1 Load { 1 wooden stair Maryport { 4 Loads 5th Round Lt Pattison R.A. moved 2 elephants from FRESQUIN D Farm L" Lennuxville Farm with 9 totalled beyond – were busy A/T relieving elephants in RED House – returning for cement work – Are below erecting elephant at LUNNAVILLE – No 3 section concreting elephant at LA TURQUE – About Bridges – whom by we concreting. Dronters Farm – Are below Sundries + Cement issues	
do	July 2nd		No 1 section – Continues – Red H&D Elephants – built two yesty to LONER No 3 section – Completed concrete of elephants up LA TURQUE No 2 section – Continued elephants at LUNAVIELE Farm. Are section – Chicken – Six men under Lieut Dorlan moved to ARROTTERÉ FARM. CAFE West yard work – merged with Captain _____ CAFOS 1/2 th Rendrays. for carriage of material to LUNAVILLE FARM	

(A5092) W. W 28591/M1293 75,000 1/17. D.D.&L., Ltd. Forms/C.2118/24.

WAR DIARY
or
INTELLIGENCE SUMMARY.
(Erase heading not required.)

Army Form C. 2118.

Place	Date	Hour	Summary of Events and Information	Remarks and references to Appendices
Att A 25 A 20 A5 63	July 3rd		No 1 2 + 3 sections had a day off - No 4 relief continued No 2 elephant in DRAPORÉ FARM with LIEUT/ANDREW - Owing to this being completed - repairing nature roads leads 5 bricks to LUNATIVILLE FARM by hand carts, hrs this place has been shored up this hut on brown tile - slots were all doubled + made twenty sturdy supported - Evening work shifting boughs this from LA TURQUE FARM to RED HQ by Local CROPPER + Aulines Det + shoring 3 bricks of stored at our own dump - Most of man went into PLPERUIGHE in the afternoon for the last have for some weeks - also him there BUCQUET says that he is still at home. Not cechi to RED HQ - No 2 section to No 2 Elephant Norman Facey, no 3 section to ESTREE FARM No 4 (6 mens) to BROSSILE FARM, last night's work shifting stain from LA TURQUE FARM to RED HQ (9 tonies) + 3 bricks of sand put in the CY dump. - RUSTIC PLAIN in dry met finished. Norman No 2 continue 12' 1' above Cg. Mr. MARIE JEAN FARM continue 12' infors 1' of the front - DRAPORE FARM content not shelter finished -	

WAR DIARY
INTELLIGENCE SUMMARY.
(Erase heading not required.)

Army Form C. 2118.

Place	Date	Hour	Summary of Events and Information	Remarks and references to Appendices
AUTHUILE Avo A 35 Avo A 63	July 5th		Work last night 5 limits of shown to MICHER and MARIE JEAN - 7 limits of shew. Lt. RUPRID item B.S.C Pt. 2t. Lieut CAUTHIER - ATKINSON - ADAMS supposed not returned. RED Ho. No2 section normal. No3 section MARIE JEAN - Lieut BRIDGER - six men Na4. No3 section and mined from Wrench's Regained Sap to Angel. CANDIDATE FARM - Change of infantry reducing handed over to motor denies. Shelter position, telec came up on 6 motor denies.	
	July 6th		Work last night 6 limits of shown to MICHER and MARIE JEAN - 6 limits to RUPRID. Ho. No2 section continued RED Ho. No3 section mined normal. No3 section mining Marie Jean. No2 Mo4 section behind CANDIDATE - Seven long trails of yards driving bag to dumpsite.	
	July 7th		No3 section continued RED HO. No2 section RUPRID HO. No3 section MICHER FARM. No4 section CANDIDATE last night only 6 limits came in lieu of 12 owing to an error - Then went to LAMBERT & yards of new carried on R.E. transport to MICHER FARM, which is retrenching completion.	
	July 8th		No3 section RED Ho. No2 section RUPRID Ho. No 16 elephants erected. No3 section Muench FARM - LAMBERT No4 section EMILIE No2 and TURNIP No 4 section finishing Emerson & began. No 1 dugout - Shew last night 2 elephants 2 upright to RUPRID Ho 6 limits to MICHER 6 limits to MARIE JEAN & current Normal to RED Ho. Load of cement AVO D HOUSE.	

Army Form C. 2118.

WAR DIARY
or
INTELLIGENCE SUMMARY.
(Erase heading not required.)

Instructions regarding War Diaries and Intelligence Summaries are contained in F. S. Regs., Part II. and the Staff Manual respectively. Title pages will be prepared in manuscript.

Place	Date	Hour	Summary of Events and Information	Remarks and references to Appendices
April 25" Aug 15 63	8th		Healths not been with Bttn - Books Quick except to shot the bombs for 10 minutes about 14.30. So far ground the Boyards.	
	9th		No 1 section Reed HO No 3 section escorted convoy out to Ypres. No 3 section finished bivouac from station Hay No 2. Damaged by shell hit, trapped La Turque, preparing Ensue (Lee Browns) to convert DHS Hay No 1 - No 2 section (less Corps Michies) CHATEAU GROUP whitewashing & strengthening jump - Stuns last nights in Ensue of bricks.) Enemy shelled EVERDINGHE heavily at various times during the day. Reed HO - a lot of air bombing JHS.	
	10th		Last night enemy attempted to raid our trenches - to shot the unds. Party prisoners have shock 12.30 AM - Casualties 2 OR. driver [478 09 GRANT J.] 478 030 CURRIE O.] are wounded seriously, 3 on animal killed 2 wounded - Capt ROSS (mounted section) were wounded this conduct was brought to the notice of the C.in.C - Work during day behaved very well. No 1 section finished AED HO. No 2 section convert 5 x 2 shelters 2/3 finished at AMMO HO No 3 section Lorry No 2 finished. LA TURQUE begged. MARIE JEAN Pelynn dry out Ypres hut visited Ensue (Lut Brown) No 2 section No. elephant shelter No. elephant shelter - Sandbagging No 1 section hutt in hand	

WAR DIARY or INTELLIGENCE SUMMARY

Army Form C. 2118.

Place	Date	Hour	Summary of Events and Information	Remarks and references to Appendices
A 10 B 62	10th		Lieut MACAULEY, 50 NFLD Cadets HQ at CHATEAU. Groups taken over Little Learnert - men returning under the Lt's finished - Bechet officers are Lieuts DISYMRAM, N°2, 2Lieut WINTER, N°3, 2Lieut LEFFINE, Mr 2 Lieuts BRISBEEN NM, 2 Lieut ATKINSON, CRUPPER, ADAMS. INTERPRETERS. PHILLIPO. MIGRANT. Medical Per, 2Lieut ATKINSON, CRUPPER. ADAMS. Sechn No. Segt BUTCHER. MYERS. BROWN. Cpl. Attached infantry Lieut MACAULEY - Section No.s Sgt BUTCHER. MYERS. BROWN. Cpl. NEWITT - Sgt GUSSETT outwork - equip etc. - Infantry working 300 men August Sections 50 NFLD Shun up the divisional last night to road no. and LANNET & & kinder relations evident - Today My Sechn LANNEY NO 1 cement & elephant NoR Sechn Read hun permeant all day N°3 Sechn Empire (Let Bram) elephant M Mobile Farm subsidiary cement walking happy MARIE JEAN . happening TURCO NoR Sechn (Last cmen & kindu) CHATEAU GROUP HER Lt MACAULEY CHATEAU BALTE HeR Lt Athinson 50 infantry on units hun PRAYON to happening RED Ho Lt CROTTER do at NORMA EMON	
	12th		Work proceeded without hitch at EMILE Camp (MB Sechin) LANNEY MED (No B) Road HR (NB) the CHATEAU comp (NR) - Lt Athinson & Adams continued 50 infantry late arriving on units	

WAR DIARY
INTELLIGENCE SUMMARY

Place	Date	Hour	Summary of Events and Information	Remarks and references to Appendices
	12th		hrs PRAVETT hint SD working at pulling on spile 6" RED 140 -the second SD at pulling lump on at NOVMA - Sgt BUTCHER IV l section proceeded on a months leave to ENGLAND.	
	13th		On the night of the 12th/13th 6 tanks carrying spile to RED 140 came under 5.9" shell fire at the junction of the sortel road with WOSTEN - ESVERDINGE Road - Four of the working party SNDs were wounded - 2 of the lorry driver Spr Jones C.M.R. No 87070 behaved with coolness and presence being in charge of the Convoy - He took the wounded in a lorry to a dressing station. Sent on 3 lorries to ROAD 140 & being unable to get on with the remaining two attempted to put in at the silt of the jump an is normally the titor at the W.R.E. Dumps and but at the coming morning and sen NOVMMA came - CRE visited the various works during morning and saw NOVMMA Road 140, RED 140, CHATEAU GROVE and BATTLE MB. Empire LANCET METER stale of which worth was in hand. Sgt. SIMPSON No 476099 was wounded to the second lient. having only returned 4 days from being wounded at MENIN.	

Place	Date	Hour	Summary of Events and Information	Remarks and references to Appendices
A 10 B 63	14th		Work proceeded. Consult north of all the Brigade is now finished. LEGRENET NO 6 Camouflage which EPPIE NO 1 being finished today - Nothing but mile farmer Cordurons at night on 12 levels	
	15th		CAMERON & DROGHEDA Farm Brigade are now complete with jails and trenches - Work proceeded to in west NORMANT Lt VINTER NO 2 cutting r 30 infantry Lt ADAMS r 50 infantry RATS HOUSE Lt McIntosh r 30 infantry RED MO Lt Gillman 50 infantry Trenches jails Lt Drummond r 30 infantry breyins & shuttering Elephant LEGRENET Lt Drummond r 30 infantry finishing No1 EPPIE MIRIES MARIE JEAN Lt EPPIE - 60 infantry Rees by Lt Cropper Rd CHATEAU GROVE finished by Lieut BRIDGEN 50 infantry CHATEAU BATTLE MR Lieut MACAULEY and 30 infantry to continue to Ellens complete trench laying wire hut walls continued - Twelve lorry loads of rails Lt BRIDGE & LEGRENET trust ramps.	

WAR DIARY
or
INTELLIGENCE SUMMARY.
(Erase heading not required.)

Army Form C. 2118.

Place	Date	Hour	Summary of Events and Information	Remarks and references to Appendices
A107/63	16th		Last night: convoy to the brigade was 12 units yds $\begin{cases} 6x \, 2'' & 13, 22, D, 52 \text{ in } NOYERS \\ 6x \, 2'' & ZARBEY \times yds \end{cases}$ in NOYERS	
			H.Q. 60 units to ÉPINE by little wagon. Lt dishonord RE Arthurton to RED Hd ARMD Hd.	
			Work Lieuts Leffling + Crippen to Épine GROUP Lt Macaulay — Chateau Group Hd VINTER + MORRIS to NOYERS Lt Bridson — Relieved start while at humidifier	
	17th		Work on Artillery dry off completed — Lieut Macaulay has no more dry off in the chateau Battle Hd — Total hit in NOYERS — 2 elephants received amount 6 pails RED Hd — 2 elephants in cellar with humidity Lobby, wh.t. also without standing Room BF 14.	
			Chateau 3 elephant repaired Road Hd — 2 light elephant complete Group 2 light elephants ZARBEY — 2 light — " DRUMLINE 1 — " MARIE JEAN — 1 — " CARDEN ÉPINE — 2 — " MONTÉ — 2 patched join LA TORRUE BRG — 1 light elephant Lorries 12 No km day 20 250 No ni ms C.F. 14 Calumite mounti	

WAR DIARY
or
INTELLIGENCE SUMMARY

Army Form C. 2118.

(Erase heading not required.)

Place	Date	Hour	Summary of Events and Information	Remarks and references to Appendices
	18th		Lieut McCauley duty at CARRIERS BATTLE HQ - Coy Gun helmet drill at 14.00. Lieut Phillips reconnoitring bridge at MOUTIERSAUX	
	19th		Lieut Macaulay + some huntsmen visit Battn HQ site - Captain Dunphy visits Divisional OC. Lt MOUTIERSAUX - Road construction in camp - Drill parade + kit inspection. Gun helmet drill -	
	20th		Drill parade at 09.00. No.2 section skirt parties to build bridge at WALAAN MOUTIERSAUX No.2 section Lieut Venter marches with Walsh with No 1 + 3 yard work in camp. Captain Dunphy & Cremi to yammendi - Baths at 2 PM COUTROVE EDITION to in training on bridges - Co. reconnaissance of proposed bridge site. Lieut bridges returned at 3 PM. Team completed the for hoisting the load tests. bridge.	
	21st		Drill parade at 09.30 - No 2 section bridging with WEAPON TRESTLE - No 1 + 3 yard work. Gun drills in the afternoon - No.2 section yarding	

Army Form C. 2118.

WAR DIARY
or
INTELLIGENCE SUMMARY.

(Erase heading not required.)

Instructions regarding War Diaries and Intelligence Summaries are contained in F. S. Regs., Part II. and the Staff Manual respectively. Title pages will be prepared in manuscript.

Place	Date	Hour	Summary of Events and Information	Remarks and references to Appendices
A10 R63	22nd		Drill parade at 9 A.M. Practice bridging with bedsteads. Trestles & plank work in camp.	
	23rd		Gas helmet parade in the evening. Captain Langley joined from Cairo with 3 servants on jobs. 2 lights changed - Lieut Loftus Vivian & Co to DUNKERQUE by march route. Sergt Smith on leave left wounded at PEPERINGHE STA.	
	24th		Parade & Gas helmet marching - yard work in camp.	
	25th		Do. - Return of party from DUNKERQUE. Admin of units with Lieut PRATT - EVANS - ELLIOT.	
	26th		Detailed reconnaissance of pont tent system. Capt. left Division pont attempts by Canadr officer for Dishonest Vivile. Heavily Captain Langley Lieut Bigham R.E. - Trek 11 Bridge still in use. Cheque about - BOTSINIE CHATEAU X Y & Lucre yamashita	
	27th		Subaltern's trek dark 3 men of their return & Captain LAMBERT 3 men of the mounted section to see the ground they marched on the 27th. Reminder Co. rest. rest in camp.	
	28th		Drill what inspection parade to A.F. & infantry at 9 A.M. - Combination of pontoon bridge by Lieut VINTER MACAULAY with No 1 & 2 sections - No 3 section complete pont trestle at the Old R.E. Dump - Infantry on yardwork. An action made a trip for learning contact.	

(A7092) W: W.12859/M.1293 75,000. 1/17. D.D. & L., Ltd. Forms/C.2118/14.

Army Form C. 2118.

WAR DIARY
or
INTELLIGENCE SUMMARY.

(Erase heading not required.)

Instructions regarding War Diaries and Intelligence Summaries are contained in F. S. Regs., Part II. and the Staff Manual respectively. Title pages will be prepared in manuscript.

Place	Date	Hour	Summary of Events and Information	Remarks and references to Appendices
A 10B 63	28th		Combined circuit at 8PM of Lt Ruding. Lander Field Coys which was a great success in spite of hostile air craft. Wait of Co & SME at Ps camp 19/X 20 D 63 to fix movement but found work on 2 day	
	29th		Heavy thunderstorm at 10 AM - No church parade - Minimum dismantling pontoon bridge of Simpson Section. Lts Jn E arrive in camp from PREVENT - Officers with the Coy 28th and Majr - CRE Lieut Lofting Bridgen Wilts Sutherland Pallister. inf. Lieut Macaulay Major Hussey Captain Cartaret, Shellar Corp Ellis Corp Lightfoot Novelle Sergts Stanley Clifford 2Lieut Perkin Evans Elliot - Capt Newitt Sergt Mylan Sergt Brown Cpl Atkinson. CRE arrived at Ps camp Section commanders & Capt Atkinson & O.C. RE went 15 army. Lunch here and catechised his camp. In the evening Captain Wp & O.C. RE new CROYSERE 12u SME about nature parties in the yard Drill parade at 0930 - Road construction in camp work at 1000 - 14,00 Parade	
	30th		of all subunit including HQRS SME Bridge Section for issue of Gas r instructions & lorgs. look - Visited XIVth Corps in the evening - Ten C.E. wagon of wood material drawn from OrdDump BARFF & parked in camp - CRE seen initials & wish boys in found material drawn from Various was woods Bros Steners	

(Apog2. Wt. W12893/M1293. 75,000. 1/17. D.D. & L., Ltd. Forms/C.2118/14.

WAR DIARY or INTELLIGENCE SUMMARY

Army Form C. 2118.

Place	Date	Hour	Summary of Events and Information	Remarks and references to Appendices
A10 B63	31st		Zero hr attack French Corps XIV Corps XIXth Corps on whole place at 0350 – Rapid work consisting of 2nd SWB, 1st Rifle Coy and Coy Pioneers cut out at 0805. Column moved into on their work at 1100 preceding by Track 11 to BECKET FARMS. Thence by FRONTIER STREET to the X line station by the continuation of Track 11 to BOESINGHE – Rapid work allotted as below Battalion 1st Canadian Cavalry – Coy Pioneers Canine 1st SYDNEY MILL – No 2, 3 sections R.E. & SWB section SYDNEY MILL 1st CACTUS JUNCTION – SWB 1st Canadian Station Wilton – Am section RE – Borith section BOESINGHE village through WHITE – Am section R.E – Borith section 1st MS CORNER Work proceeded without event – a few later were cut through 1st CACTUS Junction by 1600, when LONDON Fred Coy immediately Foundations – 2 Coy Pioneers attack – German Counter attack took place at 1500 – shelling increased soon. Shell falling on the road – Canning Casualties	

Army Form C. 2118.

WAR DIARY
or
INTELLIGENCE SUMMARY.

(Erase heading not required.)

Instructions regarding War Diaries and Intelligence
Summaries are contained in F. S. Regs., Part II.
and the Staff Manual respectively. Title pages
will be prepared in manuscript.

Place	Date	Hour	Summary of Events and Information	Remarks and references to Appendices
Roberts 63	31st		Captain Kempley set through line report of wind received by STEAM Main & his party were the first transport to cross the Canal on the Guards Div'n front. Lieut Vintin has been the first with a Shell at the trench—later, but was attended. Lot Pearson — Corporation Cpl Alcock—Evan D'n Bird Cpl Stone and Spr Youens (All wounded). A very successful days work has been done	

Bothville
Major
OC 455th W. Riding Field Co RE

C O N F I D E N T I A L.

War   Diary

of

455th (West Riding) Field Co.,R.E.

From 1st August, 1917 to 31st August, 1917.

VOLUME XVIII.

-*-*-

WAR DIARY or INTELLIGENCE SUMMARY

Army Form C. 2118.

455th (W.Riding) Fd Co RE

Place	Date	Hour	Summary of Events and Information	Remarks and references to Appendices
A to B 63	1st		Heavy rain – Field Co standing by – Nos 1,3 Sections & SWB section employed on carrying materials forward for road – took lorries back to beach – plenty bitumen for road – hut made of bad materials at 61E – Co Hd[?] for to arrange details for bitumen road – materials for Co Hd[?] moved. Trees for trees completed from Dressing Village to Cactus Junction.	
	2nd		Heavy rain continues – field Co employed as Hilton. Nos 1 & 4 sections Lieut Birdger[?] repairing road – Nos 2,3 [&] 4 sections Lieut Macaulay embanking road – Both hits bivvy[?] prep for shelters – The Lewis [?] but planks & making huts. Carried over the Canal in horse transport under Captain ploughs inwards and unloaded – German body moved – Chief Engineer & CRE bridging Lieut Peto[?] wards working – wood truck	
	3rd		Heavy rain continues all day – Field Co and infantry employed as before. No 1 HQ section Divisional No hitching road with corduroy mud silt & boulder[?]. by Birch section No 2 & 3 sections hitching road near the road bridge – stony silt	

WAR DIARY or INTELLIGENCE SUMMARY.

Place	Date	Hour	Summary of Events and Information	Remarks and references to Appendices
AMARA	3rd		Continuing as per sketch herewith.	

Sketch: pontoon/bridge diagram showing dimensions "10'" and "20'", with note "N" (north) and "? Wkend".

Unlucky shell hit & killed Sapper Machin, wounded Cpl the Swis Section. Machin moved to Cemetery in [the] evening. 20 PR. has Turkish party in the log hand — R.E. dump at Steam Mill established with description there in the boiler excellent bomb proof.

4th Held to stand by — infantry section out KAI'B. SWIS v BANKS with lights — Pont Bridge Movement. Transport tm. R.E. began collecting material.
Wire done — In, but Motion Made at Steam Mill and R.E. dump moved inside River Bridge carried 500 beach planks to the Steam Mill from Pontonier's down the elevator with little mayor & by myself assisted by Chief Engineer. The rain but weather there type of clearing Up.

WAR DIARY
INTELLIGENCE SUMMARY
(Erase heading not required.)

Army Form C. 2118.

Place	Date	Hour	Summary of Events and Information	Remarks and references to Appendices
A.70 B 63	5th		Field Coy paraded at 4 a.m. for [word] work - Subs, NCOs and Bmdrs received white arm bands. Work in teams - work accomplished No 1, 4 reclad entrance & fetterments from Steam Mill to Doutouse Ra. - No 2 & 3 reclad ditto from the ridge to Steam Mill - 5 a.m. work accomplished. Some ford work done by Lieut disturbance. Lieut Evans & Elliot escorted Lia shop on the Canal bank. Shelling Winter -	
	6th		paraded but small - Misty morning, high clear later - No casualties. Very complimentary letter received from 14th Corps Artillery on our day out work during July. Lieut MacNaught and Patton with 6 O.S. sergeants leading truck planks from Bosinghe to Steam Mill Dump - Guides convoying them across him on Dam K to the ridge & if possible on to H - Co. units 76th Guards Fld Co to take over on the 7th - Captain Langley to Esverdinghe with the handover, which will be dropped there	
Esverdinghe	7th		Lieut Poidgin No 4 section advance party like over here billets in the village leaving Forest Camp at 5.0 a.m. Co with balance of have horsepoil march	

Army Form C. 2118.

WAR DIARY
or
INTELLIGENCE SUMMARY.
(Erase heading not required.)

Instructions regarding War Diaries and Intelligence Summaries are contained in F. S. Regs., Part II. and the Staff Manual respectively. Title pages will be prepared in manuscript.

Place	Date	Hour	Summary of Events and Information	Remarks and references to Appendices
EVERDINGHE	7th		From Forest Camp at 10am march - Captain Lambert, remain for the present hutted conditions at EVERDINGHE transport - settled in camp - huts for x-men - office inside. EVERDINGHE C.H. - Men in EVERDINGHE Officers, which are hutted bombard & bombarded - excellent mess & Spanish ha afternoon.	
	8th		Parties in huts as follows. Lt Kinski N°2 section hut, one hut from B 6 A 70 to B 6 B 10.6. with 4 Coy 98th Brigade - Lt McCauley & N°3 section his shop positions Poulton - Light distribution breakdown part Not section Batteries & CRAPOUILLOT positions spraying known during afternoon - Lt Elliott, British Reg't windmill - Lt Evans Bridge work in camp - Lt Potur in reserve with KOTB section - hutted CHAMPETER Dump. Lt Brown	

WAR DIARY
INTELLIGENCE SUMMARY

Army Form C. 2118.

Place	Date	Hour	Summary of Events and Information	Remarks and references to Appendices
ELVERDINGHE	9th		Work continued on bridge - S.W.C. March 15 - No 3 section & Bridge Nolson	
			To shop work continued - No 3 section	
			Standing to parodan bridges - bringing wires also supports to the 75th Canadian	
			Rlwy Co. whose letter Lorries now working the bridges - No section completed	
			filling in in camp - SWB section slaughtering up STEENT MULE DUMP.	
	10th		No 1 section Pontoon bridge approaches. No section back into the infantry lines	
			H. No 3 section lie stage PUSSONBORTH PONTOON Mrs section Capn in bridge bridge	
			to STEEN BEEK & training huts to ADD PETT - Lieut ELLIOTT Zent Dickinson [Co].	
			Reconnoitred Tournai the STEEN BEEK stream working Fournai front Mrs Maclkean Regt	
			and Steenbeek from - In the evening the huts 2 Afrika ships & essential	
			requirements of the bridges between U20B73 and U21C79.4 , which showed	
			3 sound bridges & 3 destroyed with a certain amount of material onsite	
			Sergt GILLETT took over from CSM Ellis handed the	
			R.S.M. of 1st Staffords Regt.	

WAR DIARY or INTELLIGENCE SUMMARY

Army Form C. 2118.

Place	Date	Hour	Summary of Events and Information	Remarks and references to Appendices
ELVERDINGHE	11th		Biedersylde Pontoon bridge was damaged by shell fire yesterday evening — Not repaired. Rly lit ship was completely destroyed — 8" shell did the damage — No 2 Section continued work on the Rly decauville approach to the bridge — No 3 section did the earthwork for another lit ship SW of Pont 15 — No 3 Section did the earthwork for MD Post near HERTE MILL — SAPS No section worked on the gunting E to MD Post near HERTE MILL — SAPS section walked the Drome — CRE gave details of the work being done by the Field Coys at BIELDERDLY. Reconnoitre of the camp E of the STEENBEEK by the LUKENULLE FARM. Fork — new pontoon bridge near BAUDLE with Artillery bridge Middlesex Regiment this morning at 4.15 AM	
	12th		No 1 section — laying out tapes along BRIDGE ST. and CLAPPES ST. preparing carriage of bridges to STEENBEEK — Reconnaissance of new lit allowed by Lt Lorimer No 2 section — Repair of approaches to BUESINGHE and CRAPOUILLOT No 3 section — New lit ship at B 6 C 52 in the old British front line Pontoons	

WAR DIARY
INTELLIGENCE SUMMARY

Army Form C. 2118.

Place	Date	Hour	Summary of Events and Information	Remarks and references to Appendices
ELVER DINGHE	12th		No 4 section - Finally elephant & completing tramline to M.D. Post. No 3 } sections completing track to cars yards at Pilli Dump. Subs - Steen Both } mill dump & approaches. BATSIN GATE PONTOON - Two Crawfhalt OTR No 2 section	
	13th		Intrepid. M. Planks from DIV HQ - M.M. section laying out bridge to Triangle army Post section approached under CAMPOUFLAGE PONTOON. No 3 section let ship. No 4 section tramway M.D. post carried on No 3 section let ship. Both section trepannie with sub section with and lift laid to Lieut Loftus's party - or wheled syd.b HQ in BOESIN GATE CHATEAU	
	14th		Three men of M.M. section during night of 13th/14th with Lieut LOFTUS laid out the foot bridge across the STEEN BEEK with Bard section being slightly "Sensed" in the process - Remainder of section - shortst by L. WINTER the tramline bridge - No 2 section repaired the bridges & approaches under Sergt MYERS Lieut VINTER being sick No 3 section Lieut MACKAY finished the let ship.	

WAR DIARY or INTELLIGENCE SUMMARY

Army Form C. 2118.

Place	Date	Hour	Summary of Events and Information	Remarks and references to Appendices
	14th		Mrs Seeley Lieut BALDWIN made the route into the A.D Post at VERTE WOOD. Work commenced of the exterior MILLING S.W. of ASHER WOOD also carried by German trench mortar 1 large, 3 small completed 2 railway crossings fire 5 left to hold tanks in stations the A.D POST elephant.	
	15th		Slack day in the morning – L/Cpl JERVIS and 3 men stationed to hill near the A.D POST VERTE TUBE, which was detected the his depth Artillery + acting on German arriving tracks – 3 small TMS brought in Parade at 2.30 PM to all the Coy + all permanent made to Camp.	
	16th		In Lieut morris offensive operation. Company paraded at 4.30 AM in lightly order with 14 pack mules carrying the necessary stores – One lorry came down at 4.45 AM.	

WAR DIARY
or
INTELLIGENCE SUMMARY.

Army Form C. 2118.

Place	Date	Hour	Summary of Events and Information	Remarks and references to Appendices
ELVER DINGHE	11/5/17		Marched off at 5 PM. Rendezvous at B.6.B.63. Sections detailed as follows.	
			No Section - Lost Lepping - In reserve at rendezvous with Pioneer section & Lieut Elliott	
			No 2 section / Lieut Vardie — Right slung point construction SWB section \ Lieut Evans 97th Present at U.21.B.15	
			No 3 section Lieut Macaulay — Bridge span at U.20.B.7½.3½.	
			No 4 section Lieut Bridger — Left slung point construction Vivas section Lieut Parker 62th Present at U.15.C.3½.2	
			Germans shell had being apparently high sells on the line Forward roads	
		— CAPTAINS farm checked L" front on a nr up to the known permit	
			with every thing except the seems —	

WAR DIARY
INTELLIGENCE SUMMARY

At 8.15 the situation was still obscure & Bns HQ at SENTIER FARM did not know whether the C.O. had sailed fwd him . Wired up Nos Section to Brigade without reply — meanwhile I-Cline had sent up Nos Section tm after tm in doubt - 09.55 Bn km Subtly Wrote on Bridge stating tm apply tm return - also asked Captain outline of country & wish Nos Section to work in good approaches - Posts Section to various Nos Section to work in good approaches - Reconnoitred left hand S.P. when M.C. was hit at time had the left flank. Nos Section came up about 11 - now got into B5 site of work by spoke tm still hrs I-till hrs doing which Lieut PATON was hit - Bridge was went on well - German ASS gun teams all falling back. E - XXX Nos Section consolidated their firing point in advance of the Books LANGEMARCK line near MONTMIRAIL FARM at U15 D.12.3.

WAR DIARY
or
INTELLIGENCE SUMMARY
(Erase heading not required.)

Army Form C. 2118.

Place	Date	Hour	Summary of Events and Information	Remarks and references to Appendices
			No 6 section killed to complete their S.P. whilst finishing everything except revetment with a lip the wiring. No 2 section finished their complete revetment with a lip to the langemark line. The bridge was made fit for buses. Spent the approach went forward. A very successful day. Lieut Evans SW13, Sgt Myles, No 2 section labored with great enthusiasm – Carried his kitbag Pte [?] MR. Smyth wounded (mainly severely) thro' the stomach.	
Ex Ver Duron	17th		No 1 section carpenters little bridge No 2 section wiring N.W. section Mrs section wiring until evening Booster section dick work. Smyth wiring Mr 3 is spent to MT section at 12 noon – Lt Macaulay in charge in time of reconnaissance of the Brown Creek. Lt Dickinsed shifting logs from a pole bridge to a trunk bridge at Brown Copse. Man travel with Lt Lyly.	

WAR DIARY
or
INTELLIGENCE SUMMARY.
(Erase heading not required.)

Army Form C. 2118.

Instructions regarding War Diaries and Intelligence Summaries are contained in F. S. Regs. Part II. and the Staff Manual respectively. Title pages will be prepared in manuscript.

Place	Date	Hour	Summary of Events and Information	Remarks and references to Appendices
RAVENSBRAIE	17th		Lt Birkshaw directed the work of 4th infantry carrying duck boards to PRIMROSE STREET C.T. Lieut Bridgen & 12 men ran reclin successfully boat work. Their wiring party went in the RAVE LINE S. of RAVINE and finished the lot — The S.P. was amply except for B head man T. FARM & finished the lot — a station.	
	18th		No. 1 section continued the bridge over the tunnel E. of CAMBRONNE POSTERN 2 section " " " " at 9 AM being checknails in the tunnel 3 section had check woodwork along BRIDGE ST. an hr or so SMILES FARM 4 section. Putting alfla in-put work MORS section Bridges Sap's section fixing checknails by night Bomb section carrying duck boards towards I SMILES FARM Sergt MYERS Corpl THATCHER recommended 2/Lieut LIEUTENANT LEFERE Corpl MAHLATE awards. Also Corpl MAHLATE Kerss reclin	

(Ap92). W1 W2859/M1293. 75,000. 1/17. D. D. & L, Ltd. Forms/C.2118/14.

WAR DIARY
or
INTELLIGENCE SUMMARY.
(Erase heading not required.)

Army Form C. 2118.

Place	Date	Hour	Summary of Events and Information	Remarks and references to Appendices
	18th		From which material was taken from the big ghat-work to VERTE MILL apparently they had been captured by the Huns themselves. One 17 cmt. the other 9 cmt. small ones.	
	19th		No.1 section — continue bridging the canal at CAPPENULLOT PONTOON	
			No.2 section — check work by night	
			No.3 section — check work by day and bridge on the SYPHON RIDGE at V20B for 62.4	
			Park Rigt [?]	
			No.4 section — Move to ST DENIS church for the consolidation of roads	
			South section — check work by night	
			Works section — bridges	
			Powder section — checkworks by day	
	20th		No.1 section ⎤ continue Cappenullot Bietle bridge — All Bietle pieces in position works ⎦ Difficulty with mud softer	

WAR DIARY
or
INTELLIGENCE SUMMARY.
(Erase heading not required)

Army Form C. 2118.

Place	Date	Hour	Summary of Events and Information	Remarks and references to Appendices
	20th		No 2 Section } Spotting Staff Section } No 3 Section } Duck walk Bridge thrust — Taping for same done to the Ponton Section } STEENBEEK — Duck walk 200' beyond PONTOON FRONT — Repaired & approaches to both pontoon bridges some chockwalks at night were missed by 2nd Lieut OWEN 40 infantry carried duck walks at night onto missed (?) loads	
	21st		No 1 Section } Carpenters' yard work — all the butcher stock normally when loaded Brath Section } - it will be recurring C: hill dive No 2 Section } Dictionar Lais & pyramid up to 290° beyond FOURCHE Staff Section } Farm No 3 Section } ALLEBY Pyramid approaches to BEAUMONT HAMP london No A Section } also to the shop & bedshop. Duck walk vicinity shelling up which troops	

Army Form C. 2118.

WAR DIARY
or
INTELLIGENCE SUMMARY.
(Erase heading not required.)

Instructions regarding War Diaries and Intelligence Summaries are contained in F. S. Regs., Part II. and the Staff Manual respectively. Title pages will be prepared in manuscript.

Place	Date	Hour	Summary of Events and Information	Remarks and references to Appendices
			Tout Disposition of r 7 OR. plow up obtaining hits on the Lewis Gun Camp – W DJFM Rgft	
			No 2 – Officers with Ofs Master Miller Allitchie Lieut Evans – SWB	
			Captain Humphry Lieut Macaulay – Essex	
			Lieuts Parker (in attachment at ord Dunn) Lieut Elliott – Border	
			Martlet 2nd Lieut Dixon – Monmouth Pioneers	
			Ashford	
			Brinkley (on attachment at CRE HQ)	
			C.S.M. – Capt Gillett	
			No 1 Section – Sergt Richie	
			2 Section – Sergt Mystic	
			3 Section – Sergt Brown	
			4 Section – Cpl Thatcher	
ELVERDINGHE	29.3		No 1 Section } Carpenters hatts – pile driving Cam bridges	
Belgium			No 2 Section } Bell frames at G.H.Q. Battery attendants	
			No 3 Section (horse) Lt Dishforth attending byes stocking up motor lorries on cannon farms	

Army Form C. 2118.

WAR DIARY
or
INTELLIGENCE SUMMARY.
(Erase heading not required.)

Instructions regarding War Diaries and Intelligence Summaries are contained in F. S. Regs., Part II. and the Staff Manual respectively. Title pages will be prepared in manuscript.

Place	Date	Hour	Summary of Events and Information	Remarks and references to Appendices
		Evening	Nor section [illegible] 2 duckboards for home = 290 yards which should reach STEENBEEK or nearly so	
			Sup section Centre section 60 - 20% in hands	
	23rd	Continued	Began the Bridge — laying duckboards — Mud but being considered to width from to the bridge.	
		E. of the STEENBEEK — Stick road 100' across the WIJDENDRIFT	
			Party 6 duckboarders employed —	
	24th	Zero Hour was — Lt Bodan obtained from ENDYKE leaving 12 OR. ULC	
			in Union St.	
	25th	Last night & most before relief — Lt Birkmial reconnaissance to the STEENBEEK — MG section Yser bridge — No 2.3 as below yards from bulk truck back in the morning	

Army Form C. 2118.

WAR DIARY
or
INTELLIGENCE SUMMARY.
(Erase heading not required)

Instructions regarding War Diaries and Intelligence Summaries are contained in F. S. Regs., Part II. and the Staff Manual respectively. Title pages will be prepared in manuscript.

Place	Date	Hour	Summary of Events and Information	Remarks and references to Appendices
	28th		Drill parade – Inspection of billets – lectures	
	29th		do	
	30th		do	
	31st		do	

B. T. Wilson
Major R.E.
O.C. 483rd (W. Riding) Field Coy R.E.

WAR DIARY
or
INTELLIGENCE SUMMARY.

(Erase heading not required.)

Army Form C. 2118.

Instructions regarding War Diaries and Intelligence Summaries are contained in F. S. Regs., Part II. and the Staff Manual respectively. Title pages will be prepared in manuscript.

Place	Date	Hour	Summary of Events and Information	Remarks and references to Appendices
ELVEDERENT DEFENCES	25th		M.G. section arrived in CAMPUSET RAILS at 2 p.m. & finished up the clearances bunks. Lt Macaulay with No 3 & 5 M.G's r Border section finished up the clearances (Evans Shaw) as far as not Nutt & the Lamgeuven Line. Lt Evans carried on to Bourne Path till the top marks past down the morning. 300 [illegible] to Bourne Path till the top marks past down the morning.	
PILGRIM CAMP EGCA Pt. No W of PROVEN	26th		Transport under Captain Farmley & Lieut Brohurst left at 10.45. M.G. Coy & Bn LMG own trailers at 10 am. Sappers & labor by 76th Field Co R.E. marched to PROVEN camp nr PROVEN. Left by train at 3.30 pm r arrived Conbertene Camp nr a ½ mile NE of PROVEN. APMC independently by forced march. Large farm.	
	27th		Rain. No parades all day. Manifests have been kinded. Government Guidance cards have been made out - Sergeant Whitford received MILITARY MEDAL from Corps Commander in gallantry in the field. Many prepares to entraini.	

CONFIDENTIAL.

War Diary

of

455th (West Riding) Field Co., R.E.

From 1st September, 1917, to 30th September, 1917.

VOLUME XIX.

-*-*-*-

Army Form C. 2118.

4/5th (W Riding) Field Coy

WAR DIARY
or
INTELLIGENCE SUMMARY.
(Erase heading not required.)

Instructions regarding War Diaries and Intelligence Summaries are contained in F. S. Regs., Part II. and the Staff Manual respectively. Title pages will be prepared in manuscript.

Place	Date	Hour	Summary of Events and Information	Remarks and references to Appendices
Albert Camp	1st Sept.		Drill parade — Company drill under Co. in the afternoon — Divine Service daily at 2 p.m. — Attached infantry returned to their units.	
Nr Pernoy	2nd		Church Parade 10 am in Bull's Appricot — Details to Ceremonial parade being arranged.	
	3rd		Ceremonial Parade for presentation of medals by Corps Division (Gen. de Lisle) 87th Aerodrome Camp — (Col. Lukas C.M.G.). Fine day. His Spectacle. Sergt H. Myers received the military medal and Capt Williams M.C.S.B. (attached infantry). Strength on parade 130 OR + 4 officers.	
	4th		Half an hour drill parade. Steady hard training by No 4 section — recreation in the PM.	

(A5093.) Wt. W28599/M1293. 75,000. 1/17. D. D. & L., Ltd. Forms/C.2118/14.

Army Form C. 2118.

WAR DIARY
or
INTELLIGENCE SUMMARY.
(Erase heading not required.)

Place	Date	Hour	Summary of Events and Information	Remarks and references to Appendices
PILCKEM CAMP	12th		Transport still in marching order. Fine but cold. Lt. Graves paraded with four horse cleaned. Capt Howie & Lts Wheeler employed in the Sports Ground. No 3 section on fatigue.	
Pa Ave Nr P[?]55	13th		Russia Troops. No section employed. Greaves Rifle inspected with an before Work. Continued on numbers & sports ground. Lifle Fatigues Sports. Great success achieved by company. No 3 and squad parade completed & moved here for Sports parades especially the Drive Events in the Heavy race. Some prizes specially to numbers in detail. Won by the Company who were very much admired. They the Music for the Sports by the Lights Hopping & Bridges & to Lighter from the Front. Two 1st Bullock carts by Liluli's won by the Company from Riley Reg 1st Prize. by Lieut Bridges Events: 1st, 2nd prize fancy dress made jack & caterpillar were a scream Ripped up a Prize – Lieut Wheeler & 1st Gr XII Corps School (Corporal Gayton) a ford on Capt T Wells.	
	14		Work No 1 + 2 sections the march. Review Ground Sports Ground. Bichi Review for SMS.	

WAR DIARY
or
INTELLIGENCE SUMMARY.
(Erase heading not required.)

Army Form C. 2118.

Place	Date	Hour	Summary of Events and Information	Remarks and references to Appendices
	14th		Coff. room purtish for Margaret parade. Thanks for file on a first crops left to know	
			team the parade & Captain Hill & 29th Division Gen Rehot	
	15th		Parade Inspection parade Monthly bit Epidemical N.3 section looking on	
			Had Battles & yours. Lieut F.D Martin assumed to the Company from N.3	
			Section Bath No. - Major Wilson WMJ.33 now from Leave	
			Church Parade at 10.00. N.3 Sector looked on the bathy parade	
	16th		Peace Drill in the morning. N.3 Section looked on the Ritter perged -	
			Archery team won vs Ritcheyd the Seconds - Robert Brackley, Wm.CO Cpl Jones	
			Archery team won vs Ritcheyd Hill AC	
			Fought Manoeuvres landed at 3 PM. March past of the Company and a	
	17th		Inspection & sport. Shooting competitions. Semi Finals - Combat CAPELLE	
			Consonants 1st Runner Coys' and the inspecting officers in parade with Coy	
			Major Wilson Captain Lambert Lewis Loftus + Matthias	

(A7692) W1 W12839/M1293. 75,10.9. 1/17. D. D. & L., Ltd. Forms/C.2118/14.

Army Form C. 2118.

WAR DIARY
or
INTELLIGENCE SUMMARY.
(Erase heading not required.)

Instructions regarding War Diaries and Intelligence Summaries are contained in F. S. Regs., Part II. and the Staff Manual respectively. Title pages will be prepared in manuscript.

Place	Date	Hour	Summary of Events and Information	Remarks and references to Appendices
	13th		Beyond Bruce Hyde Bishop Smith Corporal Topes x my regt. Cpl G.M.T.	
			Gnr. Brown Wynn & Burn Lewis	
			Richards. Knight. Hall	
			Carried inwards Jarvis Hall Licht. Lee. Edward McDonald	
			Wireless Station on lost Ross.	Florida
				SWB. M Burdle C Hundred hit Sergt. Smith	
			Appendix	
ELVEADINGH /9			" No. 5	
Cortena			Lewis howitzer at 11 AM	11.30 Bulls Bay Hts
			Elveadingh Interior 2 Aistin Holt. W. g. 70l. Canteen Guards.	
			In M & 770	
			Are stations at 5 PM. Tuesle Sitri N of the Peach sold. A11A	
			Control officers pass lost sub of car movement (Sadler) menos name	
			Rustico	
			Arrival. Sectional on Arrest list. men	
						Ber.Davin. Duff. Rommary. Gilbert
				Sectional	Linkenim Steven Nicholas k.t. Meer Lesinsonke Howard Innes
			Wright arch Richard manning. Corps Breck office. I-th Sten regt.	
	20th		on Cherri Renje Stairs — Chief of Civilian	

WAR DIARY
or
INTELLIGENCE SUMMARY
(Erase heading not required.)

Army Form C. 2118.

Place	Date	Hour	Summary of Events and Information	Remarks and references to Appendices
	20th		Attended Sham Fight up to about 1170 hrs — with Phoenix — Puffs Sharp Cake then £400 was the [illegible] a coy in [illegible] & company Epaulemst [illegible] [illegible] in huts — Remounts took over billets	
	21st		No 1 sections at OTT-DRNK taking on huts — " — No 1 & 4 sections OTT-DRNK huts — Remainder No 2 section Cannonflage No 3 section current shelters at SMULETS FARM. Repair of Duckboards, upkeep of STEENBEEK bridges Infantry section having dumps of mud & camouflage on the STEENBEEK Boundary attack by enemy aeroplanes 3 animals killed 5 wounded — 2 drivers wounded	
	22nd		No 1 section Hutting scheme at Lipting also in Ex. Eng of the scheme for 57th Brigade huts " 2 Brigade Hqts 1 A.F.A bivouacs 1 A.F.A bivouac A.T. 2 D.A.C Nm section Cannonflage on the WIDJENDRAFT road No 3 section Duckwalks E of STEENBEEK Nissen huts SNB — Running huts Dump at STEENBEEK — Making No 2 section Cannonflage dump STEENBEEK Bridge — Carrying cement Sand gravel to SMULETS FARM Casualties 2 O.R wounded	

WAR DIARY
INTELLIGENCE SUMMARY.
(Erase heading not required.)

Army Form C. 2118.

Place	Date	Hour	Summary of Events and Information	Remarks and references to Appendices
	22nd		Innuiskilling — Bringing dead home — Lt Stichfund wounded. Hent Minourie. Every Particulars. for carrying by night. S.W.R. — 10.R. wounded.	
	23rd		Sunday. This section has been the hole time in canon E. ENVERDINGHE Mend African Section. To the R.E.D. no trenching the Elephants in ambushelled in the cellars Chinese Road. Lt Buckley. — Clean armi inspection — Bombing yard 5 horses killed N°2 section bringing dead home & sandbagging ON Duer hatting schemes E. of the STEENBEEK. opening Nissen hut. N°3 section repairing shock holes.	
	24th		Camouflage preparing SAULES FARM for concrete Reconnaissance WITDEN DRIFT. for M.R. N°4 section Sandbagging & Framing road dumps Zilat Goss. Mammouth drain Brittain reconnitri position Maindis section Lieut Mathers 1st FOREST AREA Bridn. & Inniskilling section Cement material. 15 SAULES FARM	

WAR DIARY
INTELLIGENCE SUMMARY

Date	Hour	Summary of Events and Information	Remarks
24		KRUIS section moving known ammo Dumps	
25		No 1 section ordinary hostile scheme. No 2 section camouflage WIEDENDRIFT road	
		San pump dam. 3 ENGINEER FARM. Duckwalk ypres. Whipping ends of Bdy Cmth	
		No 2 section Cmult No Elephant SAULES FARM. No 1 section ammo Dumps	
		by night in the support line. Sound trapping kitten hut by Bdy. KRUIS section	
		ammo Dump at STEEN BEEK Brake. Tramlaying camouflage Dump. STEEN GREEN	
		SNOS hmmed ammo Dumps by night	
26		Attack in the light division front with barrage by our coming artillery much	
		a tough morning if it in the forward area – No 2 section due E Cmult	
		camouflage at WIEDENDRIFT was not got this but completed San pump down	
		SENTIER FARM No 3 section continued cmult work at SAULES FARM	

WAR DIARY
or
INTELLIGENCE SUMMARY.

(Erase heading not required.)

Army Form C. 2118.

Place	Date	Hour	Summary of Events and Information	Remarks and references to Appendices
	26th		No shells in now finished No 2 shelter in hand No 13 section do 15 enemy mm LTM's hvened dumps could not get thro' dust 1 killed 5 wounded Posts. Minimising section killed some trps at J camp - struck 750 at OVDYKE yards for the junction Sus work in camp with No section No 2 section shelling scheme No 2 section machine mining - mi by night No 3 section not section	
	27th		Carry on with No Stephens Scores from No creeker machine mining mm by night No 13 section carry mm at night elast bus Minimising completion No 13 section Bush Bathe carried Ireast the Shelter opened Men hvened dumps new successfully completed obry Day night The mining of the Support line U.21.B.7.0 the line U.15.C 6.0. - U.15.C 4a.3 - U.15.C.6.0. - U.21.B.0.7. - U.21.B.7.0 Done between 12 midnight & 3 am. - Clear mm - no shelling - Sappers ohs 600* Hammersbehw Rft 600* up 5* HUNTER STREET	

WAR DIARY
or
INTELLIGENCE SUMMARY.
(Erase heading not required.)

Army Form C. 2118.

Place	Date	Hour	Summary of Events and Information	Remarks and references to Appendices
	28th		at SAULES FARM. There was not sufficient material at site for a No 3 section, who were employed on repairs to Duckwalks, erection of camouflage for the Artillery near the German guns on the WIEDENDRIFT road (U20B.6.5½), repair of camouflage, reconnaissance of the STEENBEEK for obstacles to plan - Gun point done MONT MIRAIL FARM Coy HQ. Border & Inniskilling sections carried gravel camd XPM to 1st Saules Farm - No 1 Section Ordnance huts. Nos 2 & 3 section not after mining. Mills KIOSKS & SWB	
	29th		No 1 section - Ordnance huts. No 2 section - Repairs to Camouflage E. of STEENBEEK. do do duckboards. M.C. dugout MONTMIRAIL FARM Gun Demm No 3 section - Saules Farm Elephants No 4 section - Preparation of Camouflage & dump E. of Gun Demm WIEDENDRIFT HQ F.O.O HQ SWB } - Push gravel Cement XPM to Inniskilling } SAULES FARM KOBS - Put camouflage mat by No 4 section Border - Camouflage & Mistur huts in camp.	STEENBEEK

WAR DIARY
INTELLIGENCE SUMMARY
(Erase heading not required.)

Army Form C. 2118.

Place	Date	Hour	Summary of Events and Information	Remarks and references to Appendices
	30th		Sunday. Only Brien tection employed - Usey carry 30 that RMM - 120 bags sand	
			2 OS seven part 6" Smuggles Farm - Church Parade 11:30 Padre Rev Arden -	
			OC. & Lieut Lorimer visit hutting Scheme - CRE conference 3 PM CHATEAU ELVERDINGHE	
			No night work. Officer with CRE MAJOR WILSON RE SMS - NIL	
			Captain Langley transited site 26th inst. Lieut Matthews RE KOSB - Lieut McDonald	
			Lieut Vintis XIV Corp school. Lieut Loftus RE Borts - Lieut Elliott	
			Lieut Bridges Field Engineer Provost Lieut Buckley RE Inniskilling - Lieut Lees	
			Lieut Drummond RE	
			Attached Lieut Macaulay	
			In been Sergt Myers Recruit Cpl Gillett - Sergts Brittain - Brown - Thacker.	
			Sergt Clifford Cpl Ingram only No 2 section	
			Weather during September excellent - Cold nights with morning mists - Full moon 30th/1st	
			Being anything his less than last time up - Rest time to work 12 midnight - 3 am	
			f Down till 11 am. BT Wilson.	
			Major RE	
			OC 48th W Riding Field Coy RE	

War Diary.

455th. (W.R.) Field Coy. R.E.

Volume XX

Volume 20.

WAR DIARY
or
INTELLIGENCE SUMMARY.
(Erase heading not required.)

Army Form C. 2118.

453rd (Mx & Bucks) Field Coy R.E. (T)

Place	Date	Hour	Summary of Events and Information	Remarks and references to Appendices
ELVERDINGHE 28NW U15 c 27	Oct 1st 1917		No 2 Section — Additional Accommodation WIDEN DRIFT Bn HQ. Repair camouflage duckwalks. Liaison but Gen. Doms U15 central. No 3 Section — Continue Elephant SAULES FARM. Gen Doms to GOC & Ypres L. Cement of hut dugout. SubS } Lieut Gass & McDonald Kors } reconnoitre proposed positions of camouflage dumps. Muddie hui — Gas at night running mist joins at about 7.30 am Parade at 5 AM. No 2 section — Preparation of 700' of camouflage in line CANNES FARM — MONTMIRAIL FARM. No section — Ordnance hut. Border — Pushing panel board cement re L. SAULES FARM. Section worked in camp huts by day — lorry by night.	
	Oct 2nd		No 1 section — Hutting scheme ORDNANCE. No 3 section — Continue SAULES FARM. Prepare Coys 3 dugout huts. No 2 section — Cork HUT WIDEN DRIFT BRITISH Gas Store — Repair Camouflage & duckwalks. No 4 section — Making standing covered ways L. STEENBEEK	

WAR DIARY
or
INTELLIGENCE SUMMARY.
(Erase heading not required.)

Army Form C. 2118.

Place	Date	Hour	Summary of Events and Information	Remarks and references to Appendices
	4th		KORB] Carrying camouflage by night to Dumps in the LANGEMARCK line SWB] Border Carrying gravel sand & cement L-SAVIES FARM. Inniskilling carrying camouflage by day to the STEENBEEK - roof silk evacuated. During night 4th/5th erected 300ft of camouflage 200ft North of the line CARNET PAPPY - MONTMIRAIL FARM - Carrying by Border SWBs erection by No 2 & 3 of SWB Work during day without sandbagging. making camouflage and ½ erecting.	
	5th		Working by the majority of the Company - KORB SWBs carried materials 6" SAVIES FARM aftermoon mat making, camouflage sandbagging Milsen hut - marking road in front of Company Dump. WHITE 110 ELVERDINGHE - RSM Macaulay & Sanches reconnoitered the new section nothing LANGEMARCK.	
	6th		No section ordered buddy scheme No 2 section Repairs D-DICKEBUSCH Clapper Street, Bridge Street thornyhop - L Tournalopu.	

WAR DIARY
or
INTELLIGENCE SUMMARY.

Army Form C. 2118.

Place	Date	Hour	Summary of Events and Information	Remarks and references to Appendices
	6th		Gun doors completed – Grants Div RE takes over the work today. No 4 section continued camouflage along the WIDENDRIFT road joining up with that not making much progress – No 3 section making much progress St. Croning – that erected Quiet morning – t Camouflage in camp – C.O. reconnoitred Battleground & RETIRED AVENUE Wieltje – Bridle tracks around yards tracks by Lieut Marchant. Very quiet work – For the last 3 days weather has been bad & much colder morning – Parade for work 2Ell at Staff. Shown him Slates installed in the men – Parade for work 2Ell at Staff. Best time to work 2Ell Steen L- changed to work time night 6th/7th. be from dawn till 10 A.M.	
	7th		Sunday – Cold + overcast – Parade Staff. For all section except No 2 section, who make Camouflage in camp – work No 1 section – Skilling No 2 section – Camouflage in camp No 3 section – Repair RETIRED AVENUE No 4 section – E. of STEEN BEEK.	

WAR DIARY
or
INTELLIGENCE SUMMARY.
(Erase heading not required.)

Army Form C. 2118.

Place	Date	Hour	Summary of Events and Information	Remarks and references to Appendices
No 2 Section	7th		Built camouflage on our own section E. of Alle Hundes St.	
Kurts Suns			Carry camouflage. Built camouflage. } Carry duck boards & Trench mortar Dumps. Ammunition.	
No 1 Section	8th		Werried hidges on the STEENBEEK S. of the STADEN R.W. at U.28.A.12.4½	
No 3 Section			Werried upon RETREAT AVENUE duckwork E. of the STEENBEEK Sergeant Brown of No 1 section (Light Distinued) was unable to work	
			Slightly wounded in the leg - Late arrived of the Whistle reposed him BARCANT CAMP - When on camouflage waiting to the loaded they later loaded with burst bombs and sent to IRON CROSS (No NP)	
No 2 Section			were not arrived, they later loaded with burst bombs and sent to IRON CROSS (No NP)	
& Lieut Distinued			made camouflage in camp - In the afternoon 10 men of No 2 section pulled 2 pairs of of the hund on the hund from 17th	
STEEN BEEK known on			RETREAT AVENUE - On the night of the 7th/8th No section	
20 string			carried Duck boards to make a Duck board walk from E. of	
LANGEMARCH			EMPEE TRENCH. Walked today from Paris in the morning, rain in the afternoon.	

WAR DIARY or INTELLIGENCE SUMMARY

Army Form C. 2118.

Place	Date	Hour	Summary of Events and Information	Remarks and references to Appendices
	9th		The day of another attack on the front of the 5th & 2nd Armies. Zero hour at 5.20 a.m. Company paraded at 5 a.m. - Following were the work allotted.	
			No. 1 section - Up-keep of 4 bridges in the STEENBEEK under Lieut Macaulay Essex Regt.	
			No. 2 section - 10% reserve in camp	
			No. 3 section - Carrying duckboards	
			No. 4 section - Up keep of Canal bridges { N12 street CACTUS TRESTLE & IRON CROSS 190 N	
			Three little parties or our limber carried Duckboards to IRON CROSS. The under carried Sandbags, shovels & chickenwire to IRON CROSS. 3 Sappers of No. 2 went with 10 G.A. men of 176 R.E. under LIEUT Goss 142 RE under DAVIES St. to the heighbourhood of the STEENBEEK on Minnenthshire Regt. with 6 Sappers + 12 SWB laid the chicken up of DAVID LANE from BROSE trench to front N.E. of that MOUSE within 300* of the front line - 1 Sapper was blown up but not injured & this party went think & considerable amount of shell fire - Capt Hill was Y/c N/T12 Sappers - The allotted infantry of	

WAR DIARY
or
INTELLIGENCE SUMMARY.
(Erase heading not required.)

Army Form C. 2118.

Place	Date	Hour	Summary of Events and Information	Remarks and references to Appendices
RUTLOWEI CAMP 27/FIELD A. Sz.	10th		KONIS Brides & Inniskilling Regiment. Each made three trips up the line from STEENSTEIN to Essex hutch — KONIS but 2 O.R. wounded. Relieved 1st camp about 6.30 P.M. — First day — rain at night. Itonering on 1st. The 93rd Field A.E. 17th Division at RED Ho. Sappers and attached infantry handed over at 11.30 & returned some other 12 noon to PROVEN area — Mounted section left at 12 noon and reached RUTLOWES camp near the CRAPOUTRE — POPERINGHE road about 3 o'clock — Attached infantry returned to their Battalions. Lieutenant Macaulay Essex Regt instructed — The Army Commander Sir Hugh Gough wished the troopers entraining & asked several questions about our work etc — Fine day	
	11th		Drill parade at 9 A.M. setting up billets — Making approaches to 1st camp. Cleaning horses, making latrines, improving horse lines, cleaning & spanning higiene. Light Bridges returned from Field Engineer Depôt. — Rain during day	
	12th		Drill parade 9 A.M. — Light Vehicles returned from XIVth Corps School — Fatigues same as for the 11th inst. — Rain during day.	

WAR DIARY
or
INTELLIGENCE SUMMARY.

(Erase heading not required.)

Army Form C. 2118.

Place	Date	Hour	Summary of Events and Information	Remarks and references to Appendices
	13th		Drill parade 9 a.m. followed by short march - Kit inspection at 11. Lieut Dishunt & the other parade went to the Rest Camp at EQUIHEN parading at 6 a.m. - Visit of other Adjutants with with Sergeant Stanley at 3 P.M. Sergeant MYERS in Dr Chapman & Parsons - Rain & storms at intervals - Officers who advance reprissentative left with others of the 87th Brigade Amy - NCO + CSgt GILMITT Ors. Major Wilson - Lieut Mathews, Buckley, Leffler, Bridger, Winter - Sgt Bristol, Myler, Brown, Capt Newitt. - D.A.V.S. inspected horses yesterday opined that they had him off since his last inspection - 12 remount arrived on the 10th October all lit light - Drivers are short in the mounted section -	
	14th		Sunday. Voluntary church parade 10.30 A.M. Army Church that proved has been a success here.	
	15th		Passing of 1st Battalion at HOUPOUTRE. Train leaves 8.45. Entrainment carried out without incident.	

WAR DIARY
or
INTELLIGENCE SUMMARY.

Army Form C. 2118.

Place	Date	Hour	Summary of Events and Information	Remarks and references to Appendices
BLANGY-VILLE 9 Kilos S.W. of ARRAS	16th		Arrived at BEAUMETZ LA RIVIÈRE at dawn - Comfortable detrainment with break fast on the station - first keen morning air very much like those in FLANDERS. BLANGYVILLE is in the devastated area, but a comfortable camp huts & Men employed in the afternoon in making billets comfortable.	
	17th		Drill parade at 9 A.M. Continuing improvement & drill.	
	18th		Company paraded drill order at 9 a.m. and worked on, horse troughs and standings, dismissed. Baths and various jobs on camp. Lecture in the afternoon to all officers & N.C.O's gymnastic section on how to fatting of horses.	
	19th		Paraded at 9 a.m. for half hours drill. Nos 1,3 & 4 sections worked on cleaning the 2 Nissen huts for reerection in officers camp. Also worked on horse troughs and Bath. No 2 Section completed proceed by road to AUENS-LE-COMTE, under Lieut Buckley. Billeted there the night for practical emergency. Lieut Hopkins proceed on Leave Home.	

WAR DIARY or INTELLIGENCE SUMMARY

Army Form C. 2118.

Place	Date	Hour	Summary of Events and Information	Remarks and references to Appendices
BLAIRVILLE	20th		No's 1, 3 & 4 Sections paraded at 6.15 am in full marching order, 10 rounds of blank ammunition per man and marched under sealed orders to SIMENCOURT under Lieut. Mathers. Orders were opened at 12 o'clock and the party marched to intercept No 2 Section on road BASSEUX – BLAIRVILLE and prevent their transport – supposed demolition party – from getting to BLAIRVILLE. The three sections took up a position directly east of Basseux, and No 2 section found it impossible to move their transport out of that village, until "Cease fire" was sounded by Major Wilson. Lieut. Brooks & 15 men of No 2 were left in enemy rear camp.	
	21st		Rifle inspection 8.45 a.m. and Church Parade at 9. a.m. Football in the afternoon, mounted section v No 3. – No 3 won. Major Wilson entertained on Leave.	

Army Form C. 2118.

WAR DIARY
or
INTELLIGENCE SUMMARY.
(Erase heading not required.)

Instructions regarding War Diaries and Intelligence Summaries are contained in F. S. Regs., Part II. and the Staff Manual respectively. Title pages will be prepared in manuscript.

Place	Date	Hour	Summary of Events and Information	Remarks and references to Appendices
BLAIRVILLE	22nd		No. 4 Section proceed with all small bridging stores and erected a covering ring for the 87th B.Le. under Lieut Bridgen.	
			No. 2 Section prepared field works for the future instruction of Infantry Officers of 87th B.Le. under Lieut Santer.	
			No. 1 & 3 Sections on the improvement of HENDICOURT camps and theatre.	
	23rd		No. 1 Section pulled down some Roden huts for to conversion to be used on the HENDICOURT camps.	
			No. 2 Section continued on field works commenced on 22nd inst.	
			No. 3 Section erected new dressing rooms at Latts.	
			No. 4 Section worked on the theatre under Lieut Bridgen.	
	24th		Paraded at 9 a.m. and continued work as on the 23rd inst.	

Army Form C. 2118.

WAR DIARY
or
INTELLIGENCE SUMMARY.
(Erase heading not required.)

Place	Date	Hour	Summary of Events and Information	Remarks and references to Appendices
BLAIRVILLE	25th		Nos 1 & 3 Sections worked on HENDICOURT camp — chiefly flooring huts. No. 2 & 4 mounted sections proceed at 4 a.m. under the orders of that Brigade, to BAPAUME where they will be joined by the remainder of the mounted section of other field cos. and H.Q. R.E. mounted section — to proceed the following day further north — exact destination unknown. No 2 & 4 dismounted men left, under Lieut Vinter in bus lorries for ARRAS station, where the will entrain for the "destination unknown" as about above. Company with other field cos. and personel of HQ R.E.	
	26th		Nos 1 & 3 Sections carried on the works at HENDICOURT camp under Lieut Doatnal.	

WAR DIARY
or
INTELLIGENCE SUMMARY.
(Erase heading not required)

Army Form C. 2118.

Place	Date	Hour	Summary of Events and Information	Remarks and references to Appendices
BLAIRVILLE	27th		No 1 & 3 Sections worked on HENDICOURT camps, flooring the mens huts	
			20 men of No 3 section under Lieut Distinal proceeded by lorrie to 29 th Div depot. Lataluini, to assist in the erection of huts for the next few days. Tool cart also went.	
	28th		No 1 section & H.Q. section clean arms inspection at 9 a.m. afterwards proceeded on to work on camps as on 27th H.Q. section commenced painting the tracing wagons.	
	29th		The oc remaining section No 1, worked on HENDICOURT camps and tents, HQ section on wagon paintings. Lieut Matters acting Captain, opening in todays orders.	

WAR DIARY
or
INTELLIGENCE SUMMARY.

Army Form C. 2118.

Place	Date	Hour	Summary of Events and Information	Remarks and references to Appendices
Blendecq	Oct 30		Work for No 1 & H.Q. sections as on 29th. No 3 section returned Div Depot Nocturnal 8.20 a.m. Mr Buckley & 15 men of No 2 section enlarging Nissen huts. Mr Buckley & 15 men of No 2 section rejoined from Army Rest Camp. Also 15 men of the Kent Field Co. & 15 men and one officer of the London Field Co. and a reinforcement officer for the London Co. joined us from the same rest camp, and are to work with us pending a move to their own Companies.	
	31st		Work ourself at 9 am. Nos 1 & 3 sections took on Hinchcourt Camp and the Kent & London men attached took on the stables. your own camp.	

F. D. Mathews Capt. R.E.
For O.C. 4 S.S./M.R. Bn E.R.

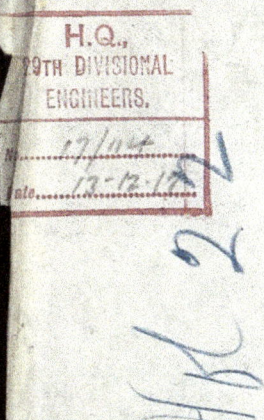

CONFIDENTIAL.

WAR DIARY.

OF

455TH. (WEST RIDING) FIELD COY., R.E.,

VOLUME 21.

(November 1917).

WAR DIARY

Army Form C. 2118.

NOVEMBER 1917
455th W. Riding Field Co RE ①

INTELLIGENCE SUMMARY.
(Erase heading not required.)

Place	Date	Hour	Summary of Events and Information	Remarks and references to Appendices
Bracelle	Nov 1st		Nos 1 & 3 sections with attached Kent & London R E work on the HENDICOURT Camps, and the 15mm of No 2 section work on an on status. Men were also detailed for work on the Divl Baths, and water supply system at BASSEUX. Two non-scouring & dump at WARLINCOURT. The Divl Cinema, and huts for the D.A.D.O.S at Bazuen. Bonder guides for lorries.	
	2nd		Nos 1 & 3 Sections with attached London & Kent R E men worked as on return. No 2 Section worked on Camp improvements and on the Company dump. Lieut Loftus returned from home leave.	

WAR DIARY
or
INTELLIGENCE SUMMARY.
(Erase heading not required.)

Army Form C. 2118.

Place	Date	Hour	Summary of Events and Information	Remarks and references to Appendices
Blainville	Nov 2nd		The 15 men of No 2 section Detail of No 4 section recently returned from leave, together with attached men of the London and Kent Field Cos, and two London officers proceeded by lorries to rejoin the half Co. of Kent Fortress, and the London and Kent Companies at F.N. No 1 Section worked on the HENDICOURT Camp and No 3 section on stables.	
	4th		Parade 9 a.m. Rifle inspection. Voluntary Church Parade at 9.57 a.m.	
	5th		No 1 Section worked on HENDICOURT camps and No 3 on on stables. An officer of the Kent R.E. joined on returning from Army course.	

WAR DIARY
or
INTELLIGENCE SUMMARY.
(Erase heading not required.)

Army Form C. 2118.

Place	Date	Hour	Summary of Events and Information	Remarks and references to Appendices
BLAIRVILLE	Nov 6th		No 1 Section HENDICOURT. Camps & No 3 on outposts. Lieut Deakins proceeded to Bays & FINS to take the place of Lieut Venter proceeding on leave. By same conv also went the officers of the Kent R.E. and two batmen and one sapper of the London R.E. returned from leave. Also GM Coles went to the detached two sections.	
	7th		[illegible] ... Hugh Liken ultimate ...	
	8th		Two Deluxe at Blairville ... of holes as to be hardly [illegible]	
	9th		stated - The following Rating was ones on movers day.	
	10th		5 hole unit march in full order with 10 y made his magazine ... of the Royal [illegible] or ...	
	11th		Gen. Kavanaugh inspected ... to 2 trailer ly in gate troop in the [illegible] ...	
	12th		all ... in tell	

Army Form C. 2118.

WAR DIARY
or
INTELLIGENCE SUMMARY.
(Erase heading not required)

Instructions regarding War Diaries and Intelligence Summaries are contained in F. S. Regs., Part II. and the Staff Manual respectively. Title pages will be prepared in manuscript.

Place	Date	Hour	Summary of Events and Information	Remarks and references to Appendices
	12th		Our men still — Pack drill musketry instruction in Gos lines — Making up 2 Squad Reveille 6.30 The Regiment on Brigade at Brigadeperiont	
	14th		Funeral of George (?) Funeral parade in Berkville church today Leaving at 9.30 A.M. Service at (Trupswork's?)	
			Filed along to Launching pontoon bridge inspected by No 1 + 3 section received 2th instructor	
BERKVILLE	15th		Practised 2 days instructing + Launching pontoon bridge	
			Under 1½ section — Locate — by our in Eyed — received 2th instructor	
			before 4.30 P.M. — (Forsythe?) our to Top Hayes HEADQUART	
			Last to march — Friendly + entertaining Capt to 15 Section WAGS —	
			In the form — Buccellos on 16 steps was higher — Back Rope Gone	
			Filled buff Motor to Battalion Aid pool to the nights at AS higher. Billets in half.	
			Him Battalion off	
			Later in the day — Scotch from Leave	
SUAKIN	16		Day laying filling have her at 15 bodies of Scotch Brinma shilled for	
IN			Attached R. E. — Part 2 the evening Strech plutoon Low distance	
			orn the top — Major Halomer — Major Distance	
			Come in the push — Officers — Captain Matteson and Bridgens	

WAR DIARY
or
INTELLIGENCE SUMMARY

Army Form C. 2118.

Place	Date	Hour	Summary of Events and Information	Remarks and references to Appendices
SOMME	17th		Andre Arrived 9 am - Settling down a/c. Lunch - CRE - Corporals 2 ppl at Lunch. Field Coy Officer - Dined. Turned in at 10 by Mobile.	
			Report sent to HQ for 11.00 hours.	
	18th		Reconnaissance of VILLERS PLOUICH front line by Major Balz.	
			The whole in am - C.R.E. and various Mess of section accompanied MAJOR WILSON Captain Mathews + Lieut Disbrowe - Had lunch in an intact dugout 3rd Corps Dump - Beautiful day + hardly a shot firing - considerable activity in railway construction in VILLERS PLOUICH - 9.2" guns already mounted in VILLERS PLOUICH - Front line system well dug - Reconnoitred suitable bivouac for the night 19th/20th at GOUZEAUCOURT just north of the FINS-GOUZEAUCOURT road. Cross country track from GOUZEAUCOURT to SOTHER.	
	19th		Half Coy Painters under Captain Spencer joined from the Monmouths that night who attacked infantry Lieut GASH + CAIN - New section practised with handsaws throughout equipment of L scantal - Got timely for made Canvey 12 in all.	

(A7092) Wt W28859/M1293. 75,000. 11/17. D.D. & L., Ltd. Forms/C.2118/4.

WAR DIARY
INTELLIGENCE SUMMARY

Army Form C. 2118.

Place	Date	Hour	Summary of Events and Information	Remarks and references to Appendices
Bivouac just W. of GOUZEAUCOURT just N. of the road to FINS	19th		Lt Dishmand and 1st section advance party to bivouac to set it ready - Remaining 2 sections Infantry Personnel marched at 3.17 AM him some his Fire Lithe bivouac - Distinguish nos & section detailed to type trump on the GOUZEAUCOURT - FINS road for possible pendicing work on (2 + 1) day - this section left some in the afternoon - Camped late at the bivouac - Concentration at bivouac complete by 5.30 AM - Captain Mallion remained i/c at some Marched	
MARCOING	20th		Zero at 6.40 AM - Morning mist - Artillery barrage very brisk - Marched Nt with Nos 1,2,3 section, 12 minutes ½ company Ponies (90) - 100 infantry at 8 AM - Reached a position of vantage at Villers Plouich behind 87th Brigade at 9 AM - Drew horse shelters for the infantry from the III Corps Dump at VILLERS PLOUICH while waiting - 87th Bgde set off at 10 am - Continued after them in first form. The fight of the attack proceeding up the VILLERS-PLOUICH - MARCOING valley was very exhilarating - The 96th were on the West of the valley - the 87th Brigade	

WAR DIARY or INTELLIGENCE SUMMARY

Army Form C. 2118.

In the Evt – The tanks were the principle interest of the day & very much in evidence. Nos 1 & 2 Section R.E. the intensity altered the position provided in 3 afternoon moving in file, behind the last regiment of the 87th Brigade. By 12 noon he was close to MARCOING & was installed in billets by 2 P.M. Coy H.Q. at some German artillery H.Q. at L22.D.65 – Infantry position at L22.D.8.4. in a big barn – No 3 Section was put in the dugouts of the German gun position close to Coy H.Q. – the whole shot back – No 1 Section left post in the Rly bridge at MARCOING. Enormous explosion – leads from the from before nightfall – No 2 Section left post on the canal bridge at L23.B.1.8. & unused explosion in the same manner – Guards were put on the bridges for the night – Brigade H.Q. were temporarily established at the Villa Charmette L23.C.2½.3½ – armaments were made for their installation in a large dug out at L22.D.4.4. in a hut, & which has been handsomely contributed by the enemy to our occupation –

WAR DIARY or INTELLIGENCE SUMMARY

Army Form C. 2118.

Place	Date	Hour	Summary of Events and Information	Remarks and references to Appendices
MARCOING	21st		Two prisoners were captured by No2 section & sent back under guard to GOUZEAUCOURT with report to the C.R.E. – No2 section also took a German sniper & les magn with various other booty including a very neat Schuemacker for cutting erriais. Left behind at the Canal bridge, when endeavouring to blow it up – Stand to at 5:15 AM. In view of the incredible shelling your MR2 were extended in the Hindenburg line under Captain Matthews at R2D6a. No's 1,2 sections were sent back to your MR2 with the attacking infantry. Fourteen prisoners were sent back to your MR2 – No2 section we took at night – All transport was brought forward to your MR2. Lieut Dickenson jammed in the German gun supports with Co.MR2 made. Made of the line at MARCOING. During the day a through reconnaissance was made of the line at MARCOING & 2 retained German dumps taken over – one Pioneer Dump in the line at L26 B 65 – the other at MARCOING copse L29 A 55 in which any variety of R.E. material was found, including several cart of PERDITE & demolition charges.	

(A)6921. Wt. W12899/M1505. 75,000. 1/17. D. D. & L., Ltd. Forms/C.2118/14.

Place	Date	Hour	Summary of Events and Information	Remarks and references to Appendices
	21.3		The town of MARCOING had been left in a great hurry by the enemy & bodys of Brug Discipline had been left behind including machine gun limbers. Lewis motor lorries & anti aircraft guns at the Ville Chemicelle. Six machine gun limbers were Essentiels to Bri⁰ HQ by the company. The cooker was taken to no mans land & also to the C.S. wagons. The sketch had L23 A 59 had been used by the enemy for installing a cistern had, a trestle & Brid⁰ braces. All of which was well filled out. The catacombs near the church at L22 B/L.8 had been exploited by the Germans, but did not show signs of recent occupation nor did the large dugout used as 87th Brigade HQ. The tunnel ran in good order and being used by the service of front line and the front. The R.E. did not appear to have been used. R.19 of front line. The sidings had been shipped. There was some Bregovs near the bridge. The rails of all the sidings had been shipped. There were some Bregovs near the bridge work at L24.C. All the bridges were intact. The large wire in the brigade sector one at L23 D12 the other all around at L24 C 59. N⁰3 section during the day worked on Ryde HQ taking up trumps & improving accommodation. One prisoner was captured during the day & sent to the HQ - O.C. Coy reconnitred the	

Army Form C. 2118.

WAR DIARY
or
INTELLIGENCE SUMMARY.
(Erase heading not required.)

Place	Date	Hour	Summary of Events and Information	Remarks and references to Appendices
MARCOING	21st		Remained during the afternoon to work arrangements the following day. The attack of the 67th Brigade on the Red line, which was timed for 11 AM has not à present, taken effect. It carried ground so far on the line N edge of CH⁵⁰ TALMA Street, all'H – L18C 70 – C10A59 where junction with the 86th Brigade was effected – L18C 70 – C10A59 where junction was distributed. Orders were issued to prepare the	
MARCOING	22nd		Stand to at 5.15 daily was instituted. Captain McKean MMC Section R¹⁵ bridge – Canal bridge at L23B16 for demolition – Lieut Dishimed R E did the canal bridge leaving Sp⁵ Faith + 10R in charge, being captured enemy explosive for the Section Stations work on the R¹⁵ bridge at L23D 12 Preparing the bange at L23D 12 purpost – work also done during day – Clearing the line path near the R¹⁵ bridge of fallen tim as a foot bridge – also a Sik tram link on the Bridge Head line – Pioneer + allotted infantry cleared the canal at L23 B 3.10. 15 The line retainers designed to retain the most part already prepared canal at G.19 C 55 + blowing the line for the enemy – complete with Bellative by the enemy Bayonet	

WAR DIARY or INTELLIGENCE SUMMARY

Army Form C. 2118.

Place	Date	Hour	Summary of Events and Information	Remarks and references to Appendices
	22nd		No 1 section dry with the Princess — During the day girders were furnished to the supply of Knife rest from the German dumps & for concertina also — 100 of their being dumped at East Flank of the bridge head him to the use of the infantry in the front line — The German M.G. limber was sent to the yard during the night & some German hay collected from the street paving to use there — L/ Bridger Cpk up our London Equipment to MASNIÈRES & handed it over to the Kent F.O. Co to making a bridge there — MASNIÈRES is considerably shelled — Marcoing is comparatively free especially at night	
	23rd		Work was continued on the job mentioned for the 22nd — No 2 section worked during the day at the C.T. from the Bays foot bridge to the Bridge Head hung No 3 section as stated & richshoring ground of Grenville explosion received from Corps from Coy H.Q. to MARCOING Corpse Dump — Pusieur & mchorby shift on the Poster Head him culling & section on hillside mid & night	≠ D

Army Form C. 2118.

WAR DIARY
or
INTELLIGENCE SUMMARY.
(Erase heading not required.)

Instructions regarding War Diaries and Intelligence Summaries are contained in F. S. Regs., Part II. and the Staff Manual respectively. Title pages will be prepared in manuscript.

Place	Date	Hour	Summary of Events and Information	Remarks and references to Appendices
	24th		Various guides to Dumps to the infantry to help them in forming Dumps of material to forward work – to visit R.E. supplies from the 5th Army school at Betagzel & bringing up more picks & shovels. Work continued on Regt Hd. Bridge head line, Demolitions work. Guns put down & many wells put in MAROEUIL – L.T. Bridges Came up L.T. MAROEUIL to take over supervision of Bridge 143 line work – Distribution of Coys as follows for the remainder of time as at MAROEUIL	
			Lt Bridges { No 1 Section – Employed extensively on Bridge 143 line work at night No 2 Section – ... by day No 3 Section – Demolition work, bridges & work in MAROEUIL No 4 Section – L.T. visits – Wiring Bridge 143 line Pionecrs } Digging Att. Infantry }	

WAR DIARY
or
INTELLIGENCE SUMMARY.
(Erase heading not required.)

Army Form C. 2118.

13.

Place	Date	Hour	Summary of Events and Information	Remarks and references to Appendices
At Livry	24th		OC Coy — Captain Mallin	
at Coy HQ			Lieut Bishimut Lt Wills	attached
			Lieut Bridgen Lt Cmdr Border Regt	infantry
			No 3 Section " Cain Suns	
			Captain Spencer ⎫	
			Lieut Slevin ⎬ ½ Monmouth	
			Lieut Edwards ⎭ shire	
			Lieut Owen Regin Inf	
			CSM — Sergt Gillett	
			No 1 Section — Sergt Britcher	
			No 2 Section — Sergt Myers No. 2 ½ sections MR Rgt	
			No 3 Section — Sergt Brown	
			No 4 Section — Sergt Thacker	
	25th		Changes in bridges kindly ready for elaboration of R19 bridge, road bridge	
			here it E Canal kitch all for explain with the Captain. An infantry guard	
			was arranged to safe guard the charge under Lieut Cain with MR at L23A89	
			with Wills riders on to select of guards mining sentries re — Work on Bridge	
			Heed Line continued on for scheme — The heavy bridge at L23D 9½ 2½	
			was hindered decked over to take mule Traffic	

Army Form C. 2118.

WAR DIARY
or
INTELLIGENCE SUMMARY.
(Erase heading not required.)

Instructions regarding War Diaries and Intelligence Summaries are contained in F. S. Regs., Part I. and the Staff Manual respectively. Title pages will be prepared in manuscript.

Place	Date	Hour	Summary of Events and Information	Remarks and references to Appendices
	26th		Bridge at L24 c was prepared for demolition with supply fuzes – A broken down lorry in the road at L22 D 23 was blocking the Traffic – ordered for destruction – This was done with incendiary charge – hardly satisfactory – about 12 hours of spare time – 1 OR. evacuated sick.	
	27th		Work continued on road including laying circuits of charge – wires laid on MAZINGHIEN side and MAZINGHIEN - LE MAROCINE road and MAZINGHIEN – The spinning bracket in the Steinville line removed, as it was considered charge from the pillar of the Rly bridge was removed. Shelling morning & evening daily in Valenne – Highway.	
			They might be hit by chance shell – Additional work included repairing bridge. Work on Bridge Head line continued – MAZINGHIEN bridge on the ESCAUT near MAROCINE CAFÉ damaged by shell fire – lost bridge at G.14 c.6o. Lieut Bishivral + 4 men cut the Rly line 200x North of hut line at L18 c 7½ 7. It known that no enemy unarmed known shewed approach to chu – Bright moonlight night – work done with leads + explodes which acted side of line by British Regiment	

WAR DIARY
or
INTELLIGENCE SUMMARY.
(Erase heading not required.)

Army Form C. 2118.

Place	Date	Hour	Summary of Events and Information	Remarks and references to Appendices
	29th		Work continued without incident — Visit of CRE with CE III Corps, who complimented Coy on the steadiness of a working party t/Corpl McCormick — The Bridge Head line is now East in many places on the bank of the canal at the turning on the road to the bank of the canal at G.19.c.55 in the SE 3'x3' section throughout including a C.T. from L.24 to L.7th loop post hidden at L.23.D.12. — The line is continuous across the station yard — it is strong in the W. & weak in the East — the Sniper's loose at G.19.c.15.9. wants attending to if it is not to the loose — its top windows sweep the trench. —	
	30th		Quiet morning — At breakfast time the shooting of the line was rather brisk & delayed work — About nine o'clock Sergt. Myers arrived with his section with the surveying team, that men of the 20th Divn. was steaming northwards from NESLA Ridge during the whole of his march L. MARCOING from the HINDENBURG LINE. This was hotly confirmed with a few shots from the trees S. of our dugout Orders were given L.TWZ section, who had to aim L. VIREM L. REMIEZ and stand to — Bright was informed	

WAR DIARY or INTELLIGENCE SUMMARY

Army Form C. 2118.

Place	Date	Hour	Summary of Events and Information	Remarks and references to Appendices
	30th		of the horn of events — No 3 section was moved forward to in marching order in the smoke. W. of Brigade HQ — Bgde sent out an officer (Captain Ewbank Border Regt) to clear up the situation & demanded the stand to. In a short time (about 20') Germans in some numbers were coming over the ridge at L35 & L30. The M.G. on top of Bgde HQ opened fire did good work. The Sappers & No 3 section rolled available of two Bgde HQ lined the road to VILLERS-FAUCON, with reinforcements catching along it to make first with the support line of the third enduring Support system. The 88th Bgde in billets in MARCOING hastily debouched from the village & at once clearing the enemy, who had worked as far as the nolan caps of MARCOING COPSE — No 3 section fired for some 15 minutes at the Germans, who soon were seen sent as reinforced, leaving many dead visible through sparish shot L29 D strength of One – Lt Bishinnal & wharfs of men was this sent to visit the bridges – Lt Pritzger with the few men remaining & No 3 section –	16.

was sent to join Captain Mulholan at Rear H.Q., who was ordered to hold on to his position, evacuate transport & prepare to reinforce MARCOING if opposed - O.C. Coy on the other side of the Canal reconnoitred the PREMY ridge which found that this was clear, that the left was unaffected by the event taking place S. of MASNIÈRES. As this was a shortage of ammo Captain Mulholan was ordered by runner to send up some by himself in Captain Mulholan's own as possible - By chance he collected in the thickening him Attamine as soon as possible - By chance he collected up by Motor Ambulance + 1 Platoon Riveters (Lt Stevens) 2000 rounds, which was carried up by Motor Ambulance just short of Bgdt HQ on the During this work Sgt Binfield was killed leading from to the R.E. dump. Orders were received for the Sappers South & leading from to collect picks, shovels at MARCOING Copse & help to dig a fresh line Riveters to collect picks, shovels at MARCOING Copse & help to dig a fresh line for the Hants Regiment about the N vs grid line between L34 - L35 This was successfully done - The Riveters lost whilst BOR wounded - Spr Woollen in & the Cx runner was wounded - Spr Ellis was killed on the thickening line

Army Form C. 2118.

WAR DIARY
or
INTELLIGENCE SUMMARY.
(Erase heading not required.)

Place	Date	Hour	Summary of Events and Information	Remarks and references to Appendices
	30th		CO started work on the lyser line to the Hants mentioned above connected Brigade (Gen LUCAS) & obtained & Rear HQ's to see what had happened to Coy - hament & clean up the builder there - Situation at Rear HQ normal - Transport had been sent away in the morning under Lt White - Infantry Pioneer & RE section was all in the support line of the Hindenburg front system at R3A33 with Captain Matthew in charge - The salient work of the 57th Division on this day was seen by the FGCO CG was met interest - of the string of high times & no other and much the same which formed rear HQ's on the VILLERS-PLOUICH road now in the of triangle of the division -	

BT Wilson
Major RE
OC 455th W Riding Field Co RE

CONFIDENTIAL

WAR DIARY

OF

455th (WEST RIDING) FIELD Co RE (T)

FROM DEC 1st 1917 TO DEC 31st 1918

VOLUME XXII

WAR DIARY
INTELLIGENCE SUMMARY

Army Form C. 2118.

Place	Date	Hour	Summary of Events and Information	Remarks and references to Appendices
MARCOING	Dec 1st		Co. left L- SORREL hit Hindenburg Kring line, 'BEAU CAMP' near Gouzeaucourt L- HENDICOURT & SORREL L- ascertain what had happened L- 184th & 142 Bt MANCHESTER. CRE G.E. MILLS went up to L- SORREL on Nov 30th at QUENTIN MILL — CRE G.E. MILLS heard of which had been captured. L- MARCOING where they at SORREL 1st/2nd. Bt Manchester Pioneers were billeted L- MARCOING in the early morning of Dec 2nd — went into the Bridge Head line in the early morning about the During this day D distributed ammunition at Bgde HQ hauling wire about the bridges — Captain Mathews RE & attached infantry Pioneers — Sapper Lee the Hindenburg Line + Lieu Subjected L- Artillery fire & indirect M.G. fire — In the covering Captain Spencer & the Pioneers went across forward/00 L- MARCOING by Gen. Lucas 87th Bgde — No orders for the Sappers or infantry either he knew they were available — Co. wining L- MARCOING with the Pioneers, who only just wound in time to get into their place in the Bridge Head line —	
	Dec 2nd		Morning Quiet — A heavy battle started at about 11 am + continued all day in which the enemy succeeded nothing — The 87th Brigade across the canal — the 88th Brigade south of it	

Place	Date	Hour	Summary of Events and Information	Remarks and references to Appendices
Harcourt	Dec 2nd		No work was possible — In the evening the whole of the 87th Brigade started, 15th Brigade of 5th division being the relieving troops under Brigadier General Walker — At no field company turned up to relieve us, he was handed over to the 16th Inf Brigade in charge of the demolition of the bridge if it became necessary. The field company, that night to have relieved us and didn't was the 509th London F.Co — An advance party arrived at 9am Hd During the 2nd a small wire it came in later, when the shelling steamed (sic), but apparently the shelling had decreased sufficiently for them as they never arrived. The 16th Inf. have Take over 87th Bgde HB as they were left behind — Brigade did not Take over CO HB Lt Bishinut's CO, & 5 supper	
Harcourt	3rd		The day opened quietly — Present at CO HB Lt Bishinut's CO, & 5 supper At 10 o'clock the shelling of the town increased slightly but was not serious so we went out to make it — At 11 o'clock it became very severe & the concrete dug out was peppered with shell — At 12, Taking advantage of a lull in the shelling of No Bgde HB we removed to the	

WAR DIARY
or
INTELLIGENCE SUMMARY

Army Form C. 2118.

Place	Date	Hour	Summary of Events and Information	Remarks and references to Appendices
MARCOING	Dec 3rd	1.30pm	from the enemies dugout — While at lunch, a wounded man reported that the Germans were in the town — he went out & saw the enemy troops men in the W. edge of MARCOING COPSE. All machine guns in the dugout were turned out to line the ground in front of the sunk road E. of the dugout	
		2.30	Met report of Gen Nelson Comdg 88th Bgde Co. Went down to see Gen Nelson Comdg 16 Bgde HQ at L27.13.18 & point out exact locality in Leuzewing the ground N. of The canal (The Peninsula) — Returned by the Lt Bickmond sent to list demolition in canals — 4/capt. McCormick Sgt. Faites recommended in him exdens shelt his on the R.W. bridge — Infantry of the 16th Bgde had been in full retreat down the MARCOING bridge for some time	
		5.5	Situation Quickened down — Rifle fire audible SE of the sunken road being held — No sign of the enemy.	

WAR DIARY
or
INTELLIGENCE SUMMARY

Army Form C. 2118.

Place	Date	Hour	Summary of Events and Information	Remarks and references to Appendices
MALCORNE	3rd	6.45	Co. reconnoitred the bridges { Pty bridge at L23 A 7,0 / AT bridge at L23 B 18 / Canal bridge at L23 B 18 } c the whole of the horn. — Only bridges visible were about a span now of the Divisible equivalent at the bridge over the ESCAUT at L23 A 48. They were unable to hold the lock bridge at L23 B 18. No signs of the large 18th Inf Bgde at CRUCIFIX CORNER L22 A 66, when it was understood to was. I resolved to get definite news from him, & identification of bridges which was assuming more & more importance as a plaintiff from the Provisionals was clearly going on. There was no sign of any Germans.	
		7.05	Returned to old Bgde HQ Dry out. — Found that Sgt Thacker RE was with SSgt to search in the afternoon, when it was known that Demolition of bridges beyond the place had safely arrived — Capt Collins sent me with to meet Lt Wentworth	

WAR DIARY
or
INTELLIGENCE SUMMARY.

(Erase heading not required.)

Army Form C. 2118.

Place	Date	Hour	Summary of Events and Information	Remarks and references to Appendices
	3rd	7.15 PM	The Deeneville bridge at L23 D 9.3 reported in Enemy hands — Gen. knew arrived about now & moved across to report to CRE to make a reconnaissance with a view to be dry being E in the neighbourhood of the HINDENBURG line	
		7.45 PM	Lt. Bisbrowned RE left in charge of bridge demolition — He received orders that the bridge was Gen. knew at 10:30 PM return up the bridge after the 4th Dec. — Left the Peninsula on my car by 6 AM of the 4th Dec. 118th Inf. Bde at the R/W bridge Fortunately to meet Colonel ROSHER 14th DLI superinting the execution — Col. when the WEST Africans in the process of superinting the execution of the R/W ROSHER gave the specific hour of 1.0 AM for the blowing up of the R/W bridge, this being the time by which the execution was to be completed —	
		1.10 AM	At 1.10 AM the R/W bridge — an iron girder viaduct consisting of 4 main Trusses about 8' high each a 2' wide having 2 railway tracks of 80' between them & an abutment to abutment span, went up	

WAR DIARY
or
INTELLIGENCE SUMMARY
(Erase heading not required.)

Army Form C. 2118.

Place	Date	Hour	Summary of Events and Information	Remarks and references to Appendices

with a loss & was thoroughly demolished - It was laid with his charges laid with safety fuze - one was lighted by Lieut BISHUNNATH R.E. the other by SERGT THATCHER R.E. The charges used were pendits, which we found in the German Dump at MARCOING CAVE - it seemed we put the ordinary primer detonator in a cartridge - The charges were laid in special pits ordinarily made for the purpose by the French engineers, who built the Railway - Each charge was about 3 cwt - Sketch of bridge as below:-

[sketch of Railway Bridge at MARCOING showing:]
- 4 pillars
- 2 pillars
- R. ESCAUT
- 80'
- 8'
- 4 Booms — 2 tracks
- 3 cwt charge in special shaft made in abutment

SKEW BRIDGE
Railway Bridge at MARCOING

Lieut Bishunnath's cool & gallant behaviour throughout the period at MARCOING was rewarded by the very thorough results obtained in the destruction of this bridge.

Army Form C. 2118.

WAR DIARY
or
INTELLIGENCE SUMMARY
(Erase heading not required.)

Place	Date	Hour	Summary of Events and Information	Remarks and references to Appendices

From other bridge now destroyed previous [-] The Rly bridge - There was the Canal bridge at L.23.B.18, which was slung through & has been cleaned by tanks on Nov 20th. This was fired with an exploder from a house on the W. bank of the canal by 2/Capt HORTON, who had kept the wires intact all day in spite of heavy shell fire - The charges were arranged as sketched below:-

Span consisted of 2 heavy I beams about 14" deep carrying cross girders with Jack arches all built built in slabs.

Two charges   Two charges

The holes in the masonry were most about 18" cube in size & crammed up with panelite on which each charge had a guncotton slab & primer & an electric detonator, all four charges being fired at once.

WAR DIARY
or
INTELLIGENCE SUMMARY

(Erase heading not required.)

Place	Date	Hour	Summary of Events and Information	Remarks and references to Appendices
MARCOING	3rd		The effect of the explosion was to seem partly destroy the canal & seem partially permit the Q's spent pulling into the canal - the bridge was industrially permitted 223 D 18 (1) Estaplette 5" bridge was blown up (2) The canal bridge at A.T. near it (3) M4 was cut in the afternoon R19 bridges at 223 A 7.0. (3) by Lt Bickford. brunton road bridge near it (4) Deamville bridge at 223 D 92 (5) New (2).(5) were destroyed by Capt Caston. 3" sappers acting independently. An attempt was made to blow up an 8" RR bridge, the large at 223 D 22 but it was found in the mud - It would have been better & have exploded some traces of guncotton at the bottom of the bridge showing at the Boer re This would have opened it out like a flower - S/C Tatchell was killed during the attempt to blow the bridge - They all had been done that has possible. New section returned to new HR about 2 o'clock - Lt Bickford went to MARCOING & upset to AIREWCOURT	

WAR DIARY
or
INTELLIGENCE SUMMARY

(Erase heading not required.)

Army Form C. 2118.

Instructions regarding War Diaries and Intelligence Summaries are contained in F.S. Regs., Part II. and the Staff Manual respectively. Title pages will be prepared in manuscript.

Place	Date	Hour	Summary of Events and Information	Remarks and references to Appendices
Hindenburg Line at R3 A 32 57cNE	4th		Coc 87th Brigade – O.C. reported to Div 6 at TRESCAULT + ordered to use HQ in the Hindenburg Line – Then bivied a memorable day to the Coy – The following recommendations for immediate award were made: Lieut Dishburst A.E. Capt Allen 4/Capt Martin Sgt Thacker A.E. Sgt Fittl Sgt Hernand Quiet morning – intermittent shelling – Lieut Dishburst wounded from RIBECOURT. Waiting orders for relief, which arrived about midday. – Marched at dusk about 4.30 pm to SOREL via HINDENBURG line, BEAUCAMP, TRESCAULT, METZ + FINS. Arrived SOREL 9 pm. – Hostile air frenzy – Reunited with MT section at SOREL + Lieut Marlin – Lieut Ayre smashed company from England – Fable Jr Bridger's were two killed by shell hit en route.	
SOREL.	5th		Entrained at ETRICOURT for MONDICOURT – Left SOREL 9.30 AM in new SW13 – Mournful return	

Army Form C. 2118.

WAR DIARY
or
INTELLIGENCE SUMMARY.
(Erase heading not required.)

Place	Date	Hour	Summary of Events and Information	Remarks and references to Appendices
	5th		Proceeded by land route Lieut. Violet Ayr - Tackud train left ETAUCOURT about 12 noon arrived MONDICOURT about 6 P.M. - Billets at BERLENCOURT Distance 10 miles - It Bridgen stuck on in a long & narrow	
BERLENCOURT.	6th		billets, which he did successfully - Coy arrived 12 midnight walker detrained & stragglers left for the night at BEAUDRICOURT - No parade. Coy resting	
BERLENCOURT.	7th		MgO Section arrived about midday.	
	8th		Drill parade 9.0 am Inspection of billets - C.O.s conference at 1/E CAURY at 2 P.M. - Coy Div.ll visited company & complimented it on the good work done at MARCOING - Present at C.O.s conference Lt Smith Captain Mekbein (Kent Fe) Captain Cummings (London Fe) - 1st kind of just the taken up with steadying drills & Musical	

WAR DIARY
or
INTELLIGENCE SUMMARY.
(Erase heading not required.)

Army Form C. 2118.

Place	Date	Hour	Summary of Events and Information	Remarks and references to Appendices
BERLENCOURT	9th		Exercise in use of Lewis & Hotchkiss guns – Mishin chair & the supplies by M.G. Companies of affiliated Brigades	
	10th		Sunday. Voluntary church parade 3 PM under Senior Chaplain of Div. – Arrival Captain Parker to take charge of Brigade Field Coy. – he has his wife with us.	
	11th		Studying Drills Physical Drill	
	12th		Kit Inspection. Knots knotting	
	13th		Billet Inspection. Instruction in M.G. & Lewis Guns	
	14th		Cleaning Kit. Cleaning Magna Hanner	
	15th		Baths. Checking Orr accounts	
	16th		Captain Mathew. Lieut Britten went on a fortnight's leave on the 15th	
	17th		Weather cold – frosty at first, then not. Lieut Buckley returned from hospital on 12th inst.	
	18th		Sunday. Blizzard in afternoon – Voluntary church parade.	

WAR DIARY

Army Form C. 2118.

Place	Date	Hour	Summary of Events and Information	Remarks and references to Appendices
AUBROMETZ (Lens II)	17th		Marched at 11 from BÉALENCOURT with 67th Regt. to the FRUGES Area - Starting point X roads in ETRÉE WAMIN at 12.6 p.m. - Half an hour's delay on starting - Gen. Lucas inspected units - complicated approach on their billets out - Rounds muddy snow on the ground - freezing towards nightfall - Halted 20' W. of FRÉVENT. Advance Guard 2Lt VIPIER - Billets found - left most of wagons clear with front so an hour good halt out in the morning.	
BÉALENCOURT (Lens II)	18th	9.30 A.M.	Marched at 9.30 A.M. to BÉALENCOURT on very slippery roads with no hot tea - Extreme difficulties from VIEIL HESDIN onwards - Two trestle wagons were left behind in AUBROMETZ with 2Lent VENFEW to try and procure in r units hor delayed start - Transtennes hills up to LE PARC - Sappers were spread out between the wagons to assist in pushing - Mortars just at FM DE JAMES ALICE : men had their dinners here the latter - Continued march at 2 P.M. via AUCHY lès HESDINS with great difficulty in mounted hills at le Rieu Manleury. Six mounted 1 RUZLÉN COURT - Mon Sorella La Mon Sorella FM	

Army Form C. 2118.

WAR DIARY
or
INTELLIGENCE SUMMARY.
(Erase heading not required.)

Instructions regarding War Diaries and Intelligence Summaries are contained in F. S. Regs., Part II. and the Staff Manual respectively. Title pages will be prepared in manuscript.

Place	Date	Hour	Summary of Events and Information	Remarks and references to Appendices
BÉTHENCOURT	16th		Main body arrived at 6 P.M. with the horses greatly fatigued — Ration wagon here the wheeling party arrived at 2 A.M. — Lieut Virtue's little wagon with a day's rations the men's blankets stuck on the hill all night — sent out teams. No 2 section horses supply wagon — Numerous other transport was also stuck. Lorry under Sgt Hammond arrived safely at 8 P.M. to MAISONCELLE — Lieut Disturnal Advance Guard — BIMELE Sent down 6 teams of mules & No 3 section to the BIMELE wagon stuck in the hill at 9.30 A.M. — Divvied heavy A.S. Car in BEAUENCOURT — Got the Heths wagon up by noon — Whole column arrived at COUPELLE NEUVE by	
COUPELLE NEUVE (Hazebrouck)	16th		3.30 P.M. — Frost still holding — very cold — All animals fit, except one mule galled — Lieut Buckley Advance Guard — Billets excellent but no latrines — all animals under cover — during march cruelty of mule transport to horse very noticeable — They do not give us like horse perhaps because they are more sheepish.	

WAR DIARY
INTELLIGENCE SUMMARY

Place	Date	Hour	Summary of Events and Information	Remarks and references to Appendices
COURCELLE NEUVE	20th		Drill parade & clean arms at 9.0 am — Billet inspection at 11.0 — Pay weekly room & inspection in the line of march — very cold — gave the column & Lt. & dismounting L-to L- Kick no all ranks — C.R.E. H.Q. at HOUQUEVIERS nearly 20 Kilometres away	
	21st		Chief set is working out lists of deficiencies, which are existence — obtaining received from Ordnance twice leaving the Cambrai area — Lieutenant's important certificates — Inspection BEAUMETZ by the Brock M.G., Bombs & important Certs slow — Bought a white but for hames bs" of billets at 10:30 — Cy drill at 11.30 — Lt Virdée Cut it down with future hats for his band, which is arriving shortly — Lt Virdée cut it down with Sunday — Visit of Indn Engineer Sannaye Service to Sunday — Genl party — Route March at 10:30 L—	
	22nd		Drill parade at 9.0 am Totally laren 10.0 am the battle field of Agnicourt — Battle began October 25th 1415 by Henry V. — Lt Dishmon took 2 six horse lorries L— BEAUMETCOURT L— bring back the R.E. stuff & he had jumped there — 1 six horse lorries went to CREVONT Bage Hos & R.E. store	

Army Form C. 2118.

WAR DIARY
or
INTELLIGENCE SUMMARY.
(Erase heading not required.)

Instructions regarding War Diaries and Intelligence Summaries are contained in F.S. Regs., Part II. and the Staff Manual respectively. Title pages will be prepared in manuscript.

Place	Date	Hour	Summary of Events and Information	Remarks and references to Appendices
	22nd		London to [?] Div for most [?] to Canadian Staff — to stay night & return on completion — Visit of C.R.E. & Lieut [?] Asst, who stayed to lunch & looked round on [?] — Complete list of deficiencies now to hand — it is a long one — some of it must be [?] for by the men, who are extravagantly careless with their kit — cuts [?] ? file kilts — Driver [?] to have child dining to Canadian Union [?].	
	23rd	10.0 am	Sunday. Clean arms inspection. Church Parade 3.30 pm. — Very [?]	
	24th	9.0 am	Drill and bayonet parade at — General talk on for Scottish celebration. [?] — Cutting hay, [?]. Shapes [?] Cutting wood — [?] [?] General Smuts motor sent his best wishes to Scotch to the Div	
	25th		This continues. [?] CRE came spent [?] — [?] the men's [?] which made [?] [?] [?] about 170 men on fall [?] for a luncheon and half day entertainment [?]	

WAR DIARY
or
INTELLIGENCE SUMMARY
(Erase heading not required.)

Army Form C. 2118.

Place	Date	Hour	Summary of Events and Information	Remarks and references to Appendices
COPPEUL	26th		Snow – Lecture to men on the Machine Gun – Lecture by OC to Company on trench orders – Lieut Nimhl attached to C on two days leave to Paris	
NEUVE	27th		Lieut Drake 87th M.G. Coy arrived to instruct Company in the element of working the machine gun – Advance party Cpl Robertson + 3 men proceeded to Musketry School at NOEUX LES MINES – Afternoon whole company dug and wired the Divisional string point in an hour's work – Fatigue worked on clearing snow from roads – Lecture by Lieut Brierly on Brigade Despatches	
	28th		Lieut Bridges with Nos 3 + 4 Sections to NOEUX LES MINES ho Thirsty Bourne. Remainder of Coy on fatigue setting up tents for moving. Lecture by Lieut Burke on "Characteristics of the Machine Gun"	
	29th		Day's work modified filling in the Div. string point, removing wire returning R.E. Stores to Bgd HQ at GREBUT, clearing barrack + starting with the Vickers gun and preparing to march to-morrow. Draft of 10 O.R. arrived from Base.	

Army Form C. 2118.

WAR DIARY
or
INTELLIGENCE SUMMARY.
(Erase heading not required.)

Instructions regarding War Diaries and Intelligence Summaries are contained in F.S. Regs., Part II. and the Staff Manual respectively. Title pages will be prepared in manuscript.

Place	Date	Hour	Summary of Events and Information	Remarks and references to Appendices
COUPELLE NEUVE	30th		March postponed one day — Snowing — Clear snow mid-day only	
ELNES	31st		15 mile march to ELNES. Started 9.30 AM & moved via FRUGES, FAUQUEMBERGUES, VINCANT — Men all ranks marched with ice but knew well FAUQUEMBERGUES. Halted one hour for meal. Men did well.	BSWilson Major RE OC 458th W Riding Field Coy RE (T)

Army Form C. 2118.

455 (W Riding) Fd Co RE
Volume XXIII

WAR DIARY
or
INTELLIGENCE SUMMARY
(Erase heading not required)

Summary of Events and Information

Place	Date	Hour	Summary	Remarks
MAISON BLANCHE	Jan 1st		Company marched to MAISON BLANCHE via the RENESCURE Axe - Arq Ferry. Went on leave and reached camp at 10.10 AM arriving in very exhausted state. Left at 7.30 PM. Co. type worked by NORT BECOURT + St OMER round seen. No 3 on return at the 5th Army Thackery camp - Return of Light Vehicle - Dismount etc. been from Paris.	
PARISFORT X roads	Jan 2nd		Company marched to HEAD DEPOT Cross roads	
PUTNEY CAMP	Jan 3rd		Company marched to PUTNEY CAMP - PROVEN town	
do	Jan 4th		Park at PUTNEY Camp. - Major Wilson went Dismount to Corps Hart Station. 2nd Lt Wills recommenced a Licit - Lieut Dismount with CRE. Army Lieut Fishers arrived, reviewed by the Co for the Marconie operation. Major Wilson. 2/Lt Holt Dismount. MC Sergt Thacker 2/Lt Kitt } MM 2/Lt Ellis 2/Lt Hants	
EVERDINGHE CHATEAU	Jan 5th		Co. marched to EVERDINGHE Chateau leaving at 9.50 arriving 3.30 PM	

Army Form C. 2118.

Instructions regarding War Diaries and Intelligence Summaries are contained in F.S. Regs., Part II. and the Staff Manual respectively. Title pages will be prepared in manuscript.

INTELLIGENCE SUMMARY.

(Erase heading not required.)

Place	Date	Hour	Summary of Events and Information	Remarks and references to Appendices
Eturbrigh Chatton 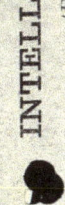	Jan 6th		Settlers into camp.	
	Jan 7th		Sent 30 carpenters & 6 cust inaster into camp on the Canal route, Kernantzh to camp – Captain McKim visited CRE Army Line	
	Jan 8th		B – Captain McKim went 2/md Army Line with CRE (Major McLean MC)	
	Jan 9th		Breaking Contrainent – Various dr worked in Cacandini in a Carneli dug out – Captain McKim went round the line with Lieut Ayres – Col Riddells RE handed over to Major GARFORTH the new CRE Army Line. Parade 7.0 AM when	
	10th		whole 2 Section Employees on the Army Line.	
			two took to PN	
	11th		M for 10th. Co. & Lieut Drummond reported from Corps Rest Camp	

Army Form C. 2118.

INTELLIGENCE SUMMARY.
(Erase heading not required.)

Place	Date	Hour	Summary of Events and Information	Remarks and references to Appendices
Elyine Camp	Jan 12th		Work on Army Lines continued – Wet & CRE Army Line – Snow at night	
	Jan 13th		Work on Army Lines continued – Lieut Dishinund directed party of 35 M.T. Coy in laying tramway – Etverdinghe Chateau completely pulled by hie – Snow lying	
	Jan 14th		Company moved camp from EVERDINGHE CHATEAU grounds, no w billet was required by 18th DIV¹ HQ – New camp in NISSEN huts near Elyine Camp where No 2 Section continued work on Army on hut moved concrete shelters last July – No 2 Section continued work on Army line by erecting an elephant ready for concrete assisted by 15 attached infantry British regiment. Lieut Smith, 30 men Border regiment relied on British regiment forming traces & cement C.G.I. – X'PTY – Trams unloading party at night unloading	
	Jan 15th		Wind & rain – No 2 Section 1st wks entrucking Mo, 2nd wks – C.G. L YPRES Lt Dishinual Lespinn – Capt Mulhern & Army line hut C.G. of L490th FWTR R.E. Captain Mulhern & Army line 1-SE 1st wks march up 7ms, 2nd wks 1 Pm Saturday –	
	16th 1/6		Wet – No 2 Section erecting elephant in Army line E of BOESINGHE – Remainder clean mess inspection & toilfier	

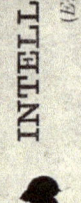

INTELLIGENCE SUMMARY

Army Form C. 2118.

Place	Date	Hour	Summary of Events and Information	Remarks and references to Appendices
	17th		Shot & Shrew - No 2 section & 15 infantry endure work Army hav - not certain supply advance party to take over from 490th R.E.E. to R.E. at YPRES & bind pontoon which was dumped at the HOP-FACTORY VLAMERTINGHE - Border attacks infantry (Lieut: Smith & Elmer) whom to their Bn in the afternoon - Lieut Veitch types to TAPEE with 2 NCO's (Sergt Newitt & Cpl Martin) & 6 OR advance party to take over work - Lieut Dickinson finishing off Army Line work - No 3 Uy returns 3E0L at NOYELLES(?)	
	18th		Preparing to move to YPRES in RED LION billets to take over from the 490th Field Coy. CO went to work & CRE in the morning.	
YPRES	19th		Moved at 10 PM whole transport & RED LION billets at 1 SA 4.5. Transport at H2.C.15 VLAMERTINGHE - Div'l HQ at DEAD END work of the Division at 83rd Brigade. Capt Matthews spent the night on GRIDIRON & in the forward area 5th/31st(?) M2.	Signals
	20th		Captain Matthews and CO went round the line to see same - Camps(?) with a long barrage of 4.2" howrs & 5.9" here at REGUE(?) N.E. SPUR which linters Coy were engaged in improving with heavy additional Grenades. Allotta conference GOC at 6.0 PM at which work in hard was discussed	

Army Form C. 2118.

INTELLIGENCE SUMMARY

(Erase heading not required.)

Place	Date	Hour	Summary of Events and Information	Remarks and references to Appendices
	21st		Night of 20/21st. Hostiles took two prisoners	Passchendaele 28 – 1/10000 Map
			1. CT to Passchendaele OP – followed by OC's inspection training for CT	
			5th R.B.M. working party – Lieutenants 2nd Lieut McCullagh Donelpmd & the relief from	
			2. Improved working platforms, reviving spoil. Gunty returns from KEIR PIELE and NS	
			Between the SPUR & VINE COTTAGE – Dr Clarke ester GOUDBERG ridge and NS	
			3. Laying wire to Beg road Rock center	
			line. [V.24 c.8.3 to D.5.B.83] Dr Brickley	
			Reconnaissance & advice on improvement of BN HQs – Brewery Brickley	
			4. Captain Matthews took survey work – The district from the line is visible to mine	
			Sp were making habit party 3 hour marching from line. Little to mine	
			at the site & took so long 3 w to been actual work smells gunned am la Dishwind	
			morning. Thus has very quiet and free from shelling	
			Relief – At 9/10 section M.G. – Dr Prid'h proceeded to NORTBECOURT (thirty trick NE 3)	
			at 9/10 section M.G. – Dr Prid'h proceeded to NORTBECOURT GUDEINE & CRUZER etticame	
			relief from 4th Army Auxiliary Group – Cont GUDEINE & CRUZER etticame	
			reliance from the 497 Field Corps in duty & healthis miles	
			Coy. Company from the 497 Field Corps in duty & healthis miles	

INTELLIGENCE SUMMARY

(Erase heading not required.)

Army Form C. 2118.

Place	Date	Hour	Summary of Events and Information	Remarks and references to Appendices
	22nd		Lt Carely (attached from Kent Field Co.) + No 2 section continued work repairing shell torn'd trench between BELLE VUE ridge and VINE COT. Lt Buckley and Hocking party started work + OC GOUDBERG defences + knocked out 4 platoon posts for an infantry support line — A Day party of 6 OR. men kept in No 5 work in the vicinity of VINE COT to 4 hour — The work in the CT to the BASSEVELT rd. in Passchendaele continued, under Lieut Gillespie. O/c west road under Commn in the neighbourhood of VAT COTTAGES making posts effort to the Friendly Literally watering our Duck board hearly at work and clearing silent in the neighbourhood of their trenches.	
	23rd		Handford attached infantry under Lieut Kirkpatrick Rfs. arrived and kheli hrd for return in the neighbourhood. No 3, 4 section under Sergeant Brown arrived from MONTRÉCOURT Hutments Camp — Nos section travelling by road in lorry transport No 1 + 2 section had alternoon with No 3 of section in funned work in the vicinity of Cetemahog on account to their lorry break E and have until .	

WAR DIARY or INTELLIGENCE SUMMARY

Army Form C. 2118.

Place	Date	Hour	Summary of Events and Information	Remarks and references to Appendices
	23rd		Lieut Kirk Patrick reconnoitred the Duckboard bridges by which his infantry are to carry on this Spinder from No 3 & 4 sections - No 3 & 4 sections in camp cleaning up in proved billets, which included whitewashing and cleaning the men's quarters. Additional accommodation for officers also granted. The O.P. job at Passchendaele continued with Lieut Gillespie & Coy Bombs section - Lieut Birthwood in charge & England.	
	24th		Three teams employed tipping up 160 tench boards to MATERLOO in trench 15 carry to the line Swifts W. of Vine Cut running a line the trench cannot end the trenchmark where 12 No 5 trench - One NC trench was opened along the march E. of Vine Cut, there were had been bogged - Lieut Ayres continued supervision with the O.P. job - Lieut Berkeley assisted the 4 Stream string parties - Captain Mattens went bomb work - Usual day party on repairing duck boards milled. Cpl Shannen - busied with in workshop & in billets	
	25th		Twelve men carried up another 160 duck boards, all of which were shipped by the infantry, who had a hard task - O.P. job continued - Supervision of Butter Pa string parties continued	

Place	Date	Hour	Summary of Events and Information	Remarks and references to Appendices
	25th		Mons 3 my Section returned here. MORTAR replacement under Lt Vivian R.E. & so not Smashin at HOP FACTORY Dugout — Lt Vivian & TOMSET killed by Brig: L-Brickley.	
			Lt VLAMERTINGHE in charge of Mounted Section. Captain Matthew found under.	
	26th		Duckboard Shelter continued L-Littsan 400ʸ of its front objective — 700ʸ has been laid in 3 days, which is good work considering the heavy camy — the bug.	
			most, OP. Jet continued — Daylight observation kept at work — OE went round all work with Major Mebbin Kent Fd Cy L- hand over the work.	
			in the forward area — Visited with him the O.P. site — had a good look at it with 2 R.E. Subalterns, who were also there.	
	27th		No 1, 2 sections to VLAMERTINGHE (HOP FACTORY) met. Lt Vivian to took on shelter track now generally — Parade at 9 a.m. No 3 to	
			Section handed in Mortars with the charm amm — in the afternoon all numbers started work on hick dugging nest home to Div HQ — Collecting timber	
			spades picks, cleaning, kit — Plan was put out during day by G.O.C.'s design.	

WAR DIARY or INTELLIGENCE SUMMARY

Army Form C. 2118.

(Erase heading not required.)

Instructions regarding War Diaries and Intelligence Summaries are contained in F. S. Regs., Part II. and the Staff Manual respectively. Title pages will be prepared in manuscript.

Place	Date	Hour	Summary of Events and Information	Remarks and references to Appendices
	27th		Company is now in the back area of the Divn. hard in the brick kiln sins Canns. Ist France. Billets in YPRES on completion	
	28th		Two sections (Nos 3&4) moved today at YPRES and allotted to the following work	
	29th		New brick making construction in Bn HQs barn. Workshop jobs – Chairs, notice boards, signs x-c. Erection of Nissen Hut at Junction Camp WIELTJE. Construction of notices Divn. chutes.	Hours 8 am – 4.30 pm with an hour for dinner
	30th			
	31st		Two sections (Nos 1&2) at Vlamertinghe Hop Factory with the Sawn timber and employed on Stables Odd jobs in Officers Club Divn Baths Drawings & Carrying approved work from Standing	

B.T. Wilson
Maj RE
OC 493rd W. Riding Field Comp RE

CONFIDENTIAL.

WAR DIARY

of

455th (W.Riding) Field Coy R.E.

From 1/2/18 to 28/2/1918.

VOLUME XIV.

VOLUME XIV

Army Form C. 2118.

WAR DIARY
or
INTELLIGENCE SUMMARY.
(Erase heading not required.)

Instructions regarding War Diaries and Intelligence Summaries are contained in F.S. Regs., Part II. and the Staff Manual respectively. Title pages will be prepared in manuscript.

Place	Date	Hour	Summary of Events and Information	Remarks and references to Appendices
YPRES	1st		Nos 1 & 2 Sections at VLAMERTINGHE under Lieut Vinden RE. Mpd section.	
			No 3 rs section at YPRES — Hours of work 8am to 4.30 PM with an hour to dinner. Work at Vlam.e-Tinghe stores, trench warfare school and "life of it."	
			Men at YPRES New Bn HQ Men Erection of Wilson Huts at Turcoline Camp. Construction of pontoon Bn's details workshop job.	
			Lieut Tibbards USA Engineer has attached 1st to on the night of the 30th Jan. Brinen 1st to the Officer Mess in ordering of Major Hilton living company, training on 1st Captain Matthew — Present	
			Major Hilton Captain Matthew Lieut Buckling Ayers Vinden	
			Rofs Ellis Corp. Light hut Sergt Thacker Sergt Mytre Carp Gillett Fourier Sergeant Simpson Sergt Nevitt Cpl Stanley Sergt Brown Sergeant Smith Sergt Clifford	
			Lieut Kirkpatrick attached his RE Lieut Tibbards USA Engineer — of very incessant training has expert —	

WAR DIARY
or
INTELLIGENCE SUMMARY

Army Form C. 2118.

Place	Date	Hour	Summary of Events and Information	Remarks and references to Appendices
YPRES	Feb 2nd 18		Nos 1 & 2 Sections at Vlamertinghe under also mounted section under Capt Venter, carrying on respiratory infantry training. No 3 & 4 sections work on new Div H.Q. at Dead End under Capt Ayres. Lieut Buckley with parties continue work on the Div Theatre and improvements of H.Q. & E.R. camp.	
	3rd		Work as on previous days till noon. Church parade at 3 p.m. Major Wilson leaves for Italy taking with him the good wishes of the whole company.	
	4th		No 2 section moves from Vlamertinghe and joins the company. Nos 2, 3, & 4 sections work on the new Div H.Q. with exception of Lieut Buckley's parties as on the 2nd	

WAR DIARY
or
INTELLIGENCE SUMMARY.

Army Form C. 2118.

Place	Date	Hour	Summary of Events and Information	Remarks and references to Appendices
YPRES.	Feb 5-18		Work for No 2, 3, & 4 Sections as on 4th. No 1 section continues on the Plumertinghe camps - chiefly deepening the drainage & under Capt. Hunter. Lieut TIBBALS U.S.A. Engineers leaves to rejoin his unit. Two hundred men of the RAMC under Captains FAZIN and AGASIS are attached to us for work on the new Div H.Q. Lieut KIRKPATRICK leaves with the attached infantry, who are replaced at the same time by another hundred, no officer.	
	6th		Parade 800 am. Work for all as on 5th.	
	7th		Work as on 5th. Lt Buckley rejoins from NORT BEQUER. Lieut Buckley leaves for the Army school FLEXICOURT	

Army Form C. 2118.

WAR DIARY
or
INTELLIGENCE SUMMARY.
(Erase heading not required.)

Instructions regarding War Diaries and Intelligence Summaries are contained in F. S. Regs., Part II. and the Staff Manual respectively. Title pages will be prepared in manuscript.

Place	Date	Hour	Summary of Events and Information	Remarks and references to Appendices
YPRES	8 Feb 18		Parade 8.00 a.m. Work for all 3 sections at Dead End. Also small repairs & additions to HASLER Camp.	
	9th		Work as on 8th inst.	
	10th		Sunday - no work parade. The whole coy including employed men paraded at 9.00 a.m. for Church Inspection. Church 10.15.	
	11th		Work as on 8th at Dead End - with exception of Cpl Dartnell and two senior NCOs from each section who proceed to WIELTJE to take over work on the Army Battle Zone from the 2nd Gallery. No 1 Section rejoins from VLAMERTINGHE.	
	12th		Two Sections parade at 8.00 a.m. No 1 Section to work on O.P.s. and Nos 2, 3 & 4 to work on the keeps in the A.B.Z.	

WAR DIARY
or
INTELLIGENCE SUMMARY.
(Erase heading not required.)

Army Form C. 2118.

Place	Date	Hour	Summary of Events and Information	Remarks and references to Appendices
YPRES Feb 18	13th		Work as on 12th not on ABZ, with exception of Lieut Bridge and six men who continue on the Div H.Q. Latrins at Dead End	
	14th		Work as on 13th for all four sections. The six men also continue work at Dead End. Lieut Bridger leaves the G Being transferred to the 587 Down AT Coy RE. and Lieut Stockton joins us being transferred from the 587 Coy RE.	
	15th		Work as on 13th inst.	
	16th		Work as on 13th inst.	
	17th		Work as on 13th inst.	
	18th		Work as on 13th inst.	
	19th		Work as on 13th inst.	

WAR DIARY
or
INTELLIGENCE SUMMARY.
(Erase heading not required.)

Army Form C. 2118.

Place	Date	Hour	Summary of Events and Information	Remarks and references to Appendices
YPRES. Feb 1918.	20th		All sections parade at 8.a.m. No 1 Section continues work on the circuit OPs, and Nos 2, 3 & 4 sections work on the keeps in the Army Battle Zone	
	21st		Work for all as on 20th inst.	
	22nd		Work for all as on 20th inst. Tool Cart men also are trained in the use of the Lewis Gun - recently issued to us.	
	23rd		Work as on 20th inst.	
	24th		Work as on 20th inst.	
	25th		Works as on 20th inst. At 3.0 p.m. the officers, sergeants & corporals attended a lecture on AIR PHOTOGRAPHY, showing that plenty of use is made of photos, and how they are read.	

Army Form C. 2118.

WAR DIARY
or
INTELLIGENCE SUMMARY.
(Erase heading not required.)

Instructions regarding War Diaries and Intelligence Summaries are contained in F. S. Regs., Part II. and the Staff Manual respectively. Title pages will be prepared in manuscript.

Place	Date	Hour	Summary of Events and Information	Remarks and references to Appendices
YPRES Feb 1910.	26th		Work in all four sections on the M32 as on 25th inst. The following party's however were differently employed.	
			Major FMcChattess Lieut Myers Lieut Desmond Sgt Brown Sgt Tucker Party Cpl Cotton Party Cpl Bailey No 1 Cpl Martin No 2 2nd Cpl Jones Cpl Whitaire L/Cpl Armstrong 2nd Cpl Chapman	
			Party No 1 left YPRES at 10.30 a.m. by bus and proceeded to AIRE, stopping for lunch at HAZEBROUCK. By the same bus sent similar parties from the Kent & London Field Cos RE.	
			Party No 2 left at 11.00 a.m. by bus, proceeded to STEENWOORDE to hear the SOC's most interesting lecture on Minor Tactics.	

WAR DIARY
INTELLIGENCE SUMMARY

Place	Date	Hour	Summary of Events and Information	Remarks and references to Appendices
YPRES Feb 1918	27th		Work for 4 sections on the A32 as on 20th inst. The party mentioned as No 1 on the 26th, visited the Bridging School, Concrete works, & Camouflage factory, all at AIRE, of which the concrete works was the most interesting. The party afterwards took the bus to St OMER & passed the night there.	
	28th		Work for 4 sections as on 27th. Party mentioned as No 1 above left AIRE at 2.10 pm and returned YPRES.	

D/Matews Major RE

ORIGINAL.

CONFIDENTIAL

WAR DIARY.

From MAR. 1ST to MAR 31ST/18.

VOLUME No XXIV

Army Form C. 2118.

WAR DIARY
or
INTELLIGENCE SUMMARY.
(Erase heading not required.)

Instructions regarding War Diaries and Intelligence Summaries are contained in F. S. Regs., Part II. and the Staff Manual respectively. Title pages will be prepared in manuscript.

Place	Date	Hour	Summary of Events and Information	Remarks and references to Appendices
YPRES.	March 1918 1st		All four sections continued the work on the ABZ. The mounted section remains at Flamertinghe until further orders.	
	2nd		Work on ABZ continued as on last out.	
	3rd		Sunday. Half of each section proceeded to the works on ABZ at 6 a.m. The remaining half of each section paraded at 9 a.m. for a full inspection, arms, ammunition etc. and rested the remainder of the day.	
	4th		The half (a) that worked yesterday were inspected at 9 a.m. to-day, and after rested. The other half proceeded at 6 a.m. to work on the ABZ.	
	5th		All four section work on the ABZ. An Officer has been received from the O. of ABZ commanding in no good rest there.	

Army Form C. 2118.

WAR DIARY
or
INTELLIGENCE SUMMARY.
(Erase heading not required.)

Place	Date	Hour	Summary of Events and Information	Remarks and references to Appendices
YPRES.	March 1918			
	6.	6ᵗʰ	Seven men proceed to erect huts at Flamertinghe and No 2 Section dug models trenches at the same place for the Divl. R.E. School of Instruction. No 4 Section worked on Camp improvements and Nos 1 & 3 continued work on the A.S.2.	
		7ᵗʰ	Sections 1 & 4 paraded at 9 a.m. and carry on with work already commenced at Flamertinghe, also 6 men for the New Divit Hqs at Dead End. Sections 2 & 3 Paraded at 11 a.m. in full marching order and proceed under Lieut Delaval to SOMME Dugouts, when they are later joined by O.C. & Lieut Steatham. Lieut Steatham having completed the handing over of work on the A.S.2. to the relieving Coy R.E.	

Army Form C. 2118.

WAR DIARY
or
INTELLIGENCE SUMMARY.
(Erase heading not required.)

Place	Date	Hour	Summary of Events and Information	Remarks and references to Appendices
YPRES	March 1918	8th	Sectors Nos 1 & 4 in YPRES under Lieut Myers continue the work which has not been in hand sometime at the New Dest. H.Q. Buildings at the Dead End. Sectors 2 & 3 with the officers already named parade at Somme dugouts at 7am. and proceed to meet working parties of Infantry at S. Pancras at KRONPRINZ at 10h and at ALL 2pm on the Divnl. Reserve Line. Constructing a line of posts 16m number eventually to be A framed and connected at to form a complete line of defence.	
	9th		Work throughout as on the 8th inst. Capt Williamson NZ joins this Coy. as Second in Command from the CRE's staff. Capt. Forbes I/Charge at YPRES but has to remain at Hdqe Runa	

WAR DIARY
or
INTELLIGENCE SUMMARY

Army Form C. 2118.

Place	Date	Hour	Summary of Events and Information	Remarks and references to Appendices
YPRES	March 1918			
	10th		Work for Sections Nos 2 & 3 on the Devl. Recent line as on 9th. The two sections at YPRES and two sections also there paraded at 9 a.m. for clean arms, respirator and other inspections, resting the remainder of the day.	
	11th		Work as for 9th not for all sections with exception of No 2 & 3 sta. coh. on till 5 a.m. getting back to billets at 6½ a.m.	
	12th		Work for all as on 9th inst. Lt. Stockham proceeds in the evening to reconnoitre a C.T. to & run from Suppts to Front line on on 87th Bde Front.	
	13th		Work for all as on 9th inst.	

Army Form C. 2118.

WAR DIARY
or
INTELLIGENCE SUMMARY.
(Erase heading not required.)

Instructions regarding War Diaries and Intelligence Summaries are contained in F. S. Regs., Part II. and the Staff Manual respectively. Title pages will be prepared in manuscript.

Place	Date	Hour	Summary of Events and Information	Remarks and references to Appendices
YPRES.	March 1918	12H	Work for Nos 9 & 3 Sections on the Divd. Reserve line as usual. Lt Byers and 20 men are employed on finishing the SOMME Dugouts Strongpoint. The remainder of Nos 9 & 3 Sections work half the day at the Dead End levees, and proceed in full marching order at 4.15 p.m. to the SOMME Dugouts, under Lieut Byers & Martin to relieve the Sections Nos 2 & 3 who go to YPRES in their tarred wagons after working all the am. on the Divd Reserve line. Lieut Dickinson goes to the Rive Luis at Poperinghe & Lieut Statham goes on leave. The O.C. is relieved & Capt Williamson on forward work.	
	13H		Sections 1 & 4 work on the Divd. Reserve line, and Nos 2 & 3 are inspected and rested.	

Army Form C. 2118.

WAR DIARY
or
INTELLIGENCE SUMMARY.
(Erase heading not required.)

Place	Date	Hour	Summary of Events and Information	Remarks and references to Appendices
YPRES	March 1918			
	16th		Sections Nos 1 & 4 continue work on the Divl. Reserve Line. Sections Nos 2 & 3 prepare a site for a new camp near Salvation Corner, with exception of 6 men who took on buildings at Dead End.	
	17th		Sections 4 & 1 as on 16th inst. also sections 2 & 3 with exception of 20 men who continue with the emptying of SOMME Dugouts. Bombing at SOMME Dugouts but Buckley arrives at Vlamertinghe from the Army school at FLETRICOURT.	
	18th		Work for all sections as on 17th inst. is completed.	
	19th		Sections 2 & 3 took on new camp at Salvation Corner. Section 1 & 4 on forward work. Work commenced on Intermediate Line between Support and Div. Res. Line. 9 Posts in all, 3 of which are already in reas. but badly in need of repair	

WAR DIARY
or
INTELLIGENCE SUMMARY.

(Erase heading not required.)

Army Form C. 2118.

Place	Date	Hour	Summary of Events and Information	Remarks and references to Appendices
YPRES March 1916	20th	night 20-21st	Two Sections at Y.P.R.E. employed on Corps Boring Bn. H.Q. The new Divisional H.Q. Building finished. No. 1 & 4 Sections employed at night on Intermediate Line, both wiring and digging. This was found necessary as the fort is on this particular part of the position. The roses supply particularly diggy and wiring.	
	21st		Nos 2 & 3 Sections, less 10 men inoculated, work at new Bde Transport Lines near 2 SALVATION CORNER. Trumpet Capt. Wilkinson took Capt. Smiths 497 (Kent) F.S. Coy, thence elsewhere to prepare for 144 Sections with 1 Platn of 1 Coy work on digging and wiring new Intermediate Line (BELLEVUE, WIELTJEMOLEN, IRON HOUSES LINE) 1 Platoon on wiring to 3 Casualties by shell fire soon after detraining.	
	night 21st-22nd		Work as usual for Nos 2 & 3 Sections. 497 (Kent) F.S. Coy relieve 2 Sections forward at SOMME Dug Outs. No 1 & 4 Section reach new H.Q. about 4.00 P.M. Defences made in preparation by Fd Coy in Rear area, handed over to Lieut Buckeley.	
	22nd		Major F.A.V.D. Matthews proceed on 1 months leave to U.K. Capt. D.R. Wilkinson acting in his absence. Lt Col MACAULEY R.K.A. becomes C.R.E. Sergt. BROWN took over details of fuses in Connection with Location and remounting of Rb fuzes.	

WAR DIARY
INTELLIGENCE SUMMARY.
(Erase heading not required.)

Army Form C. 2118.

Place	Date	Hour	Summary of Events and Information	Remarks and references to Appendices
YPRES	23rd March/18		All detraining back in Rear Work. No. 1 Section commenced work on Army Butter Zone. No. 4 Section under Lieut. BUCKLEY work on various other jobs, principal ones being Nos 2 & 3 sections on ration party, chasers hunting for ENGLISH in HQ Stables, gas doors at DIV. HQ, etc. CAMP, WIELTJE, ST JEAN DRESSING ST⁰ Baths for No. 1 & Section. Evening at Dead End Butts.	
	24th		Work as on 23rd except three men camp. No extra work at 11.00 am, and Parade 1.00 noon for Church Parade. These latter round work at 1.15 p.m. Conference of Coy Commanders at CRE.'s Hdrs... New Policy of works.	
	25th		Work as on 24th except that A/L Coy. has advanced fit of H.Q. trench Bond trick. Sergt. NEWITT report to Lt GILLESPIE at Divisional Gas Works School on instruction for a short period.	
		5.15 p.m.	Rifle Inspection and Gas helmet drill for whole Coy, followed by Clothing inspection for No. 1. Section.	
	26th	6.00 p.m.	Parade & for works as on 25th. 2 Sappers tomorrow on making 'A' frames at Bridge Dump for No. 2 Section.	

Army Form C. 2118.

WAR DIARY
or
INTELLIGENCE SUMMARY.
(Erase heading not required.)

Instructions regarding War Diaries and Intelligence Summaries are contained in F. S. Regs., Part II. and the Staff Manual respectively. Title pages will be prepared in manuscript.

Place	Date	Hour	Summary of Events and Information	Remarks and references to Appendices
YPRES. March/18	27th		Same works as on 26th	
		5.00 pm	Clothing Inspection for No. 3 lee	
	28th		Work on trench tramway divisions to relieve 510th (London) FoCoy on 30th inst. Preliminary arrangements made with London Coy for guides to take round works.	
		5.00 pm	No. 2 & 3 Sections and H.Q. proceeded to Batts at Dead End Clothing Inspection for No. 4 Section. Sergt. Myers rejoins from 29th F.A.	
	29th		Work as usual for Sections. Proceeded with Capt. Comins of 510th (London) FoCoy Re: round support Posts Right Section and then proceeded round work on PASSCHENDAELE	
	Night 29–30		Lt. Buckley and guides proceeded Posts and took over details C.T. and Mussclmarne	
	30th	6.00am	No. 1 Section continued work on Army Battle Zone. No. 2, 3, & 4 Sections drew Iron Rations, Picked Kits and blankets and stored in billets.	
		1.00 pm	No. 2.3 & 4 Sections paraded in Battle order and marched via WIELTJE DUGOUTS to Somme and Eadoo.	
		11.45 pm	No. 2 Section from No. 2 Section relieving billets in Eadoo. Ft. DISTOCK & B. OR proceeded round works on Divisional Line Hitch[?] at SPREE DUMP with LIMEFFET	

WAR DIARY / INTELLIGENCE SUMMARY

Place	Date	Hour	Summary of Events and Information	Remarks and references to Appendices
SOMME DUGOUT MARCH/18	30th	3.00 pm	Continued. All details and working men were taken over from OC London 75 Coy RE. Also all details stores in Rear Area handed over to him. Drawings being sent direct to OC 515th Coy. Regn: No 1. Pyers to hand over direct all work in Progress on MTB Zone.	SID
		7.00 pm	2 Sections and 1 Orderly Room Clerk withdrew to SOMME DUGOUTS and 1 Section at WIELTJE.	
	night 30-31st		Completion of Relief wired to CRE. Lt BUCKLEY and No 2 Section work on PASSCHENDAELE CT. and supervise 1 Platoon of 1/½ MONMOUTH PIONEERS working on MUSSELMARKE POSTS. 1 Platoon of 1/2 Monmouths working on SNIPE HALL POSTS. No 3 Section work on SNIPE HALL Post on right of BELLEVUE line, with 4 men working on Gas Proofing.	
	31st		Lt DISTURNAL with his 4 Section work on Right Sector Divisional line, having 1 Coy LANCS Fus: for work on line, and one for work on Posts. Lt AYERS and his Section move from YPRES to WIELTJE, and see details to transport Lines, MC Coy Billets being left vacant. Strops to develop point of 3 Camps in YPRES to the right on. Reported to Brig Genl Jacksen about 10.30 a.m. that nothing were special to say.	

Army Form C. 2118.

WAR DIARY
or
INTELLIGENCE SUMMARY.
(Erase heading not required.)

Place	Date	Hour	Summary of Events and Information	Remarks and references to Appendices
SOMME DUGOUTS March/18	31		Continued:- leave LT. G.C. STEDHAM returned from 14 days/r to U.K. and took charge of No. 3 Section on works.	
	night 31st/1st		LT Buckley and his 2 Sections on same work as nights 30-31st. 1 Psn. 1/2 MONS. on MUSSELMARRE POSTS 1 " 1/2 " " SNIPE HALL. Notification received from C.R.E. that 1 extra Inf. Coy will be available for work to Posts in Divisional line on 1st April. Later notification received Casualties are 3. Inf. Coy for work on Divisional line, but 1st R.A.M.C. available at WATERLOO at 9.00 a.m. for work on making Shelters in Posts.	

P. Wiremim
Capt RE
o/c 453rd (WR) F Coy R.E.
1-4-18

29th Divisional Engineers

455th (West Riding) FIELD COMPANY R.E.

APRIL 1918.

C O N F I D E N T I A L

ORIGINAL.
WAR DIARY.

> 455TH (W. RIDING)
> FIELD COMPANY,
> R.E.
> No.....................
> Date...................

From 1st APRIL. to 30th APRIL. 1918

VOLUME No. XXVI

WAR DIARY
INTELLIGENCE SUMMARY.
(Erase heading not required.)

Army Form C. 2118.

Place	Date	Hour	Summary of Events and Information	Remarks and references to Appendices
SOMME DUG-OUT	1.		Works as on 31st.	
APRIL			No. 1 Sec. — Taking over work on GRAVENSTAFEL Aid Post from No. 4. Guide for wagons from Reconnaissance of first shelter at Pole H.Q. WATERLOO PILL BOX. 2 men working. 12 men working at SOMME DUG-OUTS on improvements.	
			No. 2 Sec. — Working on PASSCHENDAELE C.T. by night (17 men) — forward portion. Lt BUCKLEY also improving 1 Post. Have working on MUSCLMARE Post — expecially No. 1 which requires much improvement.	
			No. 3 Sec. — Lt STEDHAM and 11 men working on SNIPE HALL Post by day and 1 Post 1/2 hour working on same Post by night. 1 N.C.O. and 4 men working on Gas proofing Dugouts, experience 1 man working on telephone junction to BELLEVUE P.B.	
			No. 4 Sec. — Lt DISTURNAL and section with 109 R.A.M.C. working on Shelters in Divisional Aid Posts, experiencing Posts 1, 2, 3, & 6. 2 men finishing up work on GRAVENSTAFEL Aid Post, fitting doors over to No. 1 Sec.	

WAR DIARY
INTELLIGENCE SUMMARY

Army Form C. 2118.

Place	Date	Hour	Summary of Events and Information	Remarks and references to Appendices
APRIL SOMME DUGOUTS	1st		**continued** Proceeded to PASSCHENDAELE C.T. and MUSSELMARKT POST No. 1 by day (about 10.30 a.m.) to see condition & part of flooring in wing (of) engines. The latter requires considerable amount of work to make proper, even bullet proof. The western trenches (portion of) PASSCHENDAELE C.T. requires much draining before work can be continued. Much shelling during evening at WIELTJE and towards our (front of the) 3 line (batteries) at WIELTJE Nos. 1 & 4 Sections are working very confidently. Its shelling very fresh and wide (sight). 14 Divisions & 2 Mounted Reinforcements reported transport lines are strenuous work on to the 1st Construction of C.T. over ABRAHAM HEIGHTS underway. Trench marked out as far as BERLIN. Reinforcements allotted to Sections but unable to join same owing to lack of accommodation at SOMME or WIELTJE Camp. Shells with smoke 'gray' fuse shells. Night turned out rather wet.	
	2nd			
	3rd		All sections on same work. Sapper NEWMAN returns from Hop Factory workshop. Letter (CRE) on works, instructed wishes to ground works on morning of 5th sent to Section Officers without word this O.C. was to See KOREK for w.h. AYRES and O.C. Sepn.	

WAR DIARY or INTELLIGENCE SUMMARY

Army Form C. 2118.

Place	Date	Hour	Summary of Events and Information	Remarks and references to Appendices
SOMME Dug Out	April 4th	9:00 am	Downie received 2nd party for C.T. PASSCHENDAELE for nights. Went Round works with CRE to Bde. — Dump parties issued — Lt AYERS present	
		2:00 pm	Transport Rides. On way back saw CRE to discuss a dump to be made at WATERLOO.	
		1:00 pm	Office work at WIELTJE. to PASSCHENDAELE C.T.	
		10:00 pm	G.O.C. 57 Bde telephoned & Guide to Guide for carrying party/station the said did not turn up.	
	5th	6:30 am	Sent Round fresh guide. Got telephone call from 2/Lt MOIR and Lt AYERS dumps finished for night for enquiry. On way to Office went along C.T. for nights works and subject at the 1 - see relieving the R.E.	
	6th	Evening	(No. 3) Relieved No 4 on works and at Dugout bent round works with LT BUCKLEY.	
	7th		Sent to Bde as then round Dis Res Line with LISTED HOWAT. Inspected first day's work section on HQ/M. OC 4 2 OM 237th Fuel Coy RE arrives to take over defence of work with him for night work on C.T. and on	
		4:00 pm	LT AYERS to SR 1 OM with him for night work on C.T. R.E. took as known MOSSELMARKT Posts. Then Officers Count Other Ranks STORMAN took over Storgold and Di Lines and Support system to DI STORM ever & 237 Coy issue at SOMME for night.	

WAR DIARY
or
INTELLIGENCE SUMMARY.
(Erase heading not required.)

Army Form C. 2118.

Place	Date	Hour	Summary of Events and Information	Remarks and references to Appendices
SOMME Dugout	APRIL 1918 8th		during morning Section rested & except for cleaning arms inspection. Sections busied with kits at 12:00 noon. Cooks Limbers 2:30 pm transport to Ross Group SP, ST JEAN. Lt STEDHAM sent ahead to arrange billets at CYCLIST CAMP at ST JAN-TER-BIEZEN on main WATOU Road. Lt DISTURNAL ahead to arrange entraining.	
		2:30 pm	Works and all after handed over to 237th Field Coy, RE, including Coy Relief of 2 Nos of Sections at SPREE DUMP.	
		3:30 pm	Met HQ of Sections at ST JEAN STN and proceeded by train to ST JAN-TER-BIEZEN.	
ST JAN-TER-BIEZEN			4. POPERINGHE and marched to VLAMERTINGHE arrived came camp from VLAMERTINGHE. Transport by Road from VLAMERTINGHE — transport camp & after distance about ½ hour later. Camp quite comfortable, dismount to Sanity from distance. Expect to entrain tomorrow for 13th Corps. Near ST POL & TINQUES area.	
	9th	9:00 am	Lt BUCKLEY reports to Bde and proceeds on advance billeting party in to TINQUES area inspection and Box respirator drill. Parade. Clean. Expect to entrain ROUSBRUGGE at 7:11 am 10th.	

WAR DIARY
INTELLIGENCE SUMMARY.

Place	Date	Hour	Summary of Events and Information	Remarks and references to Appendices
APRIL	9th		Continued	
ST JAN-TER-BIEZEN L.3.a.S.3. Sheet 27.		5:00 pm	Orders to move cancelled. Programme changed to - Dismounted portion now to entrain on PROVEN road at 8.30 pm - MOUNTED Section by road to MERVILLE area. Dismounted personnel, less Lt DISTURNAL, SERGT. BROWN, Cpl. ROBERTSON 9 9 of FOULDS and 10 % of other ranks, linehed 8.00 a.m - proceeded to entraining point - Coy on bicycles moved route to Mounted Section via two 10 %, proceeded by march route to neighbourhood of VIEUX BERQUIN.	
NEUF BERQUIN L.7.a.6.1. Sheet 36A	10th	2:30 am 8:00 am 11:00 am	Entrained on PROVEN Road with dismounted personnel. Detrained at NEUF BERQUIN and Coy eventually bivouaced in field, Coy proceeded to Rde. for instruction W & E of NEUF BERQUIN and Coy Rifles found to Coy in West of NEUF BERQUIN. Latter completely destroyed at LETTER	
		11:00 am 1:00 pm	Transport arrives VIEUX BERQUIN. Enemy pressed outside ESTAIRES. Footeatts and Cookers arrived with Coy at forward billets in NEUF BERQUIN then feeding in billets.	
		2:00 pm	Bde. Commander — Bde attacked. Bde. deploying in afternoon and takeing up a position in front of DOULIEU, a position maintained. Coy not offered on 'standing by' order to be reserves from CRE.	
		5:00 pm	CRE enquired for work the evening.	

WAR DIARY
INTELLIGENCE SUMMARY

Army Form C. 2118.

Place	Date	Hour	Summary of Events and Information	Remarks and references to Appendices
NEUF BERQUIN	10th		2 havings reports from CRE with picks, shovels and sandbags and dump formed in front of billet.	Officers
		7.00 pm	No7 were annoyed.	
	11th	9.00 am	Working parties for Coy to work on helping 50 Div. R.E. with their support line running front East of NEUF BERQUIN.	
		11.00 am	Nos 1 and 2 sections with Lt BICKERLEY and 2Lt AYERS. Put to work on repair of 5 bank on existing 7 NEUF BERQUIN and ast line the ESTAIRE Road of handgrenades close by with No 3&4 sections. No 3&4 sections with Lt STEDHAM & sent to a front rendezvous in front of DOULIEU as required & report back in that direction. Nos 1&2 sections having settled to their job. CRE, Maj., and OC proceeded to meet and work for Nos 3&4 sections. CRE having settled to that work we again returned with Coy to RQ	
		1.30 pm	Lt STEDHAM and OC had proceeded to meet and work, but owing enemy attack our infantry falling back on left, they were forced to take up a line with the 2 sections R.E. Later following in similar line men from M.G. Fire — 4 reinforcements.	
			including SERGT. SHAW. The front line having been re-entered by 3 & 4 sections commenced work on defences. Stray fruits which had been dug by the 50 Div R.E. to a depth of 6 inches. Took provided all night for advance. But finally stopped again by enemy M.G. Fire when infantry were again forced to retire in places. These 2 sections then took in support against further strelling. All orders to take up the line as support front line and finally had to become employed with officers men, the 2 sections were withdrawn further back.	

Army Form C. 2118.

WAR DIARY
or
INTELLIGENCE SUMMARY.
(Erase heading not required.)

Instructions regarding War Diaries and Intelligence Summaries are contained in F. S. Regs., Part II. and the Staff Manual respectively. Title pages will be prepared in manuscript.

Place	Date	Hour	Summary of Events and Information	Remarks and references to Appendices
	APRIL			
		6.30 pm	OC, not knowing conditions of affairs overnight, proceeded towards NEUF BERQUIN, but unable to get there, and returning to Bde HQ, found LISTED HAM and Nos 3 & 4 sections gone, having given permission to OC Bde, having given permission for them two sections to return to Coy. Transport lines, and LISTED HAM with Nos 3 & 4 sections made their way to G――― VIEUX BERQUIN.	
		12.00 midnight	Runner arrived at OC's Temporary lines VIEUX BERQUIN with instructions from CRE for distributing Personnel and decided to proceed to present to PT SEC. BOIS. The HQ movement to proceed with by the party to BORRE — this having already taken place.	
PT SEC BOIS E.q.c.g.1 Sheet 26A	12th	2.00 am	Nos 3 & 4 sections arrived PT SEC BOIS and were put into a barn there — all very tired and sleepy.	
		11.00 am	Nos 1 & 2 sections (less 2 Lt AYERS and CSM) reported back having been digging and fighting So of NEUF BERQUIN — casualties heavy. Lt BUCKLEY reported PT SEC. BOIS about 10.00 am having reported to CRE the condition of affairs overnight. CRE Wilson RE to take charge of Lt BUCKLEY's section. 2 Lt BUCKLEY sent	
			Received instructions that No 12 & NO section beginning 3 & 4 at PT SEC BOIS	
	11th		Enemy having founded centre of NEUF BERQUIN, Nos 1 & 2 sections retired to Coy. HQ in NEUF BERQUIN	

Place	Date	Hour	Summary of Events and Information	Remarks and references to Appendices
APR 16			11th Cont. (for 1.2 who sections) Toilets and Crates dispatches to Eng: Transport Lines	
			No. 1.2 who Sections were taken from dump in front of Ellis and dug in on 2nd side of road and rails line	
	12th		The sections has to retire during day in one has on write the front line was plate Beeuves and at the latter place dug up a position holding them.	
			The night 11/12 who sections took to Coy. GRM. dugouts but Coy. widening in killers but prepared to take up a definite position in front of PTE SEC BOIS. Two thirds sent transport. The remainder and parts were left by him with enough ammunition for night digging. Ellis and Park dying for Coy., also to include details of S.10th (Lon) F.C Coy. R.E. billeted close by. O.C. and staying party towards C.R.E. at divisional Hdqrs H.Q. MERRIS and arrangements made for O.C. to meet Coy. a little later at same point	
			In the meantime slight enemy advance and 'bosche' now a short distance outside MERRIS.	
PTE SEC BOIS	12th	12:30 pm	2Lt A. Y. ERS, R.E. a/OC. Ran C.R.E. Heavy condition of affairs and OC had to moved to new Bn HQ between STRAZEELE and VIEUX BERQUIN, and not C.R.E. proceeding with him towards BAIL O., where were
		2.00 pm 4.30 pm	Orders were sent to reverse ALL HQ to Convoy from road between STRAZEELE and CRASTRE BOIS outside the Forêt pase. (Two motor lorries of 620th (FSCoy) who also have been animals

Army Form C. 2118.

WAR DIARY
or
INTELLIGENCE SUMMARY.
(Erase heading not required.)

Place	Date	Hour	Summary of Events and Information	Remarks and references to Appendices
APRIL Bht See Bri	12th		Orders were received to work on connecting roads in front line on left of their road and about Centre of VIEUX BERQUIN E 74 & F 13 c.	Sheet 36A
		9/o.c.	was proceeded to look for Coy who should have made their way to somewhere near the rendezvous but as Re. in road Coy. had been working the Camp behind MERRIS having been shown for by C.R.E. 2 Div. The Camp having been asked by CRE to put them on the event of not finding their Servicef.	
		6.00 pm to 8.00 pm	Coy. digging on line in front face of MONT DE MERRIS in divies and the enemy little or casualties from shell fire	
		9.00 pm	Coy. now put to work on new line by Rde — night very quiet found — usefull work performed. Shovels left for parties in the line & new shovel picks up from STRAZEELE PARK on way back.	
STRAZEELE W 22 d 9 2 Sheet 27	13th	3.0 pm	Coy returned towards H.Q. first N.E. of STRAZEELE and H.Q. established then every divies — billets good. Guard posted and Coy rations.	
		12.00 noon	Enemy shell battery close by with 5.9" shells — and two to clear out billets for 1/2 hour after which period shelling ceased and Coy returned to billets. Coy made all afternoon.	
		6.00 pm	Orders received from Coy to move to work and for Transport whatever moves to ST. SYLVESTRE — details of kilo field Coy also to join	

Army Form C. 2118.

WAR DIARY
or
INTELLIGENCE SUMMARY.
(Erase heading not required.)

Instructions regarding War Diaries and Intelligence Summaries are contained in F. S. Regs., Part II. and the Staff Manual respectively. Title pages will be prepared in manuscript.

Place	Date	Hour	Summary of Events and Information	Remarks and references to Appendices
STRAZEELE	APRIL 13th	8:00 am	Coy Paraded and moved to ST SYLVESTRE with pack animals and bivouaced at Transport lines	
ST SYLVESTRE P36 2.6.6 Sheet 27	14th	11:00 am	Hot meal for Coy on arrival and tea to men	
		10:00 am	Coy Parade — Clean arms inspection — dismissed to cleaning up clothes and equipment and improving bivouacs	
			2 Sections (1 & 2nd) sent up to a field above CRE HQ as more comfortable than bivouac. 1 Section in wagon shed at farm. 1 Section in bivouac. M.I. —	
	15th	2:00 pm	Check Parade	
		5:00 am	Sgt MARTIN rejoins	
		9:30 am	Coy Parade — arms inspection (in Billets from tea) Lee. Clean arms & equipment and Billeting arrangements. Box Respirator drill by Sections.	
		11:00 am	Inspection Gaines Kit, iron rations etc in section billets.	
	16th	2:00 pm	Check Parade at Section billets	
		5:00 pm		
		9:30 am	Coy Parade — Musketry Order — Inspection — Coy drive till 10:30 am Lecture on anti-aircraft action.	
		11:00 am		
		2:30 pm	Transport arrives for a/cc to meet CRE at 5:10 pm (road) At Coy RE HQ at 3:00 pm. Orders. Coy HQ to bivouac at 6:30 pm — enemy crossing METEREN. A French Coy has already from North, and should parade in minutes to fill the gap	

WAR DIARY or INTELLIGENCE SUMMARY

Army Form C. 2118.

Place	Date	Hour	Summary of Events and Information	Remarks and references to Appendices
ST SYLVESTRE Mill	16th		Continued	
		3:30 pm	Approximate line for front system of Corps Defence Scheme marked out with tape and O/C. advised to move but no orders received.	
		6:00 pm	Coy ready to move but no orders received. No. 2 & 4 sections has ST SYLVESTRE billet. Slowly by all Coy except No. 3 Coy not moving. Arrangements made for following morning. Marking out new line; also the same arrangements infantry to dig in same on afternoon of 17th.	
	17th	12:30 am	Coy "Stand to" declared "off". Coy to work on Corps defence scheme.	
		6:45 am	LISTED HAM. R.E. & with tapping party 10 each proceeded with Lt. to K3 DISTURNAL R.E. tape out series of strong points on front of continuous line defence (the Spur Farms & Valleys) in front of CAESTRE.	
			LT. BUCKLEY R.E. and 2 LTAYERS R.E. to parade with remainder sections at 11.30 pm and await orders (drew battle order)	
		8.30 am	Taping commenced	
		9.01 am	Very heavy German Barrage fell about 600 yds to flat & remained almost continuous for 3 hours	
		11.30 am	CRE and Cap. M.G. Batts arrived and not long and tapes out — no infantry for work owing to "stand to"— CRE already ordered Commander of Coy to remove Division and no infantry arriving.	

WAR DIARY
INTELLIGENCE SUMMARY

Place	Date	Hour	Summary of Events and Information	Remarks and references to Appendices
ST SYLVESTRE	17th April		Continued	
		1.00 pm	Sappers arrive and given task of 100 cubic digging in the most important points of the drainage and to make any trifling in track.	
		2.00 pm	2nd Lt — Commander of 2nd Royal Fus — arrived on site and asked for work (Bttn) and arranged to work close. O.C. Company to carry out (work) Commander knows the work required. The infantry entrenched.	
			About after dark Lt Buckley and 2 Lt — Ayers stowed — O.C. Coys rooms Inspected portion of front system.	
	5.30 pm		Rec. Capt. Camp CRE informing that he wanted 6 Inf. Coys employed on the front as much as poss —	
	6.00 pm		Rec d/o from Lt Disturnm proceeded by car to Bde HQ and saw G.O.C. Batt —Final arrangement made and dome of Infantry to employ all Mr Coy on Coy scarps to reinforce their inspection.	
			Proceeded again to site of work and marked out new alignment having obtained — of 2/I DODDS & 2/10th (Home) Fusiliers 2/1 DODDS took over Coys portion of front system to employ to rendezvous near site and marched by Lt DISTURNM and 2 Lt DODDS.	
	9.30 pm		Infantry arrived at rendezvous near site and marched to work. Reached camp again 11.0 pm	

WAR DIARY
or
INTELLIGENCE SUMMARY
(Erase heading not required.)

Army Form C. 2118.

Place	Date	Hour	Summary of Events and Information	Remarks and references to Appendices
ST SYLVESTRE	18th		(a) 2 Section Day work (1st STEDHAM & No 3. Sec, 1st DISTURNAL & No 4 Sec) Night.	
			(b) 2 " (Lt BUCKLEY & No 2 See. 2Lt AYERS & No. 1 See.)	
APRIL			(c) [sketch]	
			No 3. Sec. — Cleaning ludges etc. and making out scheme to employ 4 Inf Coys tonight. Football.	
			No 4 Sec — Working at Support System to 2nd Zone, on line chosen earlier by G.O.C. 29 Div & CRE. 2 Infantry Coys. Continuing wire entanglements.	
			(d) No 1. Sec. relieves No 3. Sec. — 2nd Pro Battn (Haines + R.A.M.C.) arriving rendezvous new site at 6.30 pm.	
			No 2 Sec relieves No 4 Sec — 14th Pro Battn (R.R. Fus.) arriving rendezvous at 6.30pm.	
19th	8.00 am		Coy Parades — divides into pickets & divisional parties.	
	10.30 am		Lt STEDHAM proceeds to billet Coy at HONDEGHEM. Lt BUCKLEY with 1st DISTURNAL marching Coy to new billet, 2Lt VINTER bringing up the transport — Coy marching to Div. domicile.	
	2.00 pm			
	1.00 pm		O/C + 2Lt AYERS proceeded to make a reconnaissance of trench ready for the morrow — work on same line, 2nd Zone, but further South ... due E ST HAZEBROUCK to S.E. of same ... near MORBECQUE	

WAR DIARY
or
INTELLIGENCE SUMMARY.

Place	Date	Hour	Summary of Events and Information	Remarks and references to Appendices
April HONDEGHEM V.8.d.2.6 Sheet 27	19th		Continued	
		4.20 pm	Coy moved HONDEGHEM — ground fields but ditch — late Chinese Camp. Hired lorries of Flemish farmer.	
		7.00 pm	Enquiries (telephone) at CCE's HQ for work on 20th Zone	
	20th	6.30 am	4 Sections paraded — Battle order with shovels — and proceed to sites of work.	
			LT BUCKLEY with No 1 & 2 Sections work on Front System 2nd Zone LT STEDHAM " 3 & 4 " " on Support System 2nd Zone	
			Return 5th Composite Battn — Support System 2nd Provisional - 3 — Front System 68th English Lab Coy } think to be known works as for.	
		5.30 pm	Sections returned to Camp (Mule Lines Trenches S.8.d.9.4.) Chief work consists of improving trenches which have been dug too narrow & shallow (which have a tendency to slope inwards from [illeg] also wiring & completing double apron fence along front lines. Burrows etc have been dug by previous unit but dug outs are [illeg] to close to trench. Trenches shallow dug outs obtain [illeg] level.	

WAR DIARY
or
INTELLIGENCE SUMMARY.
(Erase heading not required.)

Army Form C. 2118.

Place	Date	Hour	Summary of Events and Information	Remarks and references to Appendices
HONDEGHEM April	21st		Work slightly slowed from 11th to 20th. Boundary on right has been shortened and left boundary extended to L.p. a B: Station with N° 3 Section now works on front system in front of the b B: Diamond " " " " " " No 2 " " " " " (a) No 4 and 1 Section with 2 Lt Ayers and Lt Buckley on O.P. 47 to 2 Sec Factory (b) 5th Camp Rect (b/o) (c) 1 Batt 81 R.U. 2nd Field Squadron (10-2pm) anything or everything there was everywhere in front of Fronterghem	
		3.00 pm	a/o.c attended CRE Conference at CRE Office in HONDEGHEM. The most vigilant patrolling of the following front. (a) Railway E & Central (b) Canal D & " (c) LE TIR ANGLAIS D23 " " News O.C's 497 (12 kw) FDCoy and 510th (Low) FD Coy present at Conference	

Army Form C. 2118.

WAR DIARY
or
INTELLIGENCE SUMMARY.
(Erase heading not required.)

Place	Date	Hour	Summary of Events and Information	Remarks and references to Appendices
HONDEGHEM April	23rd		Work as on 21st	
	24th		G.O.C. and C.R.E. decided on definite method of future show. Rev. crosses caused severe casualties of E.Co. one in front of the 6th and as and outside. Sapper wounded. Front work by 3 Aussie Coys.	
			Work as on 22nd	
			LT. F.W. DRUMMOND reports proceeding with C of E on Base, interns 29 LT. AVERLEY to proceed to 132 A.T. Coy 25th	
	25th	6 p.m.	C.R.E. Conference — Return of Relief of 31st Div in line F. Co. half as 1st	
		1.30 pm	MAJOR F.A. V.D. MATTHEWS assumes command from I hand the duties to V.A. and assumed command of F. Coy	
	26th		Work in Corps line as on 21st. Work and billets to be taken over tomorrow reconnoitred. Work in Corps line handed over to relieving Div.	

Place	Date	Hour	Summary of Events and Information	Remarks and references to Appendices
Au Souverain	April 27th		Men Seekers moved off in full marching order to do days work on the Cyclo line, this finished they moved to their new billets at Au Souverain. Mounted section moved to their new Camp (Brienen) at 10 p.m.	
	28th		Relief of the various sappers & sent div. in charge of road to those mines Compll. by Lieut. Buckley proceeded to join 138 A.T. Coy R.E. to Lieut Ayers to 7days home leave. No 1 section paraded at 9 a.m and went on the front of NIEPPES in front of our support line. No 3 section constructed shelters in trench near our billets for emergencies. No 2 section paraded at 8 p.m. to fell trees across road at our front line & No 4 paraded at 8 p.m. to line the extreme left of our support line.	

WAR DIARY
or
INTELLIGENCE SUMMARY.
(Erase heading not required.)

Army Form C. 2118.

Place	Date	Hour	Summary of Events and Information	Remarks and references to Appendices
Au Souverain	April 29th		Nos 1 & 3 Section work ½ day as yesterday. Nos 2 & 4 sections ½ night in Pet. Sec Bois Stony Point. The majority of sappers carrying and a few superintending ospully cassis.	
	30th		No 1 Section continue wiring left of support line ½ day. No 3 section work ½ day on cross country track to Petit See Bois Stony Points ½ day on new near Bde HQ. Nos 2 & 4 Sections work at night on Pet S.B. Stony Point as on 29th.	

M D Mathews Major R.E.

CONFIDENTIAL

WAR DIARY.

of

455th (W.Riding) Fd Coy R.E

From 1/5/18 to 31/5/18

VOLUME NO..........

Original.

WAR DIARY
or
INTELLIGENCE SUMMARY.
(Erase heading not required.)

Army Form C. 2118.

455th (W. RIDING) FIELD COMPANY R.E.

Place	Date	Hour	Summary of Events and Information	Remarks and references to Appendices
Souverain Moulin	May 1918 1st	7.00 a.m.	Parade at 7.00 a.m. Nos 1 & 3 S.H. Nos 1 & 3 take out rations and tech at Pet. Sec. Bois. clearing bridges and drains. Nos 2 & 4 Sections parade at 8.00 p.m. for wiring defences of Pet. Sec. Bois.	
	2nd		Wet and funeral so on 1st. No 3 section employed in loopholing houses within the Pet. Sec. Bois. defences.	
	3rd		Parades as on 1st. No 1 section make knife rests where trench crosses the roads at Pet. Sec. Bois. and No 3 sect complete the loophole turning. No 2 & 4 section wiring at night. We take over old CRE's dump.	
	4th		No 3 section carry on with loopholing and knife rests & clay. Also construction of War Bde. H.Q. (elephant shelter). No 1 to prepare new road nr much and H.Q. No 2 & 4 sections wiring Pet. Sec. Bois.	

Army Form C. 2118.

WAR DIARY
or
INTELLIGENCE SUMMARY.
(Erase heading not required.)

455TH (W. RIDING)
FIELD COMPANY.
R.E.

Place	Date	Hour	Summary of Events and Information	Remarks and references to Appendices
Souverain	May 1918	9ᵗʰ	Parade at 8.00 a.m. for Nº 2 Sec. Section. Work on Bole and Battalion Hqrs. Gas proof'g doors of same and thinning hedge at SWARTENBUSCH. Nº 1 & 3 paraded at 8 am & 1 pm for improvements digging R trenches in B. Bʰ Sec. Box and wiring same and Hqrs.	
	10ᵗʰ		Nº 2 Sec section work for half day only. Lath in the afternoon. Nº 1 & 3 work as on 9ᵗʰ	
	11ᵗʰ		M.C. awarded to 2/Lieut Byers W.C. and Cap. Buckley T. D.C.M. to Sergt Nevitt Bar to D.C.M. to C.S.M. Skelton. Work as on 9ᵗʰ	
	12ᵗʰ		Nº 6 Section work on Bat. & Batt. Hq. & Nº 2 Sector on Camp Improvements. Nºˢ 1 & 3 section work as on 9ᵗʰ	

WAR DIARY
or
INTELLIGENCE SUMMARY.
(Erase heading not required.)

Army Form C. 2118.

Place	Date	Hour	Summary of Events and Information	Remarks and references to Appendices
May 1918	5th		M.M. awarded to 2nd Cpl Jones C.H.R.	
			2nd " L/Cpl Biggins W.H.	
			2nd " Sapper Garlick C.G.	
			L/Cpl Mustard S.W.	
			Sergt Meyers H.	
			Bar to M.M. " Sergt Meyers H.	
Au Souverain			No 3 section fixed 600 m and continue loopholing & making knife rests for Petite Bois defences. Also Bde HQ.	
			No 1 section finished 800 ft tramway bdge in front of support line	
			" 25 4 " " Wervy or Petite Bois	
	6th		Work as on 5th	
	7th		Work as on 5th Pontoons are dumped at C.R.E's dump	
	8th		Work as on 5th for No 1, 3 & 4 sections. No 2 section being relieved	
			from night work, rests & clays in camp on intrenchments	

Army Form C. 2118.

WAR DIARY
or
INTELLIGENCE SUMMARY.
(Erase heading not required.)

Instructions regarding War Diaries and Intelligence Summaries are contained in F. S. Regs., Part II. and the Staff Manual respectively. Title pages will be prepared in manuscript.

Place	Date	Hour	Summary of Events and Information	Remarks and references to Appendices
May 1918 Souverain	13th		Parade at 9:00 am for Nos 2, 4 & H.Q. Sections. Clean arms. Iron Ration and Respirator Inspection followed. S. & Co. kept in camp. No. 1 & 3 sectors paraded at 1:30 pm for similar inspection. No night work. M.O. visits & carries for first field dressing & respirator attend.	
	14th		No. 1 section work on wiring defences of SUMPTENBOSCA, supervising the digging, clearing the hedges in front of Support line. No. 2 section on the construction of a new camp. The approach of a large arming mounted gun making present awn impossible. No. 3 Supervises the work of 270 men of the Reserve Bde digging on the Reserve line, and 30 men of Reserve Bn digging strong point, all in Pel Sec Bois. No. 4 Section construct Bde HQ 20 inf pnfg, 1 Bn HQ 20 inf/pnfg and another Bn HQ 16 inf wiring party.	

Army Form C. 2118.

WAR DIARY
or
INTELLIGENCE SUMMARY.
(Erase heading not required.)

Place	Date	Hour	Summary of Events and Information	Remarks and references to Appendices
May 1918	15th		Nos 2 & 3 sections drew many of No 3 superveneing myth cart of Pcd Sec Bns Hoads at 7am & marching order, moved to new camp and went there. No 1 section went on their various jobs as on 14 returning to camp for tea and march at 6.p.m. to new camp. No 1 section left its night work at SUMPTENBROUCH return to new camp. Hq moved to new camp at midday.	
Hazebrouck	16th		Nos 2 & 3 (less men on Refsec Bns work) went on new camp during the day. No 1 section as on 13th. No 1 section continued its night work at SUMPTENBROUCH and thinning of hedges by ledges of Support lines.	
	17th		No 2 section only went on camp, remainder of No 3 Jump out flowed parts of Reserve line, and put in Sap Colt doors to M.G. Bn Hedd Qurtrs and emplacements.	

WAR DIARY
or
INTELLIGENCE SUMMARY.

(Erase heading not required.)

Army Form C. 2118.

Place	Date	Hour	Summary of Events and Information	Remarks and references to Appendices
May 1918 Hazebrouck	18th		New draft of 10 sappers sent with their sections today. Orders for contact on 19th. Lt Drummond with 20 nt ranks sales so asked tarau from STRAZEELE Dump.	
	19th	9 a.m	Parade at 9.0 a.m for section No 2, 4, H.Q. and men of No 3 not on night work. Clean arms and Box Respirato, inspection & drill after 5 days in the Camp.	
		1.0 p.m	Parade at 1.0 p.m. for remainder of No. 3 and No 1 Section Inspection as above.	
	20th	8 a.m	Inspection as above for all men out on works on 19th. Sections 2, 3 & 4 Parade at 8.o. a.m for works Section No 1 parade at 7.30 a.m. for work in Ret Sec Bois 5 Secretenlarch	

Army Form C. 2118.

WAR DIARY
or
INTELLIGENCE SUMMARY.
(Erase heading not required.)

Instructions regarding War Diaries and Intelligence Summaries are contained in F.S. Regs., Part II. and the Staff Manual respectively. Title pages will be prepared in manuscript.

Place	Date	Hour	Summary of Events and Information	Remarks and references to Appendices
May 18	21st		Parade. Pass at No 2 sector for clearing thorns infront of Reserve line. No 3 sector for preparing gun for M.G.s. No 4 for constructing B.G.s Bats H.Qs. (Telephone ability) Parade at 7.30 a.m. for No 1 Sector to rake on tanks and swing 1 Plat. See Bom 3 Smokescreen.	
MEESBOUCQ	22nd		Parades and work as on 21st atroust.	
	23rd		Parades and work to do on 21st with exception of No 2 who dismantle and prepare for village on oil engine & hand cart a Grand. See Bom	
	24th		Parades & work as on 21st. A new draught of eleven sappers are posted to section.	
	25th		Parade at 8 a.m for Sector No 1 for bridge across in R.S.Se. Line at Colley 134 H9. for work in camp. Directing oil engine & hand cart. No 3 for wiring Saps in Reserve line. No 4 parade at 7.30 p.m. to reinforce. Staying & wiring at R.T. See Boms, Reserve Line, to Sim Ant trench. A further draught of 74 sappers arrive.	

WAR DIARY or INTELLIGENCE SUMMARY.

Army Form C. 2118.

(Erase heading not required.)

Place	Date	Hour	Summary of Events and Information	Remarks and references to Appendices
HAZEBROUCK	May 18 26th		Parades noon 25th. No 1 Section work on B.b 5th Br. M.R. Elephant Shelters. No 2 Contact knife work in the Trifford Line. No 3 Cut 8 Road Signs in the line at Pet. Sec Borr. No 4 work as on 23rd inst.	
	27th		Except for a few men who meet the usual working parties. Parade at 9.0 a.m. for all sections. Clean arms ammunition and accpt Field Dressing Inspection. Box respirator drill, and parade 0.5 am t from 10 - 12:00 am for camp fatigues.	
	28th		Parades and work as on 23rd with exception of men who worked on 27th who parade at 9.0 a.m. for inspection & so above. 8 2nd Cpl Findlay regain the coy after an absence of more than a year on	
	29th		Parades and work as on 25th. Cpls Sumner, Faulds & Beale go to Sos and Luis Sam Courses	

WAR DIARY or INTELLIGENCE SUMMARY

Army Form C. 2118.

Place	Date	Hour	Summary of Events and Information	Remarks and references to Appendices
HAZEBROUCK	May 18 30th	8.0 am	Parade at 8.0 am for Nos 1, 2 & 3 Sections. No 1 Section on construction of elephant shelter for Bde & Bn HQ. No 2 on P.O.W. cage and complete the erection of oil engine stand and (to oil engine hut to stop of the ignition device missing, and we had to make a hot tube – also other parts not as intricate.) No 3 Section continue work on the time N. Pat Sec Box & Reserve line. No 3 cooks Parade 2.30 p.m. to next working parties, and organise digging at the two strong points Pat Sec Box and Search direct. Also a few men for work on Reserve Line.	
	31st		Work & parades as on 30th. No 2 section succeeded in getting the oil engine to work. Though it still needs a bit of understanding.	

FD Mathers
Major RE.
O.C. M552A (W.R.) Field Coy. RE

– ORIGINAL –

CONFIDENTIAL

WAR DIARY.

455TH (W. RIDING)
FIELD COMPANY,
R.E.

From 1/6/18 to 30/6/18

VOLUME No XXVIII

WAR DIARY
or
INTELLIGENCE SUMMARY
(Erase heading not required.)

Army Form C. 2118.

Place	Date	Hour	Summary of Events and Information	Remarks and references to Appendices
HAZEBROUCK	1918 June 1st July	8 a.m.	Paraded at 8 a.m. for section No 1, 2 & 3. No 1 Section work on dugouts & shelters. No 2 on works over camp not on whole. W.O.P. exp. No 3 section wire strong point and Reserve Line. No 4 section reference work on strong points and Reserve Line.	
	2nd		Paraded at 8 a.m. 8 hrs work. Parades for all sections at 8am with exception of the necessary men detailed to supervise night working parties by the section officers. Three Lieut. Bynes & No 1 section are in charge of all building works forward such as Head Quarters and M.G. posts. Lieut. Drummond No 2 Section, all work on SHUTTEN Bosch strong point. Lieut. Stockham No 3 Section all wiring & wiring of the Reserve Line. Lieut. Distorval No 4 Section all works on the Petree Line, strong front.	

Army Form C. 2118.

WAR DIARY
or
INTELLIGENCE SUMMARY.
(Erase heading not required.)

Instructions regarding War Diaries and Intelligence Summaries are contained in F. S. Regs., Part II. and the Staff Manual respectively. Title pages will be prepared in manuscript.

Place	Date	Hour	Summary of Events and Information	Remarks and references to Appendices
HAZEBROUCK June 1918	3rd		On the night 2nd–3rd a Minor Operation was carried out by the Div. 2 Sappers were lent each to 6 attacking platoons for the purpose of clearing wire and other obstacles. The following men were armed with 1 Bangalore Torpedo, 1 hand axe, 2 heavy wire cutters. Cpls Stanfield, Reeves, Sappers Bridge, Simmonds, Jampson, Lamb, Larson, Peacock, Potts, Johnston, Mills & Ramsden, all of No. 2 section with Cpl Toye in a report centre established in the Support line. The operation was successful and RE reported themselves well.	
			Work for the day of the 3rd was as on the 2nd inst.	
	4th		Parade and inspection at 9 a.m a.m, no further parade.	
	5th		Work as on 3rd.	

Army Form C. 2118.

WAR DIARY
or
INTELLIGENCE SUMMARY.
(Erase heading not required.)

Place	Date	Hour	Summary of Events and Information	Remarks and references to Appendices
HAZEBROUCK				
June 1918	6th		Parades and work as on the 3rd inst. The workshops are complete and the bandsaw will take a "timber" well. No 3 in addition to work on Reserve line, also supervise the mines. (for which there a non-men permanently billeted away forward) and a permanent Charge Pm 5 of 18 mm	
	7th		Work and parades as on 3rd.	
	8th		Work and parades as on 3rd. No. 4 Section have now the whole of Pot See Bois strong point wired and in a fightable condition.	
	9th		Work and parades as on 3rd inst	
	10th		Work and parades as on 3rd inst	
	11th		Work in camp now finished, as there are ample billets for all men, a well fitted up workshop, and work such as riveting up timber is being undertaken for other field units. Section work as usual.	

WAR DIARY
or
INTELLIGENCE SUMMARY.

(Erase heading not required.)

Army Form C. 2118.

Place	Date	Hour	Summary of Events and Information	Remarks and references to Appendices
HAZEBROUCK June 1918	12		Parade for all sections at 9.00 a.m. General inspection and a short parade at 10.00 am for one hour. No work this day being on Sunday, one had Church parade at 6.30 A.M.	
	13		The following parties are recommended by the 4 Coy. N°1 Section two parties of 10 and 20 men twice a day on Hop. shelters. N°.2 section 50 men daily on SWARTENBROUCH defences. N°.3 section 100 men daily on Reserve line digging, and 200 men each night, also ½ Coy. of Pioneers revetting same and ½ coy of Pioneers every 4th day. Also a permanent drainage party of 12 men, rations by day. No.4 section ½ Coy of Pioneers revetting Batt. Sec Bris along front, 14 connected posts in all, 1/Platoon of Pioneers arranging and 50 infantry digging to trenches three by night.	

Army Form C. 2118.

WAR DIARY
or
INTELLIGENCE SUMMARY.
(Erase heading not required.)

Instructions regarding War Diaries and Intelligence Summaries are contained in F. S. Regs., Part II. and the Staff Manual respectively. Title pages will be prepared in manuscript.

Place	Date	Hour	Summary of Events and Information	Remarks and references to Appendices
HAZEBROUCK. June 1918.	14th		Work and Parades as on 13th with exception that no working party for No 3 section to night.	
	15th		Work and Parades as on 13th. The mounted section has for some days past been suffering from an epidemic of influenza, a similar complaint, necessitating numerous removals to hospital. This is not spreading to the dismounted men.	
	16th		Work and Parades as usual.	
	17th		Work and Parades as usual.	
	18th		Work and Parades as usual. Lt Byers M.C. with C.S.M and thirty other ranks visit Concrete Block Factory at ARQUES for motor lies. In addition seventeen dismounted men and three mounted men are evacuated to hospital, besides others sick and remaining at duty – all with influenza, making it very difficult to carry on with work.	
	19th		No work. Usual inspection parade at 9.00 a.m. and church parade at 5.30 p.m.	

Army Form C. 2118.

WAR DIARY
or
INTELLIGENCE SUMMARY.
(Erase heading not required.)

Instructions regarding War Diaries and Intelligence Summaries are contained in F.S. Regs., Part II. and the Staff Manual respectively. Title pages will be prepared in manuscript.

Place	Date	Hour	Summary of Events and Information	Remarks and references to Appendices
HAZEBROUCK	June 1918 20th		We received orders that we are to be relieved by 31st Div. Three advance parties arrive at 9.30 a.m. and take over ammunition dumps etc. By 2.00 p.m. at which time the Coy move off, being the mounted section moving up as the officers pass the line over. Three officers Cpls Vickers, Dishevel and Drummond are evacuated each Left. Williamson is only just recovering from a week's illness in bed and Major Mattering also suffering from influenza. All H.Q. section are sick, the C.S.M. only remaining with the Coy. We arrive at our Billets at BARRINGHEM SBANDRINGHEM at 6.30 p.m.	
	21st		The whole day spent in general clean up of camp and men. Fatigue parade at 7.00 a.m.	
	22nd		Company parade in F.D. clean fatigue at 8.00 a.m. for squad drill. Being the beginning of a signal training programme for the time the Coy are in Rest.	

WAR DIARY
or
INTELLIGENCE SUMMARY.
(Erase heading not required.)

Army Form C. 2118.

Place	Date	Hour	Summary of Events and Information	Remarks and references to Appendices
BINDRINGHEM June 1918	23rd		Parade 8.00 a.m. for one hours squad drill without arms, one hours instruction in Lewis gun & Machine gun, and one hour coy drill with arms.	
	24th		Parade as on 23rd instruction today in musketry as well as Lewis and Machine Gun and a battln parade in afternoon.	
	25th		A guard is mounted by day only. Also today a lecture by C.S.M. on Discipline & Saluting at 3.00 p.m.	
	26th		Parade for training as on 23rd. The men recently evacuated for influenza are now returning. Five reported to the coy today.	
	27th		Parades today included a practice parade for the C.R.E's inspection due on 29th inst. The Divl. Band played on the parade ground at 6.00 p.m.	

Army Form C. 2118.

WAR DIARY
or
INTELLIGENCE SUMMARY.
(Erase heading not required.)

Place	Date	Hour	Summary of Events and Information	Remarks and references to Appendices
RANDRINGHEM	June 1918 28th		The training programme for today was as follows. ½ hour Physical drill. ½ hour lecture on my health. One hour training in musketry by R.S.M. ½ hour lecture on Reinforced concrete. One hour making model in ground from a map. Today another six men to hospital with influenza. First ten men return cured and rested.	
	29th		Parade for Physical & Bayonet parade at 9.30 am in full marching order for inspection by C.R.E. at 10.30. The inspection lasted three hours and was most very favourably commented on. March past for the General's inspection on July 2nd was practised	
	30		Sunday. Church parade for C of E at 5.30 p.m. and for Non conformists in the morning. Also a lecture by C.R.E. to Officers and NCOs of this and another field Co. R.E. on Reconnaissance and Reports. After a short discussion on R.E. Stunts which will probably be held on 7th July.	

War Diary.

(Original).

Volume No. XXVIII

for July 1918.

Unit :- 455th. (W.R.) Field Coy. R.E. (T.F.)

B.E.F.

```
455TH (W. RIDING)
FIELD COMPANY,
R.E.
No. A.F. C. 2118.
Date 31-7-1918
```

WAR DIARY
INTELLIGENCE SUMMARY

Army Form C. 2118.

Place	Date	Hour	Summary of Events and Information	Remarks and references to Appendices
BAND RING MT M.	July 1918 1st		Training for dismounted sections consisted of the whole morning on the rifle range. Shooting was better than we might have expected. Fatigues in the afternoon getting ready for RE sports to be held on 7th inst. and inspection tomorrow.	
	2nd		First parade for mounted men at 6.am as usual and dismounted men at 9.00. March off in full marching order at 9.15 and arrived at parade ground at 10.15 a.m. General inspection at 11.15 a.m. consisted of general saluté, inspection and march past in col. of route. Cy commanders of 455 & 510 & (16293 were adjt. present being on leave) were called each by Gen. Cayley and congratulated. The 455th Cy undoubtedly went past in very good style.	
	3rd		Training today in Road Repairs, demolitions, Shoeing anchors, Use of Field Level, and drawing of fuzes for Demolitions and a lecture on Standing orders for Mounted men.	
	4th		Training today – Shooting, men were made to shoot wearing steel helmets.	

WAR DIARY
or
INTELLIGENCE SUMMARY
(Erase heading not required.)

Army Form C. 2118.

Place	Date	Hour	Summary of Events and Information	Remarks and references to Appendices
BANDRINGHEM				
July 1918	5th		Training of dismounted men - morning's punterring on canal at	
			BLARINGHEM. The following were found safe. Wedge a bent	
			foot and Wedge grouts line 2cm long and above tray were	
			done in 15 minutes.	
	6th		Training for front line in the morning. Revetting, Water supply	
			Influenza has ceased to cause casualties in the Coy.	
			RE Sports of whole programme attended	
	7th		Sunday church parade. Football officers beat Coy. Coy.	
	8		Parade at 8.10 am to clears fatigues for 2 days work on getting	
			ready the of sports ground.	
	7th		Sunday and RE Sports Programme is attacked. Though three coys	
			entered the majority of prizes were carried off by this coy including	
			the Tool Cart drive. No 2 Section making a tie with the London Coy.	
			and in going round a third time did a clean funnel.	
	9th		Parade at 8.00 am. Clear fatigues for 2 days work in preparing the	
			Sports ground for the Divl Sports also to take place tomorrow.	

WAR DIARY
or
INTELLIGENCE SUMMARY.
(Erase heading not required.)

Army Form C. 2118.

Place	Date	Hour	Summary of Events and Information	Remarks and references to Appendices
BANDRINGHEM	July 1918	9th	Divisional order. No parades today, in order that men may attend success, many old friends of the Div turning up.	
	10th		All officers N.C.O.s and mounted N.C.O.s took part in CRE's staff ride and exercises in constructing bridges over the canal at WANDRECQUES. Remainder of coy clean up ground etc after the recent sports.	
	11		Training as usual. Lectures by Section Officers in Bridges and Types of Trenches. 30 men of the coy are inoculated	
	12		The day was to have been spent in carrying out a scheme but on account of bad weather all ranks remained in billets	
	13		All ranks took part in a coy scheme of marching out to a line given on map and laying out the final lines for a defensive scheme	

WAR DIARY
or
INTELLIGENCE SUMMARY.
(Erase heading not required.)

Army Form C. 2118.

Place	Date	Hour	Summary of Events and Information	Remarks and references to Appendices
BANDRINGHEM	July 1918	14th	Sunday. Day of rest. Church parades. The O.C. and three subalterns rode over to the Kent Farm Cy on the East HAZEBROUCK line and arrange to relieve them on 16th. The line appears to run through all the back Junk gardens in HAZEBROUCK.	
	15th		Parade of whole Cy in full marching order at 10.00 a.m. and march off to new camp at EECKE HOUT CASTEEL arriving there at 2.00 p.m. The marching of the Cy was not good, partly on account of the long waiting.	
	16th		Sections 1, 2, & 4 paraded at 6.00 a.m. and rode off by Lesule wagons to East H. Cosrs. returning again by about 9.00 p.m. Commence work on said relaying various forge above & cables. No 3 Section work in camp constructing various forge above & cables.	
	17th		Work as on 16th except parade for Section 1, 2 & 4 is at 7.30 a.m.	

WAR DIARY
or
INTELLIGENCE SUMMARY.
(Erase heading not required.)

Army Form C. 2118.

Place	Date	Hour	Summary of Events and Information	Remarks and references to Appendices
EECKE HOUT CAMP.	July 1918 17		Parades and work as on 17th except that No 3 Section carry on training scheme – marching by various routes to & from – instead of fatigues in camp.	
	19th		Parades & work as on 12th. Training of No 3 Section in road construction in addition preparation of plans & sections.	
	20th		Parades & work as on 12th. Training for No 3 Section in Ramp making. Using Lewis Gunnery. This looks to becoming important as the coy now has an additional Lewis Gun per section making 5 L.G's establishment = 1 M.G. which at camp amplies to establishment. Lieut S Callan on leave 6 to 10th Aug 1918.	
	21		Work and training as on 18th except that No 2 Sect change places with 3.	

WAR DIARY or INTELLIGENCE SUMMARY

Army Form C. 2118.

Place	Date	Hour	Summary of Events and Information	Remarks and references to Appendices
MORTEN (near)	July 1918 21st		Parade at 2.30 and march off to work as usual. Known also as usual.	
	22nd	7.45	Arrive at 7.45 for work. Parade in full marching order at 11.45am and move off to St MARIE CAPELL area. However two companies to be a great muddle about billets and Lieut Dickinson who went forward billeting secured billets at P.35.d.01	
			of sheet 27 YPRES.	
	23rd	8.0am	Parade at 8.0am. Remainder of day spent in billets on account of very bad weather. Raining all day. Lieut Finlay reports two visiting orders.	
	24th	10.00am	Parade in full marching order at 10.00am and proceed in col. of route to camp at R.1.d.9.5 sheet 22. As there were no signs of forward billeting party to guide us in we stopped for midday feed and water at GODEWAERSVELDE – marching improving.	
	25th		Look of new work for X corps and improve our camp – Everyone under canvas.	
	26th		Nos. 1 & 2 Section 6 350 in depth on elephant shelters. Letting them into a bank on MONT des CATS.	

WAR DIARY
or
INTELLIGENCE SUMMARY.

(Erase heading not required.)

Army Form C. 2118.

Place	Date	Hour	Summary of Events and Information	Remarks and references to Appendices
GODEWAERSVELDE July, 1918.	27th		No. 3 Section parade at 6.0 a.m. to No. 3 at 12 noon to work in shifts on the new elephant shelters on Mont des Cats. No's 1 & 2 Sections parade at 8.0 a.m. and work on H.T. track leading forward from neighbourhood of BOSCHEPE.	
	28th		Work & parades as on 27th.	
	29th		Work & parades as on 28th. The night was rather disturbed by the enemy's long range shelling.	
	30th		Went as on 28th. Last night two men were slightly wounded by the shelling and as we are out of our safe area, at work to camp to a site we have already prepared. As we expect to move tomorrow work on track is handed over to 6th Bn. S.W.B. Pioneers and the almost completed shelters on Mont des Cats are carefully camouflaged up to left.	
	31st		Standing by. Waiting orders to move. Wagon cleaning and much needed bathing. 18 men on at the abandoned C.C.S. baths in neck field.	

G.H. Mathews
Major RE
OC ostens in full army RE

Original.

War Diary.

of

455th. (W.R.) Field Coy. R.E. (TF).

for

August 1918

Volume 29.

Army Form C. 2118.

WAR DIARY
or
INTELLIGENCE SUMMARY.
(Erase heading not required.)

Place	Date	Hour	Summary of Events and Information	Remarks and references to Appendices
GOED Aug 1918	1st		Coy stands to in camp ready for move. Officers sent out to take over in new sector.	
	2nd		Coy. Parade 7.00 a.m. full marching order and move off with 20 x carts intervals to new Camp at Le Peuplier. 1st two Sec. Pioneers Camp. As the Australian Coy had Co Field eng. re working at one time we take over work from the Pioneers as we are Coy in Reserve for the first time since Nov 1915.	
	3rd		Parade for all Sections 7.30 a.m. No 1 Section went on full forces at to CURFEW House and ESTAMINET corner. The late bridge was found to have been blown to pieces though only 50lb finished. No 2 Section work on the Cornette Pump House for water supply at HAZEBROUCK, taking it over about 60% complete. No 3 Section take over all prepared demolitions in the area. No 4 Section erect hut at St SYLVESTER CAPPEL at CRE. H.Q.	
	4th		Works parades as yesterday. 1 N.C.O & 3 sappers attend commemoration service.	

WAR DIARY or INTELLIGENCE SUMMARY

Place	Date	Hour	Summary of Events and Information	Remarks and references to Appendices
LE PEUPLIER	Aug 1918. 5th		Work carried on as on 3rd - by 2 & 3 sects. 2nd Company moved to the following billets. H.Q. & No 2 section to HAZEBROUCK Brick works (on the Borre road) No. 154 Section join No. 3 section for billets at BORRE. No. 154 Seators work in two C.T.s NORD St & MERRIS St. These are to be fenced out and A framed and shot boarded in the usual manner	
	6th		Some of No 3 section who were employed in CRE's workshop return to coy. to join Hq. section temporally for work near the HQ camp. These still remain 30 of the section on mines.	
	7th		Work as on 5th working parties from Div Nucleus Bn report as follows 100 OR for each C.T. under 154 sect. Two shifts of 20 each on Pump House, 15 on mines, and 12 for packing stone at Caëstre for the concrete for the Pump House	

WAR DIARY
or
INTELLIGENCE SUMMARY.

Army Form C. 2118.

Place	Date	Hour	Summary of Events and Information	Remarks and references to Appendices
HAZEBROUCK	1/5/1918	8th	Work as on 7th inst. Also a party of 6 men ny of chairinval theatre in a barn and coll tent to construct seats there.	
		9th	Work as above. Party of 50 R.A.M.C. report daily for repair of roads under supervision of No 1 Section. No 2 Section working on Concrete Pump house supply 6 men to reconstruct a camp of LA CROIX KREOLE for Bde Hd	
		10th	Work as above.	
		11th	Work as on 7th. No 2 Section supply 1 NCO & 2 OR to take part in the another commeration (sur) service. Also present. The King and troops from an American Div.	
		12th	Work as on 7th. The Diil theatre is finished. Capt Stansfield rejoin from a months leave.	

Army Form C. 2118.

WAR DIARY
or
INTELLIGENCE SUMMARY.
(Erase heading not required.)

Place	Date	Hour	Summary of Events and Information	Remarks and references to Appendices
HAZEBROUCK. Aug 1918	13th		No 184 Section work on C.T.s as before. Also on stopping shelters from Pill Boxes at CURFEW & TIFILIS House. No 2 Section continue on Pump House and complete Bde HQ. No 3 Section hand over all Secured mines to other two field coys RE and move out of BORRE to coy HQ. Note. No 184 section moved out of BORRE yesterday to the camp of Kent Field Coy at W13 b cent (27 SE).	
	14th		Work as on 13th. No 184 section change time of their working parade from 8 p.m. to 5 a.m. Casualties. 7 O.R. proceed to rest camp at AUDRESSELLES. 9 O.R. including 2 Drivers reinforcements from Base.	
	15th		Work as on 13th except No 3 section work at CRE's workshop – constructing concertinas.	
	16th		Work as on 15th.	
	17th		Work as on 13th. Party from 2nd Army Rest Camp return to Coy.	

Army Form C. 2118.

WAR DIARY
or
INTELLIGENCE SUMMARY.
(Erase heading not required.)

Instructions regarding War Diaries and Intelligence Summaries are contained in F. S. Regs., Part II. and the Staff Manual respectively. Title pages will be prepared in manuscript.

Place	Date	Hour	Summary of Events and Information	Remarks and references to Appendices
HAZEBROUCK	Aug 1918 18th		Work as on 15th for Nos 1,2,5,4. Stations. No 3 section 5 Mounted men made for inspection and baths.	
	19th		Work as on 15th.	
	20th		Work as on 15th.	
	21st		Work as on 15th. except that a party of our own type set work for the construction of new Div H.Q.	
	22nd		Work as on 15th. Work on new Div H.Q. is cancelled, and tools collected.	
	23rd		Work as on 15th. No 2 section completed the HAZEBROUCK Pumping House. The engine and pump are tested, and it was found that the engine, a Peter Junior, has not sufficient power to work the pump against no head. This of course reflects nothing on No 2 section who only had the evening and Sunday to do — and did it well.	

Army Form C. 2118.

WAR DIARY
or
INTELLIGENCE SUMMARY.
(Erase heading not required.)

Instructions regarding War Diaries and Intelligence Summaries are contained in F. S. Regs., Part II. and the Staff Manual respectively. Title pages will be prepared in manuscript.

Place	Date	Hour	Summary of Events and Information	Remarks and references to Appendices
CONGO COPNER Aug 1918	23rd		No 1 & 4 Sections continue work on Roads and C.T.s as before. No 2 & 3 Sections parade in full marching order and move with Coy H.Q. to forward Billets at W.13.B.5.5. (Sket 27) Transport this morning at V.20.a.7.9.	Nos 2&3
	24th		Work redistributed slightly. No 1 Section take over repair of roads forenamed of D.G.T. line with a working party of 100 R.A.M.C. and 6 G.S. wagons. No 2 act. with in camp. No 3 also in camp. No 4 act take over work Menin St. and Hood St. C.T.s which are now extra. A general overhaul of checkboards in timber and making fire bays in trestles throughout. Work carried on in timber and making fire bays throughout.	
	25th		Work as on 24th except that Nos 3 & 4 Sects. under Lieut Dartnall work at BORRE putting damaged houses in order for Div. H.Q. which will probably move in on 29th.	
	26th		Work as on Sept 25th. Mounted section moved up to H.Q. Billets.	

Army Form C. 2118.

WAR DIARY
or
INTELLIGENCE SUMMARY.
(Erase heading not required.)

Instructions regarding War Diaries and Intelligence Summaries are contained in F.S. Regs., Part II. and the Staff Manual respectively. Title pages will be prepared in manuscript.

Place	Date	Hour	Summary of Events and Information	Remarks and references to Appendices
CONGO CORNER				
Aug 1915	27th		Work as on 25th. Got all Lathom joints in from Base.	
	28th		Work as on 25th	
	29th		Work as on 25th. A draft of four sappers arrived from Base.	
	30th		Work as on 25th. Div HQ at Borre is completed. Today also the enemy withdrew on the Div. front, burning everything he came across. We are ordered to put the road MERRIS – OUTERSTEENE in order, including bridge over the Meteren Becque, & to put Divisional main recovery reconnaissance in order.	
	31st		Coy works in shifts on road and bridge as above. Commencing at 4.30 a.m. The works consist in laying 150' of plank road and making a new track and abutments (the old one was mined) at the Becque, and filling the enormous shell holes in MERRIS with which – the road was only just passable for infantry before we took over. Officers and NCO's & 284 rectors made up to MERRIS and put out parties for 2½ miles	M.F.F.C. Maj

Vol 32

Original.

War Diary

of

455th. (W.R.) Field Coy. R.E. (T.F.)

for

month of September 1918

Volume 30.

455TH (W. RIDING)
FIELD COMPANY,
R.E.

No.
Date 5-10-1918

Army Form C. 2118.

WAR DIARY
or
INTELLIGENCE SUMMARY.
(Erase heading not required.)

Place	Date	Hour	Summary of Events and Information	Remarks and references to Appendices
MERRIS Sept. 1918	1st		The whole Coy and Divl Nucleus Bn. work in plyts on the plank road, and road generally between MERRIS & OUTERSTEENE. Also look after supplies in neighbourhood.	
	2nd		No 1 & 3 Sn section complete the work above, and a water cart filling point in MERRIS. No 2 is treated on to make an artillery bridge at A.11.d.28. (the line running along 500x & Lood) and No 1 & 3 Sn move up to new camp at VERITY Crossing and complete a plank road round the crater there. Capt Williamson rejoins from leave.	
	3rd		Sections 1 & 2 commence a bridge at A.10 central on main road 18"G span to carry double Corps traffic. Remainder work on roads from OUTER STEENE to STINTJE and points for water in that area.	

Army Form C. 2118.

WAR DIARY
or
INTELLIGENCE SUMMARY.
(Erase heading not required.)

Instructions regarding War Diaries and Intelligence Summaries are contained in F. S. Regs., Part II. and the Staff Manual respectively. Title pages will be prepared in manuscript.

Place	Date	Hour	Summary of Events and Information	Remarks and references to Appendices
VERITY CROSS F5c 2.6.	8 Sept 1918	4th	Up the Div captured Hill 63 today we moved forward again. No 2 pct. take on a Ridge (10 tin ante 510' span) at A.17.c.87. No 4 continue on bridge at A.10 central, remainder on roads up to A.10 cent. The whole camp moved at noon to A.10.d.0.6 (STEENWERK)	
STEENWERK		5th	Work as on 4th	
		6th	Bridges as above and completed, and No 21 mctr with 1 coy of pioneers fell in mud crater which unexpectedly blew up at 6.0 p.m. yesterday evening at road & railway crossing at La Creche A.6.c. 6.7. No further progress much by infantry and our billets was troubled by long range shell fire at night but no damage.	

Army Form C. 2118.

WAR DIARY
or
INTELLIGENCE SUMMARY.
(Erase heading not required.)

Place	Date	Hour	Summary of Events and Information	Remarks and references to Appendices
STEENWERK	Sept 1918			
	7th		No 1 Section the over STEENWERK dump, removing Bombs etc and building huts. No 4 rest and remainder work on road running East & West through La CRECHE.	
	8th		No 2 rest, remainder of Coy work on La CRECHE road as above. Also dismantle a temporary bridge at STEENWERK station and put in 30 ft B 2 ft diam drain pipe (cement) also brewery had blown in the large culvert.	
	9th		Coy continue work as on 8th and also build a horse watering point at WHISKER Bridge A11d 38.	
	10th		Work as on 9th. Also work on new water point at TROIS ARBRES.	
	11th		All work handed over to 31st Divl RE. Coy moves back to HAZEBROUCK. Roads very bad, rain continuous, march about 18 kilometres but no men fell out.	

Army Form C. 2118.

WAR DIARY
or
INTELLIGENCE SUMMARY.
(Erase heading not required.)

Instructions regarding War Diaries and Intelligence Summaries are contained in F. S. Regs., Part II. and the Staff Manual respectively. Title pages will be prepared in manuscript.

Place	Date	Hour	Summary of Events and Information	Remarks and references to Appendices
HAZEBROUCK.	Sept 1918	12th	Day spent at Baths and general cleaning of Office as there were many holes in roofs of billets, and still much rain, repairs were effected.	
	13th		As on 12th. Lecture by CRE in evening to RE officers.	
	14th		Inspection of Coy on full marching order. Concert for the men at MARTYN'S Dump in the evening.	
	15th		Church parades only.	
	16th		Mounted recon. near Off G 9.30 a.m. and Sappers entrain at HONDEGHEM 4.0 p.m. Detrain at St Jan der Bieren and march to Sapphire camp near by.	
	17th		Men again at work to Bett DIRTY BUCKET Camp to work under CE 2nd Corps.	

Army Form C. 2118.

WAR DIARY
or
INTELLIGENCE SUMMARY.
(Erase heading not required.)

Instructions regarding War Diaries and Intelligence Summaries are contained in F. S. Regs., Part II. and the Staff Manual respectively. Title pages will be prepared in manuscript.

Place	Date	Hour	Summary of Events and Information	Remarks and references to Appendices
DIRTY BUCKET Camp.				
Sept 1918	18th		General clean up of camp in morning. Work on BRIDGE Camp during the afternoon. Repairing it for Divl HQ.	
	19th		Work for all sections as on 18th in morning. Horse Lines renewed. Cut sappers men up to B. railway & MACHINE GUN Sidings. Relieving the 16th Div, 61st Field Coy RE. 3&4 sections move to the island in most rent to LILLE Gate YPRES.	
	20th		No 1 section work on accommodation in BOOSTRY CASTLE area. No 2 " construct heavy timber bridge at I 13 a 7.3. No 3 " work on WARRINGTON road repairs. No 4 " construct a P.O.W. cage at WINDWARD HOUSE.	
	21st		All work as on 20th.	

D. D. & L., London, E.C. (A8004) Wt. W1771/M2 31 7/50,000 5/17 Sch 52 Forms/C2118/14

Army Form C. 2118.

WAR DIARY
or
INTELLIGENCE SUMMARY.
(Erase heading not required.)

Instructions regarding War Diaries and Intelligence Summaries are contained in F. S. Regs., Part II. and the Staff Manual respectively. Title pages will be prepared in manuscript.

Place	Date	Hour	Summary of Events and Information	Remarks and references to Appendices
MACHINE GUN SIDINGS				
Sept 1918	22nd		All work on on 20th	
	23rd		Nos 1 & 3 sections work in on 20th. No 4 section rests then work having been completed. 2nd Lt Dostrval returns from leave	
	24th		Nos 1 & 3 sections rest. No 2 section prepares billets at LILLE. S & for Coy H.Q. No 4 section for odd jobs and keeping WARRINGTON road in repair.	
	25th		No 4 section as yesterday. Remainder rest. Work on the LILLE Sub-dugouts.	
	26th		The new sections collect salvage, there being no work as all preparations for coming operations were completed by yesterday. Two forward sections work at LILLE Gate.	

WAR DIARY
or
INTELLIGENCE SUMMARY
(Erase heading not required.)

Army Form C. 2118.

Place	Date	Hour	Summary of Events and Information	Remarks and references to Appendices
MACHINE GUN Sidings	Sept 1917 27		No 1 Section dismantled horses for the guns in YPRES. No 2 & 3 Coys to complete preparations for Coy HQ & 2 sections billets at LILLE GATE. No 4 section improves accommodation at GOLD FISH Chateau. Jn advanced Dr HQ Coy HQ and No 1 & 4 sections move up to LILLE GATE at 7.00 pm. S road.	
	28th		29th Div attached. Zero 5:30 a.m. Men's breakfast 7.00 a.m. and standby of orders. 1st section went off at 2.30 to reconnitre following at 5 mm interval. Coy HQ New Rovers after to last section. All met on mule track A from WARRINGTON Road to CLAPHAM JUNCTION. Weather entering bad, very little shell fire to reconnitre MENIN Road as far as GHELUVELT. Did not attempt any molestation at 11.0 a.m.	

Army Form C. 2118.

WAR DIARY
or
INTELLIGENCE SUMMARY.
(Erase heading not required.)

Place	Date	Hour	Summary of Events and Information	Remarks and references to Appendices
GLEN CORSE WOOD.	Sept 1918			
	29th		No 1, 2 & 3 section work on the plank road Hooge towards HOOGE Company, including mounted section move up to GLENCORSE WOOD with new officers, the roads being bad and full of traffic. The work on the road was also much hindered by French cavalry.	
	30th		The Company works on the plank road from GLENCORSE WOOD to Clapham Junction, keeping same in best repair possible. Also on the main MENIN Road from Clapham Junction Road forward, all B Stock now kept open for horse transport.	

D. W. Mathes, Major RE
OC 455th Field Coy RE

War Diary.

of

455. W.R. Field Coy. R.E. (T.F.)

for

Month of October. 1918.

Volume. 31.

WAR DIARY
or
INTELLIGENCE SUMMARY

Army Form C. 2118.

Place	Date	Hour	Summary of Events and Information	Remarks and references to Appendices
GLENCORSE WOOD	Oct 1st 1918		Wash for whole Coy on MENIN Road. No 3 & 4 sections paraded at 7.00 a.m and were relieved at 12.30 p.m by 1 & 2 sections. The road is not in such a bad state as at first believed to be. Also the surface and of m feet thickness is dug off the road underneath is good except for a few shell holes which are filled from engine dumps of stone from enemy dumps at GHELUVELT.	
	2nd		Work as on 1st on MENIN Road between CLAPHAM Junction and INVERNESS COPSE. Coy moves to new lines in a field – when 20 bivouac sheets and four tents at GHELUVELT. Watson on 1st on MENIN road except that work is all East of INVERNESS COPSE.	
	3rd		Div. moving out of line. Coy move back at 6.0 am to their old billets in the deep dugouts at GLENCORSE SE WOOD. No works today.	

WAR DIARY
or
INTELLIGENCE SUMMARY.
(Erase heading not required.)

Army Form C. 2118.

Instructions regarding War Diaries and Intelligence Summaries are contained in F. S. Regs., Part II. and the Staff Manual respectively. Title pages will be prepared in manuscript.

Place	Date	Hour	Summary of Events and Information	Remarks and references to Appendices
GLENCORSE Ɉ 14 a 26.	Oct 1918			
	Wed		Four sections parade at 8.0.a.m. and prepare a camp for 82nd Bde. at WESTHOEK. Each section preparing a camp for a Bn. and 1 section on Bde. HQ. Work consists chiefly in making plank road-ways for cookers and car-rows for camp. Most of the men are housed in clef dug-outs or pill-boxes.	
		6th	Work as on 3rd. Special instruction teams on F.O.&B. Camp.	
		7th	Work as on 6th with exception of No.1 section which remains in camp to rebuild and clean all Hd. Transport.	
		8th	Work on WESTHOEK camp for 3rd section. No.3 &(?) 2 sections go forward with officers to reconnoitre the new Div. Sector (DADIZEELE) and works appertaining to a camp site closed for the day.	
		9th	Work as on 7th.	
		10th	Work as on 7th except No.2 section reconnoi- sit camp at Place of N.E.l	

WAR DIARY
or
INTELLIGENCE SUMMARY.
(Erase heading not required.)

Army Form C. 2118.

Place	Date	Hour	Summary of Events and Information	Remarks and references to Appendices
GLENCORSE WOOD	Oct 1918		Unit as on 7th in WEST HOEK Belt camp. Jn Nos 1,254 rank and file	
	11th		No 3 section remains in camp for rest. Men issued with winter clothing	
	12th		Unit as on 2nd except No 4 section rests.	
	13th		Parade at 7.00 am. Run fatigues for loading vehicles. Transport and No 1 section to pull marching order move off at 8.00 am	
			By SMITH'S Road to ZONNEBEKE - BROODSEINDE - BECELAERE E A 8 a 64. The remaining sections move to camp at 8.30 am	
			by direct route. The night is spent under 22 bivouac sheets and five tents. Badly shelled all night but no casualties	
	14th		Due attack in the morning with great success. However there is no work for the RE especially as the aspect is in reserve. Coy moves forward in the evening to K 12. 8. 19. Much shelling at	
			night. Suffer crater wounded slightly	

WAR DIARY
INTELLIGENCE SUMMARY

Army Form C. 2118.

Place	Date	Hour	Summary of Events and Information	Remarks and references to Appendices
LADIZEELE	Oct 1918 15th		Advance continued. Coy moves forward again at 08.30 a.m. and passes through LEDGENHAM [?] as the barrage opens up. However as enemy arty is not shelling any more we entered to 6.16 & 27 and Bn.H.Q. relieve the 2nd C.H.C. at 3 p.m. with orders to settle down for night at G.35.c.30 as there is no work. However at 6.00 we begin to get rid of the forward situation and move camp to farm houses at G.3.d.02 going via STEENE STAMPKOT. Struck up our third move for that day at 9.00 p.m.	
	16th		No work [?] rest and helps on civilian refugees. Officers made reconnaissance forward of G.H.Q. the LYS.	
	17th		At 01.00 a.m. we get orders to move up to [?] forward and by and bridges equipment of the other two coys forward and by and brigade the LYS at dawn, at or CUERNE H.Q. gets forward to reconnoitre and agrees with 88 Bde that the situation makes it impossible. Transport in the town to really form to await orders.	

WAR DIARY or INTELLIGENCE SUMMARY

Army Form C. 2118.

(Erase heading not required.)

Place	Date	Hour	Summary of Events and Information	Remarks and references to Appendices
	Oct 22 1917		The Transport enRobance further to rear when HQ RC became aware of enemies 6 gun at CAPPEL ST KATHERINE, arriving there at 10 a.m. CO gave order to get mules for the coy and transport (who had the remainder for bridging) were Nos 2,3,5 & sec H.) and finally get orders to return to camp. Before there to orders are acted on however, further orders asking by one received by 9th Div Tps that crowd the CYS. Been heavily attacked and had their bridge destroyed. OC confers with [GOC's] 88 & 27 "Bdes" are arranged. Detailes for Pengue bank & "Drie grachten" etc and there pontoons & trestle delivered. OC to Darbough — 2350 Siebens and proceeded over at 10.0pm pontoons successfully launched & west of CHICKNE at 7.30 p.m. & first of the herg paired over at 10.00 am. Read parts at that m. Pontoons retracted on wagons and returned home, from 5.0 pm & shelled considerably most of the tow ny, casualties 2 horses & 6 mules home at 3.00 am on 18th exhausted.	

WAR DIARY or INTELLIGENCE SUMMARY

Army Form C. 2118.

Place	Date	Hour	Summary of Events and Information	Remarks and references to Appendices
G3 d 0.2	Oct 1918	7 p.m.	By rest during day. At 9.00 p.m. the Lewis gun (Sporton's and the Coy's Reserve(?)) moved forward to bridge at E.25 c.8 by march. Personnel, O.C. Capt Byers M.C. & Doonborough, M.G. 23, 24 sections (Lieut Sellar & Farley being on leave) Right spent on road at H.7.b.9.2 the men getting some sleep in farm at that spot. At dawn the situation not being favorable information very meagre back half a mile to farm at H.1.d 33 at little rest is obtained. For the remainder of the day's meals are sent up from C Coys H.Q. O.C. reconnoiters the crossing of W.Pt Dr at COURTRAI and arranges with O.C. 497 Field Coy a mutual crossing for 80 Bde which is effected at 6.00 p.m. on Ponton being sent to Lt Brodgeg(?) Recy as an adv't depot more forward and unit all night for instructions to permit crossing.	

WAR DIARY
or
INTELLIGENCE SUMMARY

(Erase heading not required.)

Army Form C. 2118.

Place	Date	Hour	Summary of Events and Information	Remarks and references to Appendices
H.1.d.8.3 Oct 19.18	19		Situation permits Bridge being commenced at 2.0 p.m. at H.21.d.75-35 and it is completed at 8.00 a.m. with only one casualty by Shrapnel. That Lot. artillery cross at 10a.m. Bridge consisted of 4 pontoons and three trestles, the fifth pontoon was of plank by a skill on being the trestles of from CURTRAI.	
	20		Coy moves up to STACEGHEM at H.29 Central, billetting out in the villages there who received us most kindly. Only work is the maintenance of the bridges over the L.Y.S. viz 1 Pontoon bridge, 1 Barrel pier & bridge, and one heavy bridge to take light traffic over HARLEBEKE Lock.	
STACEGHEM H.29 central Sh.24.29	21st		General cleaning up. Bridge commenced (Axe trees 10 tons) at H.30. c. 6.5 over Canal, Materials all on site. Moved to billet at H.21.d.95.90 over Pontoon. The B. Sec. remained as permanent maintenance party on the pontoon bridge and on the trussel pier bridge.	

WAR DIARY
or
INTELLIGENCE SUMMARY.
(Erase heading not required.)

Army Form C. 2118.

Place	Date	Hour	Summary of Events and Information	Remarks and references to Appendices
Oct STA CEG-HEM H.24.c.ent Sheet 24.	22		After stand-to Coins were at work, bridge at H.30.e.65 is taken over by 2 L/Coys, and one was with its men. The remainder Coinies- continues to huge Enemy Pioneer Park at F.20.C+D and pontooning bridge with light-Field-Bridge. 1 Coy sent to bring away a load of this stuff destroying with carried out no enemy wagon.	
	23rd		Work in camp. Coy proceeded on leave. LI Stedman Stephens home leave	
	24		Coy on general camp work and on retrieves.	
	25th		Three sections work in rebuilt concerting bridge qp= 5½ tons Area load at H.20.c.05, Bridge is also canal and is shelled to Pel Rd. 181. Line transport by shelter went through COURTRAI after relief Bridge complete by 4.00 pm. men finishing off the men went by lorry to VLA.	
	26th		OC (MAJOR F.A.V.D. MATHEWS M.C. RE) proceeded on Command of Coy. taken over by Capt. D.R. WILLIAMSON R.E. & ten men employed on finishing bridge at H.20.c.0.9. Remainder in park on preference vehicles ready for Leave the next day.	

WAR DIARY or INTELLIGENCE SUMMARY

Army Form C. 2118.

Place	Date	Hour	Summary of Events and Information	Remarks and references to Appendices
TOURCOING X.30 Central Sheet 28.	27th		2 Lt DARNBROUGH and 4 Cyclists proceeded on a Cycling party and reconnoitring in the outskirts of TOURCOING as instructed by Bde. Group to TOURCOING was excellent. All men they intend are billets in an house.	
ST ANDRE K.8.d.10.15 Sheet 36.	28th		Coy prepared to move tomorrow to ST ANDRE area. 2nd Lt AYERS and party of Cyclists proceeded at 10.45 with Coy stores by Bde Group Motor Lorries, arriving ST ANDRE at 15.30 Coy leaving TOURCOING 10 w.m. marching. Transport & men in empty houses as houses have stables up loft thick walls.	
do.	29th	09.00	Inspection of Fortifications and Gas Helmets.	
		10.30	Drill Order — Inspection of Man and Shortclothing etc. After dismissal General cleaning up of weapons, clothing etc and Trench cutting.	
do.	30th		Nos. 1.2 and 3. Sections leave camp at 06.30 and proceed to L.13.e.3.6. to report to A. Coy 10th Cab. Railway Batt at 7.00 am. Returns worked on by above party until new dimensions received by throwing up the bridge. (The dimensions of Tube, Hard Rd. Rails, used for screw 8 approx. 4ft or above main Road by two large blocks of wood 75ft)	
CROIX L.16.d.0.5 Sheet 36	→		No. 4. Section assists transport to move to CROIX area (L.10 d. 0.5) which will be nearer the work. houses in empty tram lines — been in empty houses, there window being rather narrow which often looking to be Field Officer in each.	

Place	Date	Hour	Summary of Events and Information	Remarks and references to Appendices
CROIX L.10.d.0.2 Sheet 36	31		Nos 1 & 2 arm & Section work on railway as yesterday. Work still difficult from sentries firing frequently at 10/78 own rifles from top German Batts. Several found asleep. Railway Division sent to — Leave early 07.00 — Return 14.30. No 3 Sec parade 08.00 for work on weapons and General cleaning up. R Davies Capt RE O/C 431st (1st R) Field Coy. RE. 1-11-18	

Original

War Diary

of

455th (West Riding) Field Coy. R.E. (TF)

for

month of November 1918

Volume 32.

Army Form C. 2118.

WAR DIARY
or
INTELLIGENCE SUMMARY.
(Erase heading not required.)

Place	Date	Hour	Summary of Events and Information	Remarks and references to Appendices
CROIX (nr ROUBAIX) E.10.c.05 Sheet 36.	NOVEMBER 1st		Work continued on making road to main line diversion at L.13.d.ii. Coy used on finishing left Culvert and good work done. Same hours 07.45 on works till 21.11.00 and dinner work at 14.00 hours. No. 2 Section remaining in camp, carrying out gas drill, rifle inspection, cleaning up lines &c and billing up dugouts.	
	2nd		No. 1. Section went under Lt. DISTURNAL proceed by Lorry to WARNETON and then met 2 lorries with 4 Pontoon wagons & Pontoons with preparation of detachment filled these wagons & returned to Camp. Train carried 3 hours before return to Camp. Remainder of Section were in ordinary line activities i.e. all billets to be cleaned out, Picket to mount, ranges and one party of 40 per day Section was 2 + 3 Sections to work on railway helping the Canadian Construction Engineers to lay down track. They work well and good progress was made, taking into account the fact that all had did two trips to lay the enemy's about 450 yards of track laid. No. 4 Section remains in camp and undertake to any sine job about Camp.	
	3rd		No. 1, 2 + 3 Sections same as on yesterday, working from same hours 07.00 am proceed to Railway and came on with same work. Returned at 7.00 pm
2.LT. P.E. FURLONG
A.C. MURPHY Major

WAR DIARY or INTELLIGENCE SUMMARY

Army Form C. 2118.

Month: **November**

Place	Date Nov.	Hour	Summary of Events and Information	Remarks and references to Appendices
CROIX 6.10.c.0.5. Sheet 36.	4th		Nos. 1 and 4 Sections proceed to Railway and are employed on delying MENADA from bogs, bringing timber for railway sleepers, and then in general making a small siding. No. 2 Section remains in camp. No. 3 Section under 2Lt. P.E. FURLONG proceed to The ASYLUM, SIANDRE (K.14.a.) for work on water supply to 57th Inf. Bde. Sections find billets at K.g.d.1.1.	
	5th		No.1 Section remains in camp and works on cleaning up this piece of ground and loading same. Only 1 trestle and 1 pontoon wagon complete equipment was drawn. Nos. 2 and 3 Sections continue work on water supply. No Section mail. No.3 Section returns and comes to camp at about noon. No 3 Section received orders that the billets at The ASYLUM were unsanitary. After dinner No.3 Section to report to billets on 6th. 9 in previous orders cancelled.	
	6th	21:00	Capt. FURSE cancels billets orders sent to No.3. See to move unnecessary after dinner.	
		08:00	Orders sent to No.3 See to go to Coy H.Q.	
		15:00	No.3 See departs back to Coy H.Q. Runner sent to remain with 57 Inf. Bde.	
TOURCOING	7th		Coy moves with 87 Bde to TOURCOING and is billetted in Jardin. 2Lt. FURLONG proceeds forwards with advance billeting party to be prepared to report to CRE at ROLLEGHEM and join from on the morrow.	
	8th	07:45	Coy proceed to ROLLEGHEM and have proceeded on O.C. a reconnaisance of proposed areas near the River ESCAUT by.	

WAR DIARY
or
INTELLIGENCE SUMMARY.   NOVEMBER.

Army Form C. 2118.

Place	Date	Hour	Summary of Events and Information	Remarks and references to Appendices
From O.25.c.8.3. Sheet 79.	8th	08.00 09.30	**Continued** Coy. Parade for loading vehicles. Arrived at 9th Pole Group and proceeds to farm at 36/Ex. Very heavy Shell fire which Pole has damaged, one stretched along one side of our march. Great difficulty in getting lorries along one side of the Coy arrived at field. The Coy Company's front bridge to 15th line Armagh over Coy. to Bypass. Escape of Pontoon. The two ends on any Loco. Escape of Pontoon. Pole were making a "stand" on the which the first Pole was making a "stand" — any type of early reconnaissance necessary. bridges, but Pontoon [illegible] and 2nd Lt. FURLONG with one mounted N.C.O. proceeds forward OC. and 2nd Lt. FURLONG with one mounted N.C.O. proceeds forward	
	9th	07.30	OC to make a reconnaissance of site to front on bridge. Reconnaissance commenced by 07.30 YUT, but attempts to bridge were continuous. Staff are ready. On patrol at 07.00 a trace was put between the Div. Boundaries on patrol at Purth: I was informed that the enemy Advance lorries and 2 Tk's tank in area behind OC. reconnaissance of enemy vehicles. HQ and to commence with. The Runner immediately taken, HQ and to commence with proceeds immediately taken. light OCE. riving 08.00 Orders received to construct Pontoon bridge of ½ Pontoons Pack animal traffic and Bridging Equipment within two	
		09.15	1, 2 & 4 Sections. Picking up Pontoon 97/97 (Kent) NCC, on way proceed to site at U.24.b.4.6 Sheet 37.	

WAR DIARY
or
INTELLIGENCE SUMMARY.   NOVEMBER.

(Erase heading not required.)

Army Form C. 2118.

Place	Date Nov	Hour	Summary of Events and Information	Remarks and references to Appendices
Farm 29/0.25.c.8.3	9th	09.15	Remainder of Coy. prepare to move & commence loading.	
		0800	Bridge for Pack Transport completed at 37/U 24.6.6.6. Work of same nature continued also on a barrel pier bridge at 37/V.13.c.6.3. whilst Engineers working for Permanent (timber trestle) bridge at 37/V.23.c.6.7.	
		20.00 21.00	Nos. 1.2 & 4 Sections return to new billet at 37/U 23.c.6.7. leaving maintenance party on bridge. Remainder of Coy. arrive at new billet — leaving Lt. G.E.A. DISTURNAL & working party on bridge.	
Farm 37/U.23.6.67			'B' Coy. 1/2 Monmouth Regt. (Pioneers) assisted Coy. during the day, in digging ramps to both bridges and endeavouring the same. No. 3 Section under 2Lt. P.E. FURLONG proceeded to bridge site and remove as mounting as possible from battle trestles and carry out improvements on same. Nos. 1 & 4 Sections proceed to work on 1/2 pontoon Nos. 1 Section worked on. bridge at V. 24.6.6. and Enfilading Trenches on Ridges & forming Rubble for same. Remainder of Coy. dismantling and defending old bridge at V.13.0.6.3. & rebuilding as it into a Pack animal bridge.	
do.	10th	0700		One Copy of known trace. @ @

Army Form C. 2118.

WAR DIARY
or
INTELLIGENCE-SUMMARY. NOVEMBER
(Erase heading not required.)

Place	Date Nov	Hour	Summary of Events and Information	Remarks and references to Appendices
57/U.23.6.6/	10		No. 4 Section work on a Bridge to foot-bridge in GRAND COURANT at V.20.a.8.5. (Maintenance) and Securing foot bridge at U.20.a.2.2. Maintenance of foot-bridge at V.30.d.3.7 & Pack bridge at V.30.d.3.7 over GRAND COURANT. Two bridges put over GRAND COURANT. Two bridges put Infantry on old bridge were causing delay.	
			At V.30.d.8.5. communication cable crossing of foot-bridge at V.30.d.8.5.	
		18.00	Bridge at V.30.d.8.5. Sec't position left at side, not in the section front of Nos. 1 & 2 sections & bridge is above & Men and 2 N.C.O's of the 37th relieving party of Nos. 1 & 2 sections & maintenance party.	
	11th	06.30	O.C. with 2 Lt. AYERS and 2 Lt. FURLONG proceed forward to make a reconnaissance, having in front D/RWER RHONEY under orders of Inf Division to advance forward at ANIEEES. 37/E. 24. Convoy left at 07.30. The 2 Sec. proceeded under Sergt MYERS under orders to Division then ½ pontoon Bridge at V.24.b.6.6. under orders on Div. R.E. pontoons divisible high load drawn on contention of loading advance to firm coy on contention of loading Nos.1 and 4 Sections proceed to Area at MNIÈRES. Men to assist order from O.C.	
		07.00	No. 3 Sub. proceed with Cor. Bridge wagon to assist in loading.	

WAR DIARY
or
INTELLIGENCE SUMMARY. — NOVEMBER

(Erase heading not required.)

Army Form C. 2118.

Place	Date Nov	Hour	Summary of Events and Information	Remarks and references to Appendices
	11th		*Continued* O.C. with two officers proceed to make a road reconnaissance after on the RENAIX-MESSINES Road. 2 Lt. W.C. AYERS proceeds further to make a reconnaissance of troops billets & billeting area in KESTING. Whilst on this recon. the rumours of the completion of an ARMISTICE with GERMANY, which is confirmed about 09.30 when G.O.C. sends G.S.O.I. Div passing on however, to inform O.C. that hostilities cease at 11.00. Nos 1 and 4 Sections continue work with Section A.T. front arrive at dusk on which the 510ᵗʰ (Lond) Fld Coy have commenced temporary work. Heavy rain prevents work over the Siten.	
Bridge 7 E.20.6.7.4		12.00	O.C. dissatisfied for car in a farm at 14.00 are officers & large farm mementos house & dine over tea after the 1 Sec transferred. It evident that Proceeds with traff Cut to site of a storm of culvert at F.16.c.6.3 Sh 37 and commences training.	
37/F.20.e.6.4 Farm		14.00	1 Coy of ½ Hanover'n Regt under retransmission 40 o.c. commence work on filling in a large crater northward to STATUEUR halfway through the night & Field of tale (F.20.6.9.1) 4 Sectional in billets, 4 Section arrives at 23.00 & prepares for making their 1914 Section billets on which move are walking	

WAR DIARY
INTELLIGENCE SUMMARY.   NOVEMBER

Place	Date Nov.	Hour	Summary of Events and Information	Remarks and references to Appendices
37/F.20.c.b.4	11th	2300	*Continued* — Nos. 2 & 4 complete repairs to ESCAUT. No more road material required.	
	12th	0100	Coy Pontoon Wagon etc arrive. Coy now all in.	
		0700	Nos 1 & 3 No. 3 Sections (less 10 men of No. 3 Sections) work with 2Lt. Myers. Pioneers clear fuzing Lt. See & work on repairing large craters blown in road at 37/F.20.a.8.5. Roads on east side of road are entrenchment. Fields on west side of road are flooded so water is unable to get away. Roads in this section open when tactical temporarily repaired. Lt Off. Pioneer of Pioneers assist from OP of Pioneers. No. 3 under 2Lt. FURLONG with 2 platoons of Pioneers work on roads in F.16, F.11, F.5.d. and (X 30.c (Sheet 38). No. 4. See work on Completing metalling of culvert on Road thine at F.16.c.0.3 and F.10.b.9. respectively, also of runway commence on repairing craters and removing mines along 37// F.8. c. and d. F.3.d and F.3.a area. No. 2. See still at pontoon dump - filling Cockerel/ F.6.a.8.5 1 Platoon of Pioneers work on filling Cockerel/ F.6.a.8.5 are in Handfelling road material and other material	Nos. See 9.10 of 10.3 handled by 10.30 pm works

WAR DIARY
or
INTELLIGENCE SUMMARY. NOVEMBER

Army Form C. 2118.

(Erase heading not required.)

Place	Date Nov.	Hour	Summary of Events and Information	Remarks and references to Appendices
Farm B7/Fre.e.C.4.	12th	1700	Major F.A.V.D. Matthews M.C.R.E. rejoins Coy. from leave and resumes Command	
	13th	0700	Nos. 1, 3, 4 Sections parade for work. No. 1 carries on demolition works & Op. 12.E with the addition of filling in and craters of pits and in removal of obstacles to aviation at the work. Nos. 3 & 4 every endeavour as on 12th (1 Pl. and Pioneers train with — 2 Pl. 3)	
		1300	2 Platoons 3rd and 4 G.S. Platoons report to escort No. 3 Section	
		1700	No. 2 Section rejoins Coy. from the position it had been occupying over the ESCAUT in region of from Hospital improvements it was carrying any from Ban to U.K. Officers taking of ... hours.	
	14th		Coy. moves to OGY route march. Being the first of a series of marches to the frontier. Billets in Angle farm houses	
	15th		Coy. rests in HELLS. Work general clearing up at on 15th	
	16th		Coy. moves by march route in 97 M. ale column to HELLS at	
	17th		TRIBOURIAN stoppage etene men and beasts all room each Two A.S.C. G.S. wagons are attached to us as baggage wagons for the march.	

WAR DIARY
or
INTELLIGENCE SUMMARY.
(Erase heading not required.)

Army Form C. 2118.

Place	Date	Hour	Summary of Events and Information	Remarks and references to Appendices
TRIBOURIAU	Nov 1918 18th		Coy moves with 87th Bde to LA BELLE CROIX	
	19th		Rest. General clean up	
	20th	11 a.m.	At 12R	
	21st		Coy moves by march route to VIRGINAL SAMME, Billets not good as the village is shared with Pioneers and Ambulance	
	22nd		By rests as the MSC cannot get supplies through. Day spent in cleaning up.	
	23rd		Coy moves to a large farm by FLAMANDRES, passing over the battle field of Waterloo.	
	24th		Coy arrives by march route to CHASTRÉ. No Regtl a can arrived with Coy owing to the supply had broken down however the Coy march 27 kilometres. Four men falling out.	
	25		Coy marches CHASTRE to ORBATSE into very good billets	
	26		Rest today. General clean up of wagons etc. and change of clothes for the men	

WAR DIARY
or
INTELLIGENCE SUMMARY
(Erase heading not required.)

Army Form C. 2118.

Place	Date	Hour	Summary of Events and Information	Remarks and references to Appendices
	Nov 27th 1918		Coy marches from ORBAIS to NEUVILLE LE BOIS arriving with their men with sore feet and legs all not permit them to go further. They are evacuated.	
	28		Coy marches to HAUTE SARTE passing HUY. No men fall out	
	29		Coy marches to COMBLAIN FERON via TINLOT, very few leaving. No men falls out. Kept five show signs of not being able to continue march. Arrange with S.P.H. Field Amb. to carry them. Raining all evening short.	
	30th		Orders received to march to LES COMBLES are received at 01:00 hours. Cancelled at 07:00 and repeated at 10:00. Coy marches off at 11:00 but billets short at BELLEVAUX. No Zmen fall out.	

W. Mathers Major RE
O.C. 253 Field Coyre

Original.

War Diary

of

455th. (W.R.) Field Coy. R.E. (T.F.)

for

month of December 1918.

Volume 33.

455TH (W. RIDING)
FIELD COMPANY.
R.E.

WAR DIARY
or
INTELLIGENCE SUMMARY.
(Erase heading not required.)

Army Form C. 2118.

Place	Date	Hour	Summary of Events and Information	Remarks and references to Appendices
	1918 Dec 1st		(a) Continued the advance. Raining. BELLEVAUX at 8.30. Roads very slippery with ice, and hills very bad, an hour or two got getting to starting point. Consequently we were three hours behind. Both a/c we find halted for 1½ hour just past Spa. Noticed armed German sentry at aviation aerodrome. Fed and watered at Spa and arrived ANDRIMONT at 4 p.m. Billets very good. Rested.	
	2nd		Rested the day at ANDRIMONT. (about a mile about STAVELOT) and drew the first canteen stores we have seen for some time.	
	3rd		Continued Rest. Tried to patch up men's boots but they were in most cases too far gone. Some of the men's boots (they had been given the worst) will not hold together at all. Late at night arrive all sorts of advance stores, mostly useless and most that we have entered - no boots.	
	4th		Continued march, eventually ordered to BURTENBACH but were turned off to ELSENBORN LAGER (German military camp.) We passed the German cavalry that had at 10.00 am and arrived in billets at 7.30 pm about 30 kilometers march.	

WAR DIARY or INTELLIGENCE SUMMARY

Army Form C. 2118.

Place	Date	Hour	Summary of Events and Information	Remarks and references to Appendices
1918 Dec 5th			Bg moves off at 9.30 and has great trouble getting clear of the EUPEN on account of the exhausted condition of the horses. However make MONTJOIE at 1.30 p.m. Find our billets are 2 kilos distant by railway station. Officers billet in Foerster's house. It is noticeable that billets are getting better, especially as far as officers are concerned. Our budging wagons we left at MONTJOIE to be brought on by M.T. The hills being too much for our jaded horses.	
	6th		Continue to march to SCHMIDT (billets not quite so good). It is noticeable that the Germans think they are supposed to feed as well as house us. Our chaps would be dong well if only they had more food.	
	7th		From SCHMIDT to KREUTZ (met or close with Battery RHA and very nice and comfortable too. So far we have had very fine weather but a few spots of rain today.	

WAR DIARY
or
INTELLIGENCE SUMMARY.

Army Form C. 2118.

Place	Date	Hour	Summary of Events and Information	Remarks and references to Appendices
Dec 1918	8th		From KELTZ to DIRMERZHEIM. We have very little trouble in seeing that the civilians pay the proper compliments.	
	9th		March to Schwals of Cologne about TRIER. As there is some trouble about billets we are kept waiting on the road in the rain when to finish we are marched off at 7.30 a.m. However billets are eventually good. The men occupy a school and officers a fine house at LINDENTHAL street car.	
	10th		Day spent in general cleanup. Bridging wagons fan wagon	
	11th		etc on 10th - no advance stores yet arrived. Drew two horses	
	12th		etc on 10th - Final cleanup for march past. Boats and other advance stores at last to hand, and plenty of Horny Bologna	
	13th		Rains slightly most of the day. However the civilians seem to think our march through the COLOGNE for the HOHENZOLLERN bridge worth turning out for see. Billets at BERG GLADBACH all good.	
	14		Rest in billets, nothing much done except non rains all day	

WAR DIARY or INTELLIGENCE SUMMARY

Army Form C. 2118.

Place	Date	Hour	Summary of Events and Information	Remarks and references to Appendices
	Dec 1918 15		Coy paraded at 9.45 and moved in column of route with the B Battery R.H.A. to KALTERHERBERG, arriving about 14.00. Billets not good. Sector animals out of stables or loose lines for the first time for a month.	
	16		The 87th Bde continue their march, but we are not come under CRE's orders with instructions to remain in present location. However in billets are bad, we move a kilometre into BURSCHEID. 2nd lines for all animals in a truck works it very bad of stores which we left at COLOGNE rejoins us.	
	17		Stables 6.00. Sappers parade 8.00 for general cleaning of.	
	18		Parades & Work as on 17. Started at actions, moved at orderly room to lost the 3 mobile no 1 collect the various information regarding to make out each man's Demobilisation papers	
	19		Parades and Work as on 17 except morning stables at 6.30. Up the two other field coys RE and CRE's H9 more in today. No 3 Section evacuate a billet to make room for Kent Coys drivers	

BURSCHEID

Army Form C. 2118.

WAR DIARY
or
INTELLIGENCE SUMMARY
(Erase heading not required.)

Place	Date	Hour	Summary of Events and Information	Remarks and references to Appendices
Dec 1918	20th		Such as on 12th. Work for all sections consists of camp improvement such as making horse troughs, latrines, cook houses etc. A report from the civilian in charge of work who accuses the driver with taking oats from his store, which is apparently what they have done.	
	21		As on 20th	
	22		As on 20th. Whan other jobs the Coy is taking on a bit of road work to be made into a macadam road. The sapper sections move into a school at the centre of the village which it is hoped will be the final billet for some time.	
	23		Work consists in camp improvements.	
	24		Work consists in preparing officers (regimental) mess, sergeants and sappers and drivers messes (in all) for Christmas.	
	25		Christmas day. Plenty of church parade. The promised Christmas fare of pork, turkeys etc has not turned up. The ASC ration issue was 25% to Bully Beef — however the best fare possible was kept up.	

BURSCHEID

WAR DIARY or INTELLIGENCE SUMMARY

Army Form C. 2118.

Place	Date	Hour	Summary of Events and Information	Remarks and references to Appendices
Dec 1918	26th		Yesterday a large draught of men from base, also a large party of men back from leave, in all 38 men, join the coy. Also a large amount of canteen stores arrive. The feast for a month, which is good to us we are not allowed to purchase food locally. Work carried on camp improvements. Div Comd stays at Br's coys.	
	27th		In a parol issued by S.S. Men Commandant (Cdn) we are ordered to pay the civilian in charge of the Anchworks from which coals are taken, 230 marks. This was duly paid out of canteen funds. The coy was employed today in unloading a train (42 trucks) of different R.E. stores which was taken to the siding at Bursch who is in BURSCHEID.	
	28th			
	29th		Sunday. Parade at 9.00 a.m. 1 & 2 sections complete the unloading of the train.	
	30th		Private 7.45 wounded received present gate arc. Makins & road to stables. Russian Pt. de Rowen + minerals etc.	
	31st		Work and parades as on 30th	

J.D. Matthews Major R.E.
O.C. 455 Field Coy R.E.

RHINE ARMY
SOUTHERN DIVISION
LATE 29TH DIVISION

455TH (W.R.) FLD COY R.E.
JAN - OCT 1919

Box 2065 & 2084

RHINE ARMY
SOUTHERN DIVISION
LATE 29TH DIVISION

Original

War Diary

of

455th. (W.R.) Field Coy. R.E. (T.F.)

for

Month of January 1919

Volume 34.

455TH (W. RIDING)
FIELD COMPANY,
R.E.

Army Form C. 2118.

WAR DIARY
or
INTELLIGENCE SUMMARY.
(Erase heading not required.)

Place	Date	Hour	Summary of Events and Information	Remarks and references to Appendices
	1st		Parades at 7.45 for work and 6.30 stables. Dinners at 12.30. Works chiefly consist in camp improvements. Men only drew tea ration for midday, and an attempt was made at a New Year dinner and concert in the evening.	
	2		Work & Parades as usual.	
	3rd		Work & Parades as usual. No 3 section proceed to BENSBERG for various works for 86th Bde and Div. Hd qrs as also staples pulling in limbs etc. Lieut Furlong goes out with the section.	
	4th		Work & Parades as usual. B. Chief work being getting out demobilisation papers & to return.	
	5th		Work & Parades as usual.	

WAR DIARY
or
INTELLIGENCE SUMMARY.
(Erase heading not required.)

Army Form C. 2118.

Place	Date	Hour	Summary of Events and Information	Remarks and references to Appendices
BURSCHEID	Jan 1919 5th		Church parade at 9.30. No work except for No 3 section. Football in afternoon.	
	6th		O.C. visits work of No 3 Section at BERG. GLADBACH. Work also commenced on baths for M.G. Bn. Baths - also various odd jobs for different units.	
	7th		Work and parades normal.	
	8th		New work requested at Div H.Q. ALTENBERG, DABBEN &c. All work carried in stables, huts, incinerators. Also work on and accommodation of old Div Area.	
	9th		Parades & works as usual. Also harness inspection by C.R.E.	
	10th		Army Commander comes into the neighbourhood, but any sees C.R.E. Work & parades as usual.	
	11th		Inspection of dismounted men and clean up of billets.	
	12th		Sunday. Church parade & Sports. Mens RE memorial fund committee meetings from O.C.	
	13th		Lieut Myers goes on leave, and Capt. Williamson Vermont.	

WAR DIARY
or
INTELLIGENCE SUMMARY

Army Form C. 2118.

Place	Date	Hour	Summary of Events and Information	Remarks and references to Appendices
BURSCHEID	14th		Work & Parades as usual.	
	15th		Rifle range for 88 Bde. and stables for M.G. Bn arranged for. Work to commence tomorrow.	
	16th		Work & Parades as usual	
	17th		2/Lt Stedham leaves for hospital. Work commenced at WERMELS KIRCHEN on rifle range, and on stables at DEBRING HAUSEN on stables.	
	18th		Baths & ceremonial parade for the Coy.	
	19th		Sunday. Church parade at 09.00	
	20th		Work & Parades as usual, Lieut Stedham returns to Coy. from C.C.S.	
	21st		Work & Parades as usual.	
	22nd		Work & Parades as usual	
	23rd		Work & Parades as on 21st.	
	24th		One hours physical training after 7.45 parade. The remainder of the morning spent at Baths	

Army Form C. 2118.

WAR DIARY
or
INTELLIGENCE SUMMARY.
(Erase heading not required.)

Instructions regarding War Diaries and Intelligence Summaries are contained in F. S. Regs., Part II, and the Staff Manual respectively. Title pages will be prepared in manuscript.

Place	Date	Hour	Summary of Events and Information	Remarks and references to Appendices
	25th		Drill parade and billet cleaning.	
	26th		Sunday. Church parade ong, at 9.00.	
	27th		Works as usual.	
	28th		As on 27th.	
	29th		As on 27th.	
	30th		As on 27th.	
	31st		As on 27th. During this month 2 men were demobilised whilst on leave, and 14 from the cy. no officers.	

P Matthews Major RE
OC 453rd Field Cy. RE

Vol 36

War Diary
of
455 (W.R.) Field Company R.E. (T.)
for
Month of February 1919
Volume 35

Army Form C. 2118.

WAR DIARY
or
INTELLIGENCE SUMMARY.
(Erase heading not required.)

Place	Date	Hour	Summary of Events and Information	Remarks and references to Appendices
BURSCHEID	1st Feb 1919		Coy working on various jobs. 4 men at KURTEN. 10 men at BARRINGHOVEN. 6 men at HERMES MUHLEN. No 3 section at BENSBERG on old jobs.	
	2nd		Renewed work at camp improvements. BURSCHEID furnishing 745 and working 6 12.30. No 3 section return this day. General clean up for the inspection tomorrow.	
	3rd		Works were necessary continue. Inspection by G.O.C. of men, transport, harness arrangements and medal presenting. Reuters were put to S.A.C. by the two of the men re articles they had read about demobilization.	
	4th		No 2 & 5 remainder of No 1 section go to STUMPF to complete the stables begun there.	

Army Form C. 2118.

WAR DIARY
or
INTELLIGENCE SUMMARY.
(Erase heading not required.)

Place	Date	Hour	Summary of Events and Information	Remarks and references to Appendices
BURSCHEID GERMANY.	5/2/19		Capt. D.R. WILLIAMSON. R.E. rejoined Coy from leave and took over Command on Major F.A.D. MATHEWS R.E. proceeding on 10 days leave to PARIS. Duties and Routine as usual.	
	9/2/19		Lt. G.C. STEDHAN M.C. R.E., 2Lt. R.E. FURLONG R.E. and 18 men proceed to Base for England and dispersal.	
	12/2/19 14/2/19		Lords F ? returned to refreshments back from leave. Lt. W.E. AYERS M.C. R.E. returned from Coy. marked out. At present states are in Site of hires Stables for Coy. are required to commence work again, all hutments and their assigned to stables, two billet doors of 3 Companies have to build new stables, hers billet doors of one double stable for 30 animals in BAHNHOFF STRASSE and one single stable for 45 horses in small road known as HINDENWEG. Which officers moved into is in Ann of KAISERHOF HOTEL. Then in BURSCHEID proceed to billets.	
	Saturday 15/2/19 Sunday 16/2/19		7 all men of Coy billeted in BURSCHEID proceed on Route March and Clean up billets on return.	
	17/2/19		Church Parade at 10:55 am. Work commenced on new Stables. 3 local Huns engaged to work as labourers.	

(A3475) Wt W2358/P360 600,000 12/17 D. D. & L. Sch. 52a. Forms/C2118/15.

WAR DIARY
or
INTELLIGENCE SUMMARY.
(Erase heading not required.)

Army Form C. 2118.

Place	Date	Hour	Summary of Events and Information	Remarks and references to Appendices
BUERSCHEID GERMANY	Feb/19 18/19		Works as usual. Area Labouring Party necessary in size for work on Coys. new stables.	
	19th		Works & Parades as usual. Major F.A.V.D. MATHEWS M.C. R.E. returned from leave.	
	20th		Works and Parades as usual. 12 men proceeded to BERG GLADBACH for Mullein test and will return on the 24th Feb.	
	21st		Coy continues work on stables at STUMPT & BURSCHEID. Parades as follows: 1st working parade 8.15 a.m. Dinner at 13.00. No pm tea parade. Baths at KURTEN are finished.	
	22		2nd Lieut LINDSAY joins the Coy for instruction and work from Woolwich and commences by attending to all stable duties.	
	23rd		Work & parades as usual.	
	24		Sunday church parade at 10.55.	
	25			
	26		All work and parades as on 21st	
	27			
	28			

Y.D. Mathews

Major R.E.
O.C. 455th (W.B.) Field Coy.
Major R.E.

CONFIDENTIAL

WAR DIARY.

of

455th Field Coy R.E.

From 1/5/19 to 31/5/19

VOLUME No. 38

455th Field Coy R.E.

Army Form C. 2118.

WAR DIARY
or
INTELLIGENCE SUMMARY.
(Erase heading not required.)

Vol. 38

Place	Date	Hour	Summary of Events and Information	Remarks and references to Appendices
BURSCHEID	May 1/6/19	Sun	Lt W.T. Miller rejoined unit from leave. The Company was employed on work for the Company at Burscheid	
	7/6/19	Mon	Lt W.T. Miller & 15 O.R. proceeded to Berg Gladbach. No 4 Areas has moved there. Landed over to this City as well as No 1 Area for the purpose of work.	
			Lt. D Compton & H.O.R. proceed to Kurten to give technical advice to 1st Southern Infantry Brigade in wiring the permises.	
	9/6/19	Sun	Work started on Zander's Factory for 1st Southern Infy Bdg Berg Gladbach. Latrine ablution troughs, seating accommodation etc.	
	13/6/19	Fri	Lt E.R Canham left unit for Midland Div. R.E. 16 men transferred to 497 Field Coy on 11/6/19.	
			Company employed on works at Berg Gladbach. Coys strength diminished to 60 O.R. The works at Berg Gladbach consist of building stables, cook houses etc for D.A. & at Zander's factory for 1st Southern Infy Brigade	
			All Berg new Rd services held up owing to uncertainty	
	3/6/19	Mon	as to the signing of the Peace terms	

D Meehan
Major
OC 455th Field Coy RE

Confidential

Original.

29 DIV
Southern

War Diary

of

455th. Field Coy. R.E.

for

month of June 1919

Volume 39

455TH
FIELD COMPANY,
R.E.
No.
Date 1-7-19

Army Form C. 2118.

WAR DIARY
or
INTELLIGENCE SUMMARY.
(Erase heading not required.)

Place	Date	Hour	Summary of Events and Information	Remarks and references to Appendices
Burscheid	1/6/19	Sun	Work held up on big jobs by the uncertainty as to whether the enemy will sign the Peace Terms.	
			The Company was employed on maintenance & completion of work in hand at Burg Gladbach, wiring the permanent Barracks	
			The Company was employed on additional sheds, latrines & maintenance at Zanders Factory Burg Gladbach. (Ablution Shed painted)	
			Shed to 16 horses at MX6 (1077-69) Burg Gladbach (flooring to finish)	
			A latrine of bricks at Camp Cay Sand, fire escape & 10XY book bind provided for HQ 113 Bde. RFA Q67-52. Woodwork to staff	
			of 1st SAA. BAC at Paffrath renewed & new one of corrugated iron put on.	
			fire escape built to billet. Accessory buildings to Lorry Camp	
	16/6/19	SOS	at Rifle Range Delbrook this job 75% complete	
	17/6/19	Con	"Unite" 20th June received & CRE 1st Southern Brigade	
			Operation Order mils effect, all work ceased.	
	19/6/19	SOS	Detachments report from Delbrook & Burg Gladbach & Kurten & Waterhoff	
			Coy. packed up & prepared to move on 20-th 18/6/19	

Army Form C. 2118.

WAR DIARY
or
INTELLIGENCE SUMMARY.
(Erase heading not required.)

Instructions regarding War Diaries and Intelligence Summaries are contained in F. S. Regs., Part II. and the Staff Manual respectively. Title pages will be prepared in manuscript.

Place	Date	Hour	Summary of Events and Information	Remarks and references to Appendices
Burscheid, Germany.	19/6/19	8 AM	Overhauling Stores etc. Removing surplus kit. Hilgen Standing by awaiting the word "Go" in case enemy did not sign the Peace terms.	
	20	9 AM		
	21st	2 PM	Route march.	
	6		Cleaning gear & over hauling Company transport.	
	27/6/19	2 PM	C.R.E's Inspection. Lt Campion R.E. & Lt Miller R.E. went on detachment. The former to complete the Camp at Delbrück the latter to build a hut for soda water plant at Berg Gladbach 20 O.R. 9th Gloucester Pioneers proceeded with each party.	
	28/6/19	9 AM	C.R.E's Inspection. Peace Signed.	
	29/6/19		Church Parade	
	30/6/19		"A" day. Sappers go out on to works again	

E.W. Meacham

Confidential

Original

War Diary

of

455th. Field Coy. R.E. (T)

for

month of July 1919.

Volume 40

455TH
FIELD COMPANY.
R.E.
No.
Date 1-8-19

Army Form C. 2118.

455TH FIELD COMPANY. R.E.

WAR DIARY
or
INTELLIGENCE SUMMARY
(Erase heading not required)

Instructions regarding War Diaries and Intelligence Summaries are contained in F. S. Regs., Part II. and the Staff Manual respectively. Title pages will be prepared in manuscript.

Place	Date	Hour	Summary of Events and Information	Remarks and references to Appendices
BURSCHEID (Germany)	1/7/19	9am	Works being carried out as follows. Detachment at BERG GLADBACH under Lt MILLER, detachment at DELLBRÜCK under Lt CAMPION R.E. 9ᵗʰ and 4 Sappers at HOVERHOFF. Remainder of Company at BURSCHEID.	
"	4/7/19	9am	Observed as a whole holiday in celebration of Peace by order of Commander-in-Chief.	
"	5/7/19	noon	Company Bathed	
"	6/7/19	9am	Church Parade	
"	7/7/19	9am	Works resumed by Company	
"	12/7/19	9am	Work completed on cookhouses at HOVERHOFF. Detachment there withdrawn between the BERG GLADBACH and the DELLBRÜCK detachments	
"	13/7/19	9am	Church Parade	
"	14/7/19	9am	Lieut G.M. WYNN R.E. reported for duty from C.E. II Corps	
"	19/7/19	9am	MAJOR F.V. WESTLAM R.E. assumed command on return from leave	
"	26/7/19	9am	Getting ready for sports day. R.E. Works as usual	

29/7/19

WAR DIARY
or
INTELLIGENCE SUMMARY.
(Erase heading not required.)

Army Form C. 2118.

455TH FIELD COMPANY, R.E.

No. ....
Date ....

Place	Date	Hour	Summary of Events and Information	Remarks and references to Appendices
BURSCHEID	26/7/19	Sat.	R.E. Sports Day. Company won the Tug-of-Cart, Sub. pair slipper L.D. Horses, & Sub. pair of mules.	
	31/7/19	Sat.	Works as usual. Only important work to be carried on.	

Sherborn
Major R.E.
O.C., 455th Field Coy. R.E.

CONFIDENTIAL

Original.

War Diary

of

455th. Field Coy. R.E.

for

month of August. 1919.

Volume 41.

455TH
FIELD COMPANY,
R.E.
31 AUG 1919

Army Form C. 2118.

WAR DIARY
or
INTELLIGENCE SUMMARY.
(Erase heading not required.)

Place	Date	Hour	Summary of Events and Information	Remarks and references to Appendices
BURSCHEID	1/8/19	p.m.	Work being done on odd jobs at Div H.Q., Soden Water Factory, Barracks at Saventaley, Berg Gladbach, Delbrook Rifle Range Camp. Cutting timber for Army Sports, Meat-Safe at Berg Gladbach, Huts at Silkenrath, Berg Gladbach & odd jobs on upkeep in Div. Area	
			Moved from old School billets to Felmate	
	3/8/19	am	1 Lt & A Lindsay proceeded to Berlin for attachment to 145th Infy Bgde	
	5/8/19	noon	15 men as reinforcements joined the Company.	
	10/8/19	am	1 Rider, 3 & D & 4 mules proceeded for sale in Germany (14/6/10 Lt D Campion Egypt)	
	16/8/19	am	3 O.R. proceeded on draft for Egypt. (Proceeding to England on leave)	
	18/8/19	am	Army Horse Show. Company took several places with horses & mules.	
	19/8/19	am	2 O.R. proceeded for Demobilization under new organization scheme	
	25/8/19	am	Works completed to date Delbrook Rifle Range Camp, Huts at Silkenrath, Goblets at Saventaley, new work taken Baths at Delbrook Camp, Alteration Sheds for rest Company Tilsen. Lt Millen proceeded on leave 27/8/19.	
			Lt. J. Robertson left the Coy on draft for Egypt.	
	31/8/19	noon	Works completed, Delbrook Camp & Baths & Coy Alteration Renaters.	

E.W. Neston
Major RE

Original.

War Diary

of

455th. Field Coy R.E. (T.)

for

Month of September 1919.

Volume 42.

Original

Army Form C. 2118.

455TH FIELD COMPANY. R.E.
Date: 1 OCT 1919

WAR DIARY
or
INTELLIGENCE SUMMARY.
(Erase heading not required.)

Instructions regarding War Diaries and Intelligence Summaries are contained in F. S. Regs., Part II. and the Staff Manual respectively. Title pages will be prepared in manuscript.

Place	Date	Hour	Summary of Events and Information	Remarks and references to Appendices
BURSCHIED (Germany)	29/9/19	W/m	Detachment rejoined unit from DELLBRUCK and BERG GLADBACH.	
	30/9/19	W/m	2nd Lieut L.A Lindsay R.E. rejoined from leave to U.K.	
	1/9/19	W/m	3. O.R. proceeded on draft for EGYPT. I.O.R. proceeded for Demobilization	
	8/9/19	W/m	Lieut W.Miller R.E. rejoined from leave to U.K. I.O.R. proceeded on demobilization	
	10/9/19	W/m	4 O.R. proceeded on demobilization	
	11/9/19	W/m	4. O.R. " " "	
	12/9/19	W/m	6. O.R. " " "	
	13/9/19	W/m	Lieut G.M Wynne R.E. proceeded on leave to U.K.	
	14/9/19	W/m	3 O.R. proceeded on demobilization	
	16/9/19	W/m	3 O.R. " " "	
	19/9/19	W/m	3 O.R. " " "	
	20/9/19	W/m	1 O.R. " " "	
	21/9/19	W/m	3 O.R. " " "	
	22/9/19	W/m	3 O.R. " " "	
	23/9/19	W/m	6 O.R. " " "	

Army Form C. 2118.

WAR DIARY
or
INTELLIGENCE SUMMARY.
(Erase heading not required.)

Place	Date	Hour	Summary of Events and Information	Remarks and references to Appendices
BURSCHIED (Germany)	24/9/19	WM	8 O.R. proceeded on demobilization	
	25/9/19	WM	Capt L.A. Martin M.C. R.E. proceeded on leave to U.K.	
	26/9/19	WM	10 O.R. proceeded on demobilization	
	28/9/19	WM	Major E.W. Prodam R.E. proceeded on special leave to MAINZ (Germany)	

W.P. Miller
Lieut. R.E.

Original

War Diary

of

455th Field Coy R.E. (T)

for

Month of October 1919.

Volume 43.

455TH
FIELD COMPANY.
R.E.
30 OCT 1919

Original Army Form C. 2118.

465TH FIELD COMPANY R.E.
No.
Date 30 OCT 19

WAR DIARY
or
INTELLIGENCE SUMMARY.
(Erase heading not required.)

Instructions regarding War Diaries and Intelligence Summaries are contained in F. S. Regs., Part II. and the Staff Manual respectively. Title pages will be prepared in manuscript.

Place	Date	Hour	Summary of Events and Information	Remarks and references to Appendices
BURSCHIED (Germany)	2/10/19	WM	Major E.W.McLean rejoined Unit from special leave to MAINZ	
	11/10/19	WM	1 O.R. proceeded on demobilization	
	13/10/19	WM	Major E.W.McLean R.E. proceeded to U.K. for demobilization. Lieut W.Y.Miller R.E. assumed command of the Coy.	
	15/10/19	WM	4 O.R. proceeded on demobilization.	
	18/10/19	WM	Preparatory to the disbanding of the Unit, commenced loading in surplus stores & equipment, and parking Coy vehicles and equipment at MULHEIM	
	21/10/19	WM	Completed parking of equipment at MULHEIM.	
	23/10/19	WM	II Corps report the accidental death of Lieut G.M.Wynne R.E. Whilst riding motor cycle he collided violently with a stationary motor lorry death being almost instantaneous. Court of Enquiry is being held by II Corps.	
	24/10/19	WM	Capt. W.Y.Seymour R.E. took over command of the Coy from Lieut W.Y.Miller R.E.	
	27/10/19		Lieut Miller & 30 O.R. left unit for 206 Field Coy R.E.	
	28/10/19		Captain Seymour, (Rear Party) leaving for Mulheim to sort + check Coy equipment.	